ÆLFRIC

A NEW STUDY OF HIS LIFE AND WRITINGS

BY
CAROLINE LOUISA WHITE

with a supplementary classified bibliography
prepared by
MALCOLM R. GODDEN

ARCHON BOOKS
1974

Library of Congress Cataloging in Publication Data

White, Caroline Louisa, 1849–1905.
   Aelfric : a new study of his life and writing.

   Reprint of the ed. published by Lamson, Wolffe
London, which was issued as v. 2 of Yale studies in
English.
   Bibliography : p.
   1. Aelfric, Abbot of Eynsham. 2. Aelfric,
Abbot of Eynsham—Bibliography. I. Title. II.
Series : Yale studies in English, v. 2.
PR1534.W5   1974   016.271′1′024   73–20339
ISBN 0–208–01438–1

'We have a deep concern in preserving from destruction
the thoughts of the past, the leading conceptions of all
remarkable forms of civilization; the achievements of
genius, of virtue, and of high faith.' 'Though these things
may be individually forgotten, collectively they survive,
and are in action still.' James Martineau.

[Yale Studies in English, vol. 2]

© 1898 by Caroline L. White
Reprinted 1974 with permission in an
unaltered and unabridged edition as an Archon Book
an imprint of THE SHOE STRING PRESS, INC.,
Hamden, Connecticut 06514

Printed in the United States of America

PREFACE.

The repeated efforts of scholars for the past three hundred years to discover the identity of Ælfric, show the significant place that his writings hold; no history of English culture would be complete that left out of account the century that preceded the Norman Conquest, and in that century Ælfric's writings are more important than those of any other man. Transliterated copies of his homilies made in the Middle English period show that their practical use had not ceased at a time when men could no longer read the language in which they were first written.

These writings are valuable, first, in reference to the history of English literature and English culture; secondly, in reference to the history and development of the English language; thirdly, as theological writings which throw light upon the beliefs of the church in the Old English period.

It was this third value of Ælfric's works that, in the sixteenth century, gave the first impulse to the modern study of Old English.

The attempts made by such scholars as Wharton and Mores to identify Ælfric, succeeded in bringing together a body of facts which finally proved useful in deciding the question. The modern author who has done most to illuminate this subject is Edward Dietrich, late professor at the University of Marburg, who in 1855 and 1856 published the results of his investigations in Niedner's *Zeitschrift für Historische Theologie*. His papers considered, first, Ælfric's writings; secondly, the teachings of the Old English Church according to Ælfric's writings; thirdly, Ælfric's education and character; fourthly, Ælfric's life.

Of these studies, Dietrich writes thus: 'The great ignorance as to Ælfric's life and personality which has prevailed in church histories up to the present time has led to the following investigations. They were preceded by several years' study of Ælfric's writings, and of the earlier and later Old English literature, and a long stay in England gave opportunity to study at the British Museum and at Oxford his yet unpublished works.'

The chief results of Dietrich's investigations have been accepted as authoritative by German students of Old English, and are fundamental in all subsequent German Ælfrician studies. But although almost half a century has passed since he wrote, his work is rarely noticed by English writers. Those who have studied at German universities are well acquainted with it, and perhaps many others. But in such works as the *Encyclopædia Britannica,* and the *Dictionary of National Biography* which gives references to the most important authorities on each subject treated, Dietrich's work is entirely ignored. Cockayne, whose discussion of the subject of Ælfric's identity is probably the most thorough and satisfactory of anything originally written upon it in English, makes no reference to Dietrich. Yet it is hardly to be doubted that he was indebted to him, although it may be indirectly.

This study is based upon Dietrich's work in so far as that accords with the results of more recent investigations. Whereever equally advantageous, his words are simply translated. Chapters five and six are chiefly translation. Such also is chapter seven, but with various additions, omissions and modifications, in order to bring the treatment of the subject up to the present day.

In preparing the descriptions of Ælfric's works I have rewritten as far as possible Dietrich's different divisions, omitting some things, adding others, and treating the subjects with much freedom.

The uncertainty which has been felt up to the present time as to who Ælfric was, and where he lived, and his frequent identifications with others of the same name, make it very desirable, now that the main outline of his life is known, to take him away completely from the false surroundings in which he has been placed, and, as it were, to create his identity anew. Hence the attempt has here been made to show his true relation to his age, and to embody in a connected whole the known facts of his life. As a complete biography the result is of course inadequate. Some of the data are uncertain, but the degree of uncertainty is indicated. This account of Ælfric's life incorporates the chief facts established by Dietrich, but is not a translation. In some few cases a result different from his has been reached. For instance, the view here given is that Ælfric remained at Cernel from the time he left Winchester, in, or soon after 987, until he became abbot in 1005. Dietrich's view that he returned to Winchester, and perhaps went elsewhere, is accounted for, in that he recognized no relationship between the two noblemen who were Ælfric's patrons, and considered it necessary for him to return to Winchester in order to make the acquaintance of Æthelweard. The chapter on the monastic revival is added in order to explain Ælfric's literary activity, and is not at all derived from Dietrich.

No attempt has been made to give Dietrich's account of the views of the Old English Church according to Ælfric's writings. The spirit in which he treats that subject is characteristic of all his work, and explains why the results of his studies are of permanent value. He says of the above subject: 'Whether it is Protestant or Catholic does not now concern me. I wish to ascertain from his collected expressions upon it, and through comparison of these, what that teaching is in itself, and what it is in comparison with that of the times just before and just after it.'

In the last chapter are printed the prefaces of Ælfric's writings. They afford material, not only for deciding various questions of fact in respect to his life, but when studied either separately or in comparison, they reveal much that is of interest in the character of Ælfric, the Christian man and the

1½

teacher of his people. These prefaces are complete in all cases except that of *Genesis* and the English preface of *Catholic Homilies* I. In those, the parts which are not of a personal nature are omitted. Also the autobiographical portions of the work *On the Old and New Testaments* are given, and an extract from the charter of Eynsham Abbey.

The bibliography is as complete as circumstances allow. It can hardly have failed to omit some things which should find a place in it, since its subject is an author whose voluminous works have often been printed, and about whom much has been said by many writers.

The original purpose of the present study was to render the most important parts of Dietrich's work accessible to English readers. The endeavor to fulfil that purpose showed the advisability of adding to these some of the results which have been reached by other scholars during the years which have elapsed since he published his papers. In those years nearly all of Ælfric's writings which were before unpublished have been printed, and the authenticity of some hitherto doubtful ones has been conclusively established. It should be added that the many recent studies of Ælfric's works have only rendered clearer and more certain the chief results obtained by Dietrich. In most cases where he can be shown to have been mistaken, the later judgments are derived from facts not easily accessible at the time when he wrote.

I gladly acknowledge my indebtedness to the various scholars whose works are referred to or quoted in the following pages. To Professor Albert S. Cook I am grateful, not only for criticism and suggestion, but still more for encouragement and inspiration in this endeavor to render a little more distinct the life and work of an English scholar of the past.

C. L. W.

New Haven, May, 1898.

CONTENTS.

8 *Contents.*

CHRONOLOGICAL TABLE.

449 The English land in Britain.

597 Augustine converts Kent.

597-681 Conversion of the English to Christianity.

664 Council of Whitby.   Victory of Roman Christianity.
   Cædmon at Whitby

668 Theodore made Archbishop of Canterbury.

673 Birth of Bede, died 742(?).

789-855 England plundered by the Danes.

855-897 Danes invade England and make settlements.

871 Alfred, King of Wessex, born 849, died 901.

878 Peace of Wedmore made with the Danes.

901 Edward the Elder, died 925.

925 Æthelstan, died 940.

940 Edmund, died 946.

945(?) Dunstan made Abbot of Glastonbury.

946 Eadred, died 955.

952(?) Æthelwold made Abbot of Abingdon.

955 Eadwig, died 959.

956 Banishment of Dunstan.

957 Dunstan made Bishop of Worcester, and of London.

959 Edgar, died 975.
   Dunstan made Archbishop of Canterbury.

961 Oswald made Bishop of Worcester.

963 Æthelwold made Bishop of Winchester.

970 Restoration of Ely Abbey.

972 Restoration of Peterborough Abbey.
   Oswald made Archbishop of York.

975 Edward the Martyr, died 978.

979 Æthelred the Unready, died 1016.

980-2 Beginning of Danish inroads.

984 Alphege II. made Bishop of Winchester.

987 Founding of Cernel Abbey.
988 Æthelgar made Archbishop of Canterbury.
    Beginning of Danish settlements.
990 Sigeric made Archbishop of Canterbury.
991 Battle of Maldon.
992 Aldulf made Archbishop of York.
994 Danish inroads.
995 Ælfric made Archbishop of Canterbury.
997-999 Renewed attacks of the Danes.
998 Death of the ealdorman Æthelweard.
1003 Wulfstan made Archbishop of York.
1005 Founding of Eynsham Abbey.
1006 Alphege made Archbishop of Canterbury.
     Kenulph made Bishop of Winchester.
1007 Æthelwold II made Bishop of Winchester.
1016 Accession of Edmund Ironside.
     Cnut, King of England.
1023 Ælfric made Archbishop of York.
1035 Harold Harefoot, died 1040.
1040 Harthacnut, died 1042.
1042 Edward the Confessor, died 1066.
1066 Harold elected King; Battle of Senlac; Norman Conquest.

CHIEF DATES OF ÆLFRIC'S LIFE.

Some of these dates are conjectural. The degree of uncertainty is indicated in the chapters that treat of Ælfric's life.

955 Birth.

972-987 Life at Winchester.

987-1004 Life at Cernel.

990-991 The Catholic Homilies, I.

992 The De Temporibus.

994 The Catholic Homilies, II.

995 Grammar.

998 Lives of the Saints.

997-999 The Glossary

998 Translations from the Old Testament.

998-1001 Pastoral Letter for Wulfsige.

995-1005 The Colloquium.

1005 Ælfric Abbot of Eynsham.

1005-1006 Tract composed for Wulfgeat.

1005 Excerpts from the De Consuetudine.

1006 Latin Life of Æthelwold.

1005-12 Treatise on the Old and New Testaments.

1007-1012 Sermon on Vigilate Ergo.

1014-1016 Pastoral Letter for Wulfstan.

1020 Second edition of the Catholic Homilies.

1020-1025 Death.

'If we add to the consideration (of their belief in the approaching end of the world), the recollection how imperfect was the possession then retained of the literature of antiquity, the indifference with which that literature was regarded by the majority, and the difficulties under which it was studied and transmitted, it may perhaps occur to us that the censure and the sarcasm so often directed against these ages, might well give place to something more of reverence and gratitude towards the heroic few who tended the lamp amid the darkness and the storm.' J. B. Mullinger, The University of Cambridge, p 46.

CHAPTER I.

THE MONASTIC REVIVAL.

The story of any life is incomplete which gives no glimpse of the human influences that have moulded it, and the other lives upon which it has impressed its personality. This is most truly the case when the man of whom the story is told is one who has spent his years in the service of his fellow-men. In the life of Abbot Ælfric, the greatest of the Old English prose writers, we cannot find the real man by seeking him in the quiet cell of a mediæval monk. It is only when we place him in the midst of human interests, and in direct relation to the men of the period in which he actually lived, that the true Ælfric will appear. While history has given us only a few of the minor details of his life, our knowledge of its chief events, though imperfect, is now fairly certain. Enough is told to illuminate the time in which he lived, to explain his various undertakings, and to give consistency to his literary work. But it is possible for us to understand in some measure his relation to his contemporaries, and it is absolutely essential that we should understand this in order to estimate correctly the nature and the value of his work. Therefore before recounting the story of the man himself, we will speak of the age in which he lived, and of the men whose influence upon their time made possible the activities of that life which we are to describe.

The life and writings of Ælfric belong to a cultural epoch of great significance; they are part of a movement which occupies a definite and important place in English history. We propose in this chapter to show the historical relation of this movement to earlier times, and some of its important features as it was carried on by a few earnest men in the latter half of the tenth century.

2

The childhood and youth of Ælfric fell in the reign of Edgar, the great-grandson of Alfred, a period of unwonted prosperity for England. Its few years of tranquility followed more than a century of disheartening struggles with the Northmen, when first as invaders, and then as inhabitants of the land, the Danes had been alternately defeated and victorious, and had for the time prevented the internal and social development of the nation. The unbroken peace of Edgar's reign seemed the beginning of better things.

Fortunately influences for higher culture, an intellectual and religious revival, had begun to work actively even before this, in the reigns of Edmund and Eadred, and it was Edgar's hearty co-operation with those men who were working for the moral uplift of the nation, that helped most to make the few years of his reign memorable. History represents Edgar as the weak slave of vice, and, on the other hand, as a wise and noble king. Some truth there is in both traditions. Well authenticated inconsistencies appear in the king's life. And yet good in him must have had most power, for he showed wisdom and energy as a king, and chose as his chief counsellors men of undoubted righteousness, while he himself evidently loved goodness and good men for their own sakes.

This period of earnest effort to revive letters and purify life is usually spoken of as that of the Monastic Revival. It centers chiefly in the lives of three men, Dunstan, Æthelwold, and Oswald, whose period of activity reaches from about the middle of the tenth century to the beginning of its last decade. Their names are great in the history of that day, and after their deaths they were not only canonized, but remembered by the people as worthy of all love and reverence. For us their great significance lies more in the spirit in which they worked and in the ultimate ends they sought, than in the direct means which they employed, even though the means themselves were fruitful of good. Not as revivers of monasticism for its own sake do we specially honor them, but because they loved the ideal ends which that monasticism was meant to promote, and because they laid the chief stress on the ends rather than on the means. Various causes, however, have given the monastic element an undue emphasis in the historic records. To the people of their own time they represented the higher ideals of living, and there gathered about them the men who cared for the things of the spirit, and gladly followed their leadership. Nowhere is there a better example of their power to train men to live patient, unselfish, laborious lives, than Æthelwold's pupil, Ælfric, alumnus of Winchester.

The tenth century is one of the most barren in original English historical documents. There remains much that we still need to know in order that an accurate and just understanding of the time may be possible for us. Some light is given by three early biographies of the churchmen who have been named. Each was written within a few years of the death of the man whom it describes, by one who knew him personally. While all of these biographies contain some admixture of fable, they are for the most part trustworthy, and stand among 'the memorials of the best men of the time, written by the best scholars of the time.'

In order to understand the reforms of Dunstan and his co-workers, and successors, among whom Abbot Ælfric should be counted, it is necessary to appreciate the condition of the church and of monastic life when these men began to make their influence felt. And first of all, it must be remembered that the clergy formed the sole cultured class; that in their keeping was not only all religious teaching, but also the preservation of literature and the instruction of the young; in other words, the furnishing of nearly all the mental stimulus which comes to a people through the knowledge of the past, and the use of that knowledge in the preparation for the future. The numerous sermons and other writings of Ælfric continually reminded his readers of this as of a well understood fact, and Ælfric's choice of material in most of his writings, which were designed for laymen, professedly takes this into account.

From its early days, the English Church had combined episcopacy with monasticism. The limits of the first bishoprics had corresponded with those of the different kingdoms that embraced Christianity, like those kingdoms changing their boundaries with the successes and defeats of 'the political rulers. Archbishop Theodore (688-690) sub-divided some of these large dioceses, added new ones, and gave to the church, with the co-operation of the rulers, a more complete and centralized organization. The parish system was of somewhat later origin. It grew up in this way: the land was held by owners of large tracts, and the religious needs of the tenants were commonly provided for by the owner of the township, who built and endowed the village church, and provided it with a pastor ordained by the bishop.

But from the very first, monasticism, although upon the whole subordinate to the episcopal organization, had been of great importance in England. The life of the English Church began with the founding of the monastery of Christ Church at Canterbury. The conversion of the different English kingdoms was brought about by the patient work of the monks. The Celtic Church, the great instrument for the conversion of the North, was almost exclusively monastic in its tendencies, and though the Synod of Whitby (664) decided that the English Church was to belong to the Roman communion, it did not change the ideal of holy living which Columba and Aidan and Cuthbert had set forth by teaching and example, and which the Roman Church not only did not discourage, but even promoted. Indeed, the century that followed Whitby was the great monastic century. Then were founded the monasteries of Wearmouth and Jarrow by Benedict Biscop, Glastonbury, Peterborough, Abingdon, Ely, and a host of others.

The brightest lights of this flourishing period are Cædmon and Bede, and there might be added a list of many names, not indeed of poets, like Cædmon, or of great scholars like Bede, but yet of devoted Christian adherents of the monastic houses, who fostered piety and scholarship, and made their lives powerful for good. Libraries, indispensable in a Benedictine house, were gathered together, and schools were established by the monks. Evils and abuses there undoubtedly were. A system founded on a theory of society which makes it holier to withdraw from the common life of men than to live that life from the highest motives, is in itself so unnatural that it never long maintains itself free from abuse. Yet the monasteries of early mediæval England fostered industry, set a high standard for human conduct, and kept alive piety, literature and education. Our indebtedness to them is beyond calculation.

Near the close of the eighth century began the invasions of the Danes, when, because of their wealth, churches and monasteries became special objects of plunder and destruction. Their inmates were driven away or killed on the spot, their books and other treasures were destroyed, and their walls were burned to the ground. Thus perished within a few years the monasteries of Lindisfarne (793), Wearmouth, Jarrow, Peterborough, Ely, Croyland and many others, together with many churches; while their monks, nuns and priests either abandoned their service or were barbarously put to death. At the beginning of this period of devastation England stood high among the nations of Europe in religion, education, and literary culture; at its close, the clergy, without books or teachers, were quite unfitted to be the guides of the people, and the people themselves had lost their Christian ideals and become rude like the barbarians who were now finding homes for themselves through all the northern and eastern parts of the land. The monasteries had almost ceased to exist.

It was in these distressing days that King Alfred, mindful of the wise and good men, and the great learning and devotion to the service of God which had abounded among the

English in the former days,[1] undertook to revive among his people religion and the love of letters. He made laws to check the prevailing immorality and to promote justice; he induced men of culture and piety to come from other countries to assist him; and in every way, by example and by incentive, he endeavored to repair the losses suffered, and to set at work all possible instrumentalities for educating and enlightening the church and the people. He established at Winchester a school where not only his own children, but also the sons of his nobles and others could be well instructed, and by his own study and by the work of his assistants, he furnished translations of useful books: of Bede's *Ecclesiastical History,* of Gregory's *Pastoral Care,* of Orosius' *History of the World,* and of Boethius' *Consolations of Philosophy.* He collected the annals of English history and started the *Saxon Chronicle.*

Alfred's efforts were still bearing fruit in the days when Dunstan and his friends undertook their work. His books were read by the few who could read, and the tradition of better things was by no means forgotten. But there was need of revival and reformation. One has only to read the history of Alfred's royal successors, to see that while they desired the prosperity of the church and of scholarship, their energies were of necessity chiefly absorbed in preserving and enlarging the dominion of the Wessex kingdom, which had come in the tenth century to mean the kingdom of all the English. That the work of Alfred and his immediate successors had thus failed to bring about even a tolerable state of morality and culture will appear from the following points:

First, the religious and moral influence of the clergy was to a considerable extent degrading, not elevating. Following the teaching of St. Gregory, the clergy of the English Church, except the orders below the priest, were celibate from its

---

[1] See the preface of Alfred's translation of Gregory's *Cura Pastoralis.*

foundation, and so continued until the devastations of the Danes broke up the religious houses, and scattered the monks and the secular clergy. At the time when Dunstan began his work many of the officiating priests had asserted their right to marry, and had married, though not legally, of course, for they could not marry legally. Furthermore the immoral position in which they were thus placed, made it easy for them to take the next step and divorce one wife for another whenever they chose to do so. This practice had grown out of the demoralized state of the country and the dissoluteness of life which followed the overthrow of almost all the centers of religion and culture. The practice resulted not from a conviction of its reasonableness, but from the desire to be free from restraint. The same irksomeness of restraint made the services of the church distasteful, and the priests who drew the revenues often performed their church duties by proxy. In the monasteries and cathedral establishments the services were now performed by the secular clergy, often men of dissolute lives. No more severe commentary on the church of that day can be found, than the laws of the state and the canons of the church issued in respect to the clergy.

Secondly, the education of the clergy and consequently of the people, had fallen with their morals, and from the same causes. The destruction of libraries, the absence of schools and teachers and centers of culture, had resulted in that state of illiteracy and indifference to learning of which Ælfric speaks when he says, 'before Archbishop Dunstan and Bishop Æthelwold re-established the monastic schools, no English priest was able to compose or understand a letter in Latin.' Even if this were not true without exception, it must have been generally true.

But there were many who longed for a healthier condition of affairs, and were ready to welcome and promote any change which promised to forward a better civilization. The monasteries, as has been said, were almost destroyed. It might

well have seemed to those who cherished the tradition of the
past, a feasible and promising enterprise to found anew the
abbeys and the abbey schools.   The actual change, however,
came about like most genuine reforms, not by preordained,
systematic arrangement, but by a natural train of circumstances.   At Glastonbury Abbey, perhaps the oldest seat of
Christianity in England, there still lingered a few secular
clergy who preserved the tradition of learning and piety
unbroken.   Dunstan, the son of a wealthy kinsman of Bishop
Alphege of Winchester, was born near Glastonbury about
922.   This boy, of poetical temperament, and fond of study,
was placed by his parents in the famous abbey, where he received the tonsure.   There he studied and read so diligently
that the fame of his learning reached the court of King
Æthelstan, and he was summoned thither, but only to become an object of jealousy to his young companions, who
conspired against him and brought about his banishment
from court.   At this crisis Bishop Alphege, who saw in
his young relative a man whose brilliant qualities would help
forward the cause of God and of the church, besought him to
take the monastic vow, which, in accordance with the monastic practice of the English hitherto, meant the vow of celibacy and devotion to God, but did not insist upon the stricter
regulations of the Benedictine order.

Dunstan hesitated, but a little later, when the disgrace of
banishment, and the ill treatment of the courtiers had been
followed by a severe illness, he yielded to the persuasions of
his friend, became a monk, and returned to his own abbey of
Glastonbury.   From there he was recalled to court by King
Edmund, but envy once more drove him from the king's
presence.   A little later, about 945, the repentant Edmund,
in atonement for his injustice, appointed Dunstan, then
scarcely more than twenty years old, abbot of Glastonbury,
according to his biographer, 'the first abbot of the English
nation.'   The enterprising spirit of the young monk quickly
brought disciples once more to Glastonbury who soon be-

came Benedictine brethren. New buildings were added to the monastery, manuscripts were gathered into its library, and a great enthusiasm for study possessed the abbey school with Dunstan as the teacher. The keynote of the life there can hardly have been strongly ascetic. What we see of Dunstan and his influence seems to forbid such a view. Notwithstanding the many marvellous tales which gathered around Dunstan's name soon after his death, the character of the man in its chief outlines is distinct, and we can see in this mediæval abbot a lover of literature, of music, of painting, a versatile and strong personality, wise and devout. As such, he made a lasting impression upon his pupils. We can not doubt that those early students were picked men, elect by their own hunger for higher opportunities, attracted to this spot by a man who possessed that union of imaginative power, executive ability, and devotion to ideal ends, which is of all types of character the one most universally attractive to seekers after the ideal.

But a short time passed before Dunstan's scholars were sought for as pastors and teachers in many different cities, so that the influence of Glastonbury was widely disseminated, and abbots, bishops, even archbishops, went forth from that monastery, and by useful lives, and in some instances by heroic deaths, attested the value of the instruction they had received.

Among his disciples at Glastonbury was Æthelwold, a monk of about his own age,[1] a native of Winchester, and a pupil of his kinsman, Bishop Alphege, by whom both young men had been ordained on the same day to the priest's office. It is most probable that they had also been associated at the royal court, for Æthelwold was for a long time attached to the king's retinue, where, his biographer says, 'he learned many useful things from the king's counsellors.' His brilliant record as a student at Winchester had, as in Dunstan's

---

[1] Perhaps a few years older, but probably not born as early as 908, as some have thought. See *Acta Sanctorum*, edited by Bollandus, Vol. 35, notes on Æthelwold's life.

case, led to the summons to attend upon the king. On join-
ing the brethren at Glastonbury he devoted himself to
'grammatical and metrical science' and to the study of sacred
letters; he was prayerful and self-denying, and made his influence felt among the brethren of the monastery. At length
he took the monastic vow and formally joined the Benedictine order, and still continued for some time longer at the
abbey of Glastonbury, which was up to this time the only
house of monks in England. In this quiet and holy life the
appreciation of such advantages grew stronger within him,
and he felt that he must learn more of the regular monastic
discipline, and consult sacred writings not to be found in his
own country, accordingly he decided to go abroad.

Continental monasticism had a close connection with this
new zeal in England. The foreign marriages of the English
royal house had facilitated intercourse between the Flemish
monasteries and the higher clergy of the English church, a
connection which is important to notice here. But more
than this, England, though separated from the Continent, was
yet near enough to it to share in its general course of thought
and development. The fall of the monasteries in England
had not been an isolated fact. Those of France and other
countries had also declined, and much the same antecedents
appear in all cases. [1] Three prominent causes of the decline
are the following: first, the Continent as well as England
had suffered from barbarian invasions; second, on both sides
of the Channel before the period of invasion, the church
had lost much of its enthusiasm for monastic life, and the
outward misfortunes only precipitated and rendered more
complete a change that had already begun; third, the enor-
mous gifts of land to the churches and monasteries had put
great wealth and great secular interests under ecclesiastical

---

[1] See E. Sackur *Die Cluniacenser im Ihrer Kirchlichen und Allgemeingeschichtlich-
en Wirksamkeit*, I. Introduction; also Lingard's *Hist. and Antiq. of the A.-S. Church*,
II. 217.

control,[1] and had withdrawn from the use of the kings and of the peoples too large a part of the territory of the kingdoms. It is in consequence of this that in the period of monastic decline we see the temporal rulers taking into royal ownership a large part of the lands which had belonged to the religious establishments.

As the monasteries declined in the different countries at about the same time, so the Benedictine revival in England corresponded with one on the Continent, and it can hardly be doubted that the first impulse in England came from abroad, or at least that the foreign influence gave shape to existing aspirations. The reformation of the French monasteries began not far from 910, and Cluny, and Fleury on the Loire were influential centers of reform.

Dunstan became a monk through the influence of Bishop Alphege, and Alphege's superior, Odo, Archbishop of Canterbury (926-959), had taken the monastic vow at Fleury. Both Odo and Alphege esteemed the life of a Benedictine monk the vocation most to be desired for their young kinsmen, as we have seen in Dunstan's case, and shall see in that of Oswald, Odo's nephew. Dunstan himself when he fled from the persecution of Eadwig (956), found refuge at St. Peter's abbey in Ghent, and there had opportunity for personal inspection of a prosperous Flemish monastery, in which 'secular canons had been replaced by Benedictines about twelve years before Dunstan was received there, or in 944.'[2]

Æthelwold's after life proves that his plans at Glastonbury for study abroad, had a practical aim. He was surely looking forward then to that extensive work of re-founding monasteries in which he himself was to take such an important part. When at last he made it known that he was to leave England, the king's mother, Eadgifu, the widow of

---

1 In making grants of land to churches and monasteries the donors were not influenced exclusively by religious motives, but 'chiefly by considerations of social and politica-utility.' Earle's *Land Charters and Saxonic Documents*, p. lxxxix.

2 E. W. Robertson, *Historical Essays*, p. 194.

King Edward, urged her son, King Eadred, not to permit it. Æthelwold's abilities and attainments had no doubt been reported to her since he entered upon his life at Glastonbury, and it is not unlikely that she sometimes visited Dunstan's abbey. It is certain that she would remember the promise of his early years when with other young men he was in attendance at Æthelstan's court. 'Such a man,' she said, 'must not be lost to England.' To Eadred the intimate friend and ardent admirer of Dunstan, Æthelwold also was no stranger. Eadred, prompted by his mother, saw plainly that the way to retain the energetic monk in his service was to forward his ideal ends by giving him an opportunity to put them into practice. A feasible plan was suggested to the king, and with Æthelwold's consent a new enterprise was undertaken which was singularly fitted to meet his desires and to engage his activities. Among the old-time abbeys almost destroyed by the Danes in Alfred's time, and now destitute and forsaken, was Abingdon on the Thames river a few miles south of Oxford. Some wretched buildings and a small area of land were all that remained of the once well endowed abbey.[1] It is an instance of what was to be found all through England: much of the rich land of the monasteries, the gifts of kings and of laymen in the more prosperous times, of the religious houses had been absorbed into the royal domain. But the tide had already begun to turn; King Edmund had given several grants of land to Glastonbury, and now, dating from the new endowment of Abingdon, for many subsequent years, the *Codex Diplomaticus* abounds in charters and records of the re-endowment of the old abbeys.[2]

---

[1] Cockayne is of the opinion that the abbey was not so poor as has been represented, because there are records of several grants of land to it in 930 and 931, and it was a rich abbey before Alfred's time. But these lands seem to have been under the king's control and not available for the use of the establishment until granted anew by Eadred. See Cockayne, *Leechdoms, Wortcunnings, etc.*, III. 408-9.

[2] A few donations to churches and monasteries had been made by every king who had ruled in the tenth century. In a charter signed by Edmund, Eadred and Eadwig (*Cod. Dip. A.-S.* 259-60) are these words 'Nos dei gratia reges reddimus tellures has, quas praedecessores nostri fratribus Christique aecclesia retrahere consueverunt.' The authenticity of such a document may be questioned, but the fact contained is doubtless true.

Thus we read in this case that 'it came to pass with Dunstan's permission, according to the king's will, that Æthelwold received in charge the monastery of Abingdon to promote the cause of God, and to ordain there monks serving God according to the Rule.' [1] It is to be noticed that Dunstan's permission is asked. This indicates not merely that he was Æthelwold's superior at Glastonbury; already he had become Eadred's chief adviser, and begun to take that active part in the government of the realm which did not cease for any length of time until Æthelred's reign, nearly thirty years later.

The story of Æthelwold continues as follows: 'Then this servant of God came to the place entrusted to him, and there immediately followed him certain secular clergy from Glastonbury: Osgar, Foldbircht and Frithegar; also Ordbircht from Winchester, and Eadric from London, who all put themselves under his discipline; and in a short time he assembled a company of monks, and by the king's command was made their abbot.' The importance of this step is not likely to be overestimated. Its influence appears as a beneficent one all through the subsequent history of the English until the Norman Conquest, and indirectly in later times. We of the present age owe a large part of our knowledge of late Old English history and culture to its preservation by instrumentalities set in motion by the new foundation of Abingdon. It was by the labors of monks, especially of those trained by Æthelwold or his pupils, in the monasteries founded in imitation of this one or influenced by it, that books were composed or translated, manuscripts copied, and the minutiae of secular and religious history recorded. These results of their work are the original documents which open up the details of the life of the tenth, eleventh and later centuries. The initial movement was, as we have seen, given by Dunstan at Glastonbury. His later activity in the founding of monasteries was, like his earlier work, designed to further

[1] *Life of St. Æthelwold,* in *Chronicon Monasterii de Abingdon,* II. 257.

education and religion, but not so much to emphasize the stricter Benedictine ideas. In this he was different from Æthelwold. Yet they worked together in entire harmony, and the work of each supplemented that of the other and made it more efficient.

The migration of Æthelwold to Abingdon, and the reopening of the old monastery was, we may be sure, a matter of concern to many. We have a hint of this in the different centers of interest represented by the men who followed to take part in the new undertaking: Glastonbury, London, and Winchester, as well as others, doubtless, of which we are not told. Queen Eadgifu contributed liberally of money. The king, the patron of the enterprise, gave his royal estate at Abingdon and its best buildings for the support of the new foundation. He helped too with money, and took a personal part in the arrangements for rebuilding. Coming to Abingdon he planned the construction of the new church, measured with his own hands the foundations, and decided how the walls should be built. He did not however live to see the new abbey, but Æthelwold built in a later reign. Eadred's death seems to have delayed the work, for in another writing [1] we are told that Edgar was the founder of the church. During the four years of Eadwig's reign, several grants of land were made by the king to Æthelwold for the abbey. Meanwhile, the abbot took pains to interest the young prince Edgar, and with such success that 'as soon as he was chosen to his kingdom (959) he was very mindful of his promise, which he made to God and to St. Mary, when as a young child in his princely estate the abbot invited him to the monastery.' 'He soon gave orders to have a glorious minster built there within the space of three years,' and 'commanded that same minster thus ornamented to be consecrated to St. Mary, to the praise and worship of God.' An interesting description of this round-apsed church and its parts is found

---

[1] *Leechdoms, Wortcunning,* etc. III. 430

in the history of the abbots of Abingdon. Æthelwold himself superintended its construction, built the organ, and made
the bells. Above the altar he placed a tablet adorned with
figures of the twelve apostles in pure gold and silver, at a
cost of three hundred pounds, and there were many other
beautiful and costly treasures.[1] Ælfric himself, who also
speaks of this in his life of Æthelwold, had evidently seen
with admiring eyes the completed building. The success of
the new work was now assured. In the chronicle of Abingdon there are recorded no less than fifteen royal grants of
valuable lands to the church and monastery during the years
of Æthelwold's administration, and in the few following
years, up to 975, there are seven more.

Although the abbot could not leave England himself, he
did not forget his earlier designs. It is more than probable
that the practical duties of his new office strengthened his
purpose to obtain a fuller knowledge of the rules of his
order, and of its administration in the better-organized abbeys on the Continent. Accordingly when the opportunity
came, he sent Osgar, one of his monks who had come with
him from Glastonbury, who was later his successor as abbot
of Abingdon, to the Benedictine house at Fleury, to study
the system of the order, and to fit himself to teach it to the
brethren at home. From this we must infer that the rule
observed at Glastonbury was not the fully developed system
of St. Benedict, but was derived probably from traditions of
the earlier English monasteries, perhaps with admixture of
Celtic tradition, since Dunstan's biographer says that he had
studied 'Irish books.'[2]

In 963, after about ten years at Abingdon, Æthelwold was
appointed by King Edgar, bishop of Winchester. In that
city the episcopal seat was in the church of the Old Monastery, of which the bishop always acted as abbot. It was in
the school of this monastery that Æthelwold had studied in

---

1 *Chronicon Monasterii de Abingdon* II. 277-8.
2 Cf. E. W. Robertson, *Historical Essays*, p. 190.

boyhood under Bishop Alphege. But now, when he returned
to his old home, he found the change from the atmosphere
of study and devotion in which he had been living quite in-
tolerable. Thus far there were no monks in England except
at Glastonbury and Abingdon,[1] and here at Winchester,
among the secular clergy connected with the cathedral, were
men who disgraced their office by vicious lives. Given up to
avarice, luxury, and drunkenness, their influence only
strengthened the evil in the world about them. They put
away their illegal wives and took others; they sometimes dis-
dained the services of the church, and refused to celebrate
mass in their turn. But they must have known well by
report the character of the new bishop and what his demands
might be, and with no willing mind have awaited his coming
among them. As for Æthelwold, he did not question what
he ought to do. With the king's assistance, he expelled those
of the disaffected clergy who would not take the monastic
vow, and filled their places with monks from Abingdon. We
do not know that he used persuasion or sought to appease
opposition, so that his action here appears somewhat harsh.

And now began for him a career of great activity. With
peace and good order restored to his own monastery and
cathedral establishment, he carried his reforms still farther:
in the words of his biographer: 'He expanded his wings, and
expelled the secular clergy from the New Monastery, ordained Æthelgar his disciple as abbot there, and placed
under him monks of the regular order (964).' This monastery and a convent of nuns adjoining had been founded by King Alfred. In the latter minster also, Æthelwold
established the Benedictine discipline. It is to his influence
too that we must ascribe the expulsion of the secular clergy
in the same year at Chertsey and at Milton, and the introduction of monks into their places.

---

[1] This does not mean that all of the old monasteries were uninhabited; in some of
them, as at Winchester, Ely and Worcester, the homes of the monks were taken by secular clergy, who perhaps considered themselves as filling the places of the monks.

Dunstan, who meanwhile (959) had become archbishop of Canterbury, co-operated with Æthelwold in the reforms in his diocese, and seconded his other efforts to introduce beneficial changes. As primate and chief advisor of the king, Dunstan was now able to balance the interests of church and state with a view to the welfare of both, and so long as Edgar lived no serious obstacle hindered him from carrying forward his policy.[1] Hereafter Æthelwold too appears, not simply as bishop but as a chosen counsellor of the king.[2]

At Winchester, the royal capital, the bishop occupied a position of great power in a time when church and state were very closely united; and a man of Æthelwold's character and force, bent on certain definite results to be attained, was sure to use all the influence that his position allowed him. It accords then with a reasonable expectation when we read in a contemporary writer that 'The king was instructed in the knowledge of the true King by Æthelwold, bishop of the city of Winchester, and that Æthelwold greatly incited the king, so that he sent the secular clergy away from the monasteries and brought in men of our order.'[3] In 963, when Æthelwold became bishop, Edgar was but twenty years old. We have reason to believe that the king was not the hypocrite that he has been called by his enemies. But it is also impossible to doubt that much of his enthusiasm for reform, and his personal activity in restoring the monasteries of England, was due to the careful instruction and earnest personal influence of Dunstan and Æthelwold.

The labors of the Bishop of Winchester soon extended beyond the limits of his diocese. He visited the almost de-

---

1 'If we read the accounts of the hagiologists, all is done by Dunstan, and we see nothing of Eadgar. If we trust to the scanty records of the Chronicle Dunstan is unheard of, and the glory of the reign is wholly due to Eadgar. The contemporary charters supply the explanation of the seeming inconsistency; they show so far as their evidence goes, that the work was one, but that its oneness was the result of a common and unbroken action of the primate and the king.' Green, *Conquest of England*, p. 306.

2 'Erat Athelwoldus a secretis regis Eadgari.' *Life of Æthelwold* by Ælfric, p. 262. 'Qui erat Confessor Domini Regis et secretorum conscius.' Wharton, *Anglia Sacra*, I. 603.

3 *Historians of the Church of York and its Archbishops*, I. 426-7. Rolls Series.

3

serted shrine of St. Ætheldred at Ely and found it still rich
in buildings and lands which now belonged to the royal ex-
chequer.   An arrangement was made with the king for the
possession of the abbey, and a large number of monks, with
Brithnoth, Æthelwold's pupil, as their abbot, was established
there under the Benedictine rule.' From the king and the
nobles he obtained Peterborough abbey (972), where he
found remaining only 'old walls and wild woods.' This he
founded anew under Aldulph, later archbishop of York.   At
about the same time the abbey of Thorney, not far from
Peterborough, was also re-established by Æthelwold.   From
these foundations of the two famous houses of Ely and Peterborough begins the second chapter in their history, which
continues unbroken until the present day.   Of the influence
of the first of these upon subsequent history, Conybeare says:
'The above-mentioned restoration of Ely is an event of the
first importance in the history of Cambridgeshire.   Cambridge itself would probably but for Ely have remained an
obscure provincial town instead of one of the great intellectual centres of the world.   For from Ely we shall see,
came almost certainly the earliest germs of our University
life.' ²   The prompt and vigorous action of the reformers at
this time is thus described by Ælfric: 'and so it came to pass
that partly by the advice and effort of Dunstan, and partly by
those of Æthelwold, monasteries were founded everywhere
among the English, with monks and nuns living according to
the rule under abbots and abbesses.   And Æthelwold went

---

1 Clericos quidem Monachilem habitum suscipere consentientes in Monasterium susce-
it, renuentes de Monasterio expulit. *Anglia Sacra*, I. 604.

2 *History of Cambridgeshire*, p. 71. From the same, p. 73, we take the following: ' The
revenues and jurisdiction of the Isle (of Ely) were now restored to the Church and the
ancient limits most accurately marked out afresh by Edgar, after consultation with the
leading men of the whole neighborhood.'   ' And the Isle, though for some civil purposes
regarded as a part of Cambridgeshire, has this day its own County Council, within these
same limits, and ecclesiastically is exempt from archdiaconal jurisdiction, being immediately under the Bishop as representing the Abbot of Ely.'

See the accounts of the foundations of Ely and Peterborough in the *Saxon Chronicle*
under the year 963.

about from monastery to monastery establishing their customs.'

With the work carried forward at Winchester, Ely, and elsewhere by Æthelwold and his friends, Oswald Bishop of Worcester was in full sympathy. The nephew of Odo, Archbishop of Canterbury, Oswald had distinguished himself in youth by studious tastes, had remained for a time in a monastery at Winchester either as prior or canon, living there a luxurious life among the secular clergy, and later had at his own request been sent by Odo to study at Fleury. There his earnest character and winning traits made him a general favorite; indeed, all through his life he possessed rare power to win the love of the men about him. The length of his stay at Fleury is uncertain, but probably lasted several years. The school of Fleury, later celebrated for its fine library, even at this time offered unusual advantages. Oswald entered into its life with ardent desires for the best training. There he made himself a master of the secular and religious studies of the age. There also he studied music and trained his beautiful voice to sing the services of the church. His love of justice and of noble living, which was to become a light in his own country, shone brightly in this foreign monastery. He returned to England just after Odo's death (959), made Dunstan's acquaintance, and in 961 was appointed Bishop of Worcester. In the monastery connected with Worcester Cathedral he found secular clergy who had been left there undisturbed by Dunstan, his predecessor. Neither here nor at York, of which he became archbishop in 972, did he replace the secular clergy with monks, nor did Dunstan, now Archbishop of Canterbury (959), make any such change there.[1]

---

1 ' He held the See of Canterbury for nearly twenty-seven years, and never introduced a Benedictine into the diocese. *Clerks* accompanied Æthelwold from Glastonbury when he revived the monastery of Abingdon; clerks welcomed the new archbishop to Canterbury and remained in unmolested possession of Christ Church until the time of Abp. Ælfric.' E. W. Robertson, *Historical Essays*, p. 194.

And now it happened in Worcester, just as in the early days of Glastonbury and Abingdon, that many of the secular clergy were eager for instruction. Germanus, a friend of Oswald's whom he had left at Fleury on the occasion of his second visit there (960 or 961), was soon summoned home to teach the brethren at Worcester. Before long their number was so large that Oswald provided a home for them at Westbury, a parish of his diocese, and there under the rule of Germanus they lived quietly for two or three years as a Benedictine house. But as interest increased, it was thought best to hold a council of 'all the authority of all Albion.' The king appears in the narrative as the chief actor in this assembly, but Oswald's part is suggested when it is said that the King 'acknowledged the fame of Saint Benedict through the narration of pious Bishop Oswald.' [1] Dunstan and Æthelwold were both present and took part in the deliberations. The council resulted in an order of the king's for the establishment of 'more than forty monasteries' and the charge of accomplishing this was committed to Æthelwold and Oswald. This was before the re-founding of Ely, for when Oswald asked for a suitable home for his monks, Ely was one of the places suggested by the king. The earliest life of Oswald, written between 995 and 1005, is by a monk of Ramsey, who shows how that place was at length decided upon as the site for the new abbey. This story, told with the interested zeal of one who had had a share in the benefits of the house, relates how Oswald met by chance Æthelwin, the son of the great ealdorman, Æthelstan, the 'half-king' of East Anglia. Æthelwin gladly offered Oswald a place for settlement, the offer was accepted, and with the greatest enthusiasm the new abbey was begun, necessary buildings were erected and the brethren from Westbury took possession, joined by others eager for the same religious and educational

---

[1] The king's interest is well shown in a charter of 969. Kemble, *Cod. Dip. A.-S.*, III. 40.

advantages. Able teachers were invited to the abbey-school, among them Abbo of Fleury, later abbot in that monastery, and already a thorough scholar. He came now to Ramsey and for two years gave instruction in Benedictine usages, to which he had been devoted from boyhood, and in the circle of studies usually taught in the cloister-schools. Ramsey was a favorite foundation of Oswald's,[1] but he was instrumental in starting at least seven others. A few years later his sphere was made very broad by his appointment to the archbishopric of York (972-992).

Thus in the last quarter of the tenth century, many opportunities for education were offered to the English. These were most numerous in the midland districts, where were Abingdon, Worcester, Ramsey, Ely, Thorney, Peterborough, and others only less well-known. Of the schools in the south, Glastonbury and Winchester were the most famous. 'At that time' says Wharton, 'almost none were held worthy to preside over monasteries or churches unless they had come from the schools of Dunstan, Æthelwold or Oswald,' and 'almost every one of the English bishops and abbots, from the beginning of Edgar's reign (959) till about 1000 A. D. were chosen from the three monasteries of Abingdon, Glastonbury, and Winchester.' Ælfric, who added to his name and title the words, 'alumnus of Winchester,' felt, no doubt, something of the same satisfaction in belonging to such a school, that a modern Englishman feels in his connection with one of the great English universities.

The later history of this movement is involved in the political history of the times. After Edgar's death at the early age of thirty-two, politics became confused, and the scanty records do far too little to unravel the tangled threads. The monkish historians relate much that is true but tell their story from a partisan standpoint. Fortunately the history

---

[1] 'Oswald stood in the place of abbot, and there was no Abbot of Ramsey as long as he lived.' Robertson, p. 182.

of the work of the three leaders can be determined with tolerable certainty. Oswald during the thirty years of his activity exerted a strong and elevating influence through Middle England, and in the North where civilizing and educating forces were most needed. Dunstan's work in founding monasteries has been by some writers under-rated, perhaps in part because he showed a conciliatory policy in his dealings with the secular clergy. But the new foundations owed to him much more than a passive consent. We read that in the work of reform 'the king constantly used the advice of Dunstan.' [1] Ælfric, his contemporary, speaks of him in reference to the same reforms as 'Dunstan the Resolute,' and adds: 'Dunstan and Æthelwold were chosen of God, and they most of all exhorted men to do God's will, and advanced everything good to the pleasure of God.' [2] The constructive hand of Æthelwold seems to have done more than anything else to organize and give efficiency to the labors of all three. As their personal influence waned, efforts were made to undo the results of their work. But such efforts met with only partial success because these men had left behind them pupils imbued with the love of order, of learning and of religion. It was these disciples who preserved through the long troublous period of internal dissension and foreign conquests, the continuous chain of English culture.

---

1 *Leechdoms, Wortcunning, etc.* III. 440.
2 *Lives of the Saints,* I. 470.

CHAPTER II.

ÆLFRIC AT WINCHESTER.

Among the students in the Old Monastery of Winchester, probably in the early seventies of the tenth century, was the youth Ælfric, afterwards the writer. His silence about Abingdon is sufficient proof that he was not one of the monks who came thence to Æthelwold in 964, and had he been at Winchester in the early years of Æthelwold's bishopric he would not have omitted from the life of his teacher the account of the building and dedication of the new church, the story which Wulfstan, an eyewitness, has supplied in his revision of Ælfric's biography. What we know about Ælfric seems to point to a younger man than the first monks of the Old Minster.

There is found in his writings no trace of his early home and parentage. It can hardly be doubted that he was a Wessex boy, and born not far from the middle of the century. The first date in his life that can be fixed with certainty is 987, when he was sent by Bishop Alphege to the newly-founded abbey of Cernel. At that time by his own account he was a priest, and as it is not probable that he would have been sent on such an errand if just ordained, it is reasonable to place the ordination yet earlier. If it were two years before, at the age of thirty, the inferior limit for entering the priesthood, he was born in 955, and this date or one within the few previous years is doubtless correct. The view which places his birth as early as this is confirmed by his repeated praises of the reign of Edgar as a most blessed time for the nation and the church, a time whose fortunate conditions he himself had experienced and appreciated. Thus he says in a homily, 'We can remember well how happy we were when this island dwelt in peace, and abbeys were held in honor, and the laity were prepared against their foes, so that our word spread far and wide over this land.'[1]

He seems to have belonged to a middle class of society. That he was not of high birth is inferred from the fact that he remained simply a priest until at least his fiftieth year. At that time the high offices of the church were almost exclusively filled by men of the upper class, and it can hardly be doubted that such a man as Ælfric would have been recognized by some promotion if his rank had corresponded to his ability and attainments. But, on the other hand, the absence of all servility toward those of high family or dignity, the independence of spirit joined with humility, that he maintained in intercourse with people of different ranks, lay and ecclesiastical, indicates that he was not of mean origin. He was not a child when he came to Winchester, and his social bearing was probably determined, as in most cases, by his earlier associations. So far as we know, none of those who have sought to indentify him with Ælfric of Canterbury, have found anything in his character inconsistent with the high birth ascribed to that archbishop.

He had already received some training in books before he entered the school at Winchester, for he speaks in his preface to Genesis of a certain half educated man who was his teacher. 'This teacher,' he says, 'a mass-priest, had the book of Genesis, and was able to understand some Latin, but he did not know the great difference between the Old Law and the New, nor did I at that time.' To the youth eager for knowledge, and with a deep sense of its practical value, the entrance to the Old Minster must have seemed the height of privilege. We can not fix the date of his arrival. He says only that he lived in Æthelwold's school 'many years,'[2] and as Æthelwold died in 984, it is not unlikely that he came there as early as 972, when he was about seventeen years old. Outwardly at Winchester there was much to attract the eye

---

1 Sermon *On the Prayer of Moses, Lives of Saints,* I., 294.
2 Preface to Extracts from Æthelwold's *De Consuetudine.* See ch. XIII.

in the days when he began his life there. The splendid new
church of Æthelwold was dedicated in 971, perhaps just before his arrival. The bishop himself had planned this building, and he and his monks had carefully watched its progress.
His biographer says: 'Æthelwold was a great builder, both
when he was abbot and after he became bishop.' This cathedral was consecrated with impressive ceremonies in the presence of the King and Archbishop Dunstan, and its consecra-
tion was made memorable by the removal of the bones of
Bishop Swithun—bishop of Winchester when King Alfred
was a boy—from a grave outside of the church to a new
tomb by the high altar. Many years after Ælfric wrote the
story of the removal of the saint's bones to the church, and
the miracles that followed. This very entertaining narrative,
derived in part from the life of Swithun by Landferth,[1] and
in part from the writer's personal knowledge, is full of details
that throw light upon the history of the monastery in the
days when Ælfric lived there. It shows the credulous spirit
of the age, and how fully Æthelwold shared this; it tells how
the secular canons who had been expelled shunned Æthelwold and the monks in the minster, and makes it clear that

---

[1] Who Landferth was, is uncertain. Ælfric in his story of St. Swithun gives a long
account of a miracle which, he says, was related to Bishop Æthelwold by the person to
whom it happened, and was set down in writing by 'Landferth the foreigner.' The
few years that followed the removal of Swithun's bones to the new church were not far
from the time Oswald sent for Abbo of Fleury to come to Ramsey and gathered, it is said
in his biography, teachers from various places. Landferth may have come to England at
about the same time from a Flemish monastery. Two fragments of a Latin history of
Swithun's miracles which are closely related to Ælfric's homily, are extant (*Acta S.* July
2. 292–299), but (see Ott's dissertation, p. 47 f.) neither of them can have been just the
form from which Ælfric translated the parts not original with him. Ælfric's words in the
preface of the *Saints' Lives* do not permit us to believe that he wrote the homily without
an original before him. Otherwise we should ask the question : may not these fragments ascribed to Landferth be Latin re-workings of Ælfric's homily, aided by sources
not now ascertainable ? According to his custom, Ælfric probably added something of his
own ; thus, as Ott suggests, ll. 443–463. Whatever is true as to the authorship, it is impossible to believe that Ælfric lived ' many years ' at Winchester in Æthelwold's school,
and did not know all about these stories ; and did not sing with the brethren, as the author
of this homily says that he often did; and did not see the Old Minster hung round with
the crutches and stools of the many who had been healed. Therefore it seems to us
justifiable to use as his own the words of the homily which we have quoted in this
chapter.

the reforming party in the church was gaining the upper hand.

During the early years of Ælfric's life at Winchester, when Edgar was king,[1] many reports, no doubt, came to the monks and the young students of the king's kindness to the monasteries, and well they remembered it all in the dark days that followed, for never while they lived did such prosperity come again to England. In after years, recalling his life at St. Swithun's, Ælfric writes: 'That time was blessed and happy in England when King Edgar furthered Christianity and built many monasteries, and his kingdom dwelt in peace so that we heard of no warlike fleet except that of our own people who held this land. Then moreover such wonders were wrought through St. Swithun as we have already spoken of, and as long as we lived there (?) miracles often happened.'[2]

In coming to Winchester, Ælfric entered no newly-founded school and church. For more than three hundred years the site of Æthelwold's cathedral had been devoted to the service of God. Ælfric, whose writings show a strong historic sense of proportion, and a reverence for the good received from the past, could not have been indifferent to the associations connected with this ' "Sanctuary of the house of Cerdic," and minster of the West Saxons.' A hundred years after Æthelwold's death, the Normans rebuilt his church upon a site close at hand, transferring St. Swithun's bones to the new choir. To-day as we stand in the choir of Winchester cathedral, it is not difficult to carry the thought back nine hundred years to the days when Ælfric sang there hymns to God in praise of great St. Swithun. Does it not say on the chest just before us, raised upon the choir-screen, 'in this tomb rests pious King Eadred, who nobly governed this land of Briton, and died A. D. 955'? and on the next chest, 'King Edmund, died A. D. 946'? Ælfric saw their tombs, then in the crypt, for Eadred was the king who sent Æthelwold to Abing-

---

[1] The quotation from the sermon *On the Prayer of Moses*, implies that he was in the monastery during Edgar's reign; See p. 36.

[2] And swa lange swa we leofodon þær wurdon gelome wundra. *Lives of Saints*, I, 468.

don, and died about the time of Ælfric's birth, and Edmund
was the father of King Edgar. St. Swithun's bones rested
in peace until scattered in the sixteenth century. But in
Edgar's time, and for long after, they were the great attrac-
tion of the church. Ælfric tells us that by the virtue of this
saint so many were healed that 'the burial-ground lay filled
with crippled folk, so that people could hardly get into the
minster;' and that 'the Old Minster was hung all round with
crutches, and the stools of cripples who had been healed
there, from one end of the church to the other on both walls,
and yet they could not put up half of them.'

In this minster Ælfric found a well-established school
taught by Benedictines, and closely connected with the important cathedral. This was no time of decline and abuse of
monastic customs. A strong hand and exact discipline ruled
the daily life of every person who dwelt in this establishment.
Every hour of the day was provided with its special duty.
Æthelwold had taken care that his monks should know the
Rule, and for those who could read Latin the manuscripts
containing the laws which regulated their life were at hand.
It was to serve the needs of those who could read only English that, probably about the time of Ælfric's coming, say
972-975, the Bishop translated the Rule.[1] In this orderly,
busy life Ælfric performed the duties of the lower orders of
the clergy, took part in the menial services, and learned his
daily tasks in the studies prescribed. The acquisition of
book-learning was of the greatest consequence in a Benedictine house. There are many proofs of it in regard to this
one. Here at Winchester much inspiration came from the
Bishop himself, and though his state and ecclesiastical duties
called him, perhaps daily, to the king's side at Wolvesey
Palace, and often to other parts of England, his influence did

---

[1] ' This English translation is a necessity for unlearned secular men, who for fear of
nell penalty and for love of Christ, quit this miserable life and turn unto their Lord, and
choose the holy service of this Rule.' From tract appended to Æthelwold's translation.
See pp. 160–1.

not fail to be felt in the school. He must occasionally have shared the duties of teaching, for Ælfric writes: 'It was always sweet to him to teach children and youth, both by explaining books to them in English, and by exhorting them with pleasant words to better things. It is for this reason that it has happened that very many of his disciples have become abbots and bishops among the English.' Thus Æthelwold's pupils were allured by sweet words and winning ways, and Ælfric gained much incentive from association with such a teacher and such disciples.

A literary atmosphere belonged by tradition and in fact to the Old Minster. In the scriptorium which had been founded by Swithun in Æthelwulf's reign, writing, translating and the illumination of books, flourished under Æthelwold. Here, not long before Ælfric came, Godemann, one of the monks, made a beautiful illuminated Benedictional for the bishop's use.[1] Here too was prepared a little before Æthelwold's death, the 'Tropary of Ethelred,' a MS. compiled for use with Æthelwold's new organ, which 'gives, in the musical notation of the period, the actual cadences and tones used in the services of St. Swithun's in the tenth century.' Ælfric in his schooldays, and in the time of his novitiate, was accustomed to watch the progress of such work as done by others, and since in the abbeys there was always a place assigned for the younger members, he was doubtless learning here to work on manuscripts, perhaps to illuminate them, certainly to write them in Latin and in English.

The ideal of the Benedictine monastery was that of a home, and its Rule provided for the strong and the weak, the educated and the ignorant. It was intended that under this Rule men should grow more manly and self-controlled, and more efficient in God's work in the world; and so they did

---

[1] 'This gorgeously illuminated MS. is a folio volume of vellum $11\frac{1}{2}$ in. by $8\frac{1}{2}$ in. containing 119 leaves. It contains thirty illuminations, and thirteen other pages surrounded with profusely ornamented borders. It is written in a clear Roman hand, the capitals being in gold, alternate lines in gold, red and black sometimes occurring on the same page.' This is now the property of the Duke of Devonshire. It is reproduced in *Archæologia*, XXIV.

when it was rightly administered. Unlike some forms of monachism, it sought to regulate more than to repress. St. Benedict recognized human nature in the foundation of the system. One cannot read Ælfric's *Colloquium,* which he wrote afterwards for boys who were living in a monastery just as he did at Winchester, without seeing that the cloister-youths lived a happy life, much the same as in any well-regulated school. If the requirements seem to us at first strict and severe, a little consideration somewhat modifies that view. That Ælfric could write such a dialogue shows that he had sympathy with the spirit of play natural to boyhood, and that the play-spirit was not altogether banished from the monastery. Plenty of it we know there was, for every cathedral has expressed it in the grotesque carvings of gargoyle or choir-stall, and such can not have been its only form of expression. The *Colloquium* has this interest for us at this point, that it has something to tell of Ælfric's own life at Winchester, for can we doubt that when he describes the way a boy spends his day in the monastery, he is recording one of his own days? It is a very simple narrative written for a different purpose, and leaving the gaps for us to fill in from other sources. This cloister-boy is asked how he has spent the day. From his replies are gathered these details of its author's life. He slept, he says, in the dormitory with the brethren, and at the sound of the bell arose and went with them to sing matins in the church. The drowsy boy would sometimes miss the signal that called him up thus at three o'clock in the morning, and so in the dialogue he answers just as might be expected, 'Sometimes I hear the bell and arise, and sometimes the master awakens me sharply with the rod.' At six o'clock he went to church to sing the service of prime, with its seven psalms and the litany and early mass. About nine he sang again the service of mass, and yet again at mid-day. After that came their first meal, and it is hardly to be wondered at that the boy says, 'I eat with great thankfulness vegetables, eggs, fish, cheese, butter, beans and all clean things.' But he adds that he does not have all these things at one meal. As to drink, he has ale if there is any, if not, water, but wine he says he is not rich enough to buy, and besides, 'wine is not the drink for boys, but for their elders.' According to their custom a reader was appointed each week to edify the monks while they were at their meals, and the readers were appointed according to their ability as such. Good sense marks the details of the Benedictine life. So of the reader of the week the Rule says, 'Let him not take the book suddenly and begin to read there without any consideration.' Some preparation for the task was required. The Rule says further, 'If they who are eating or drinking have need of anything, let them ask for it by a sign and not speak with the voice.' [1] After this midday meal, there was a chance for a nap, though not for a very long one. One might read if he would, but no one must make any noise to disturb the others who wished to sleep. At two they sang the service of none, and after that came a lesson hour, with study or recitation or instruction by the master. At four o'clock was the vesper service, and at seven the last of the canonical services of the day. In Ælfric's dialogue, from which we have been quoting, the master asks the boy: 'Have you been punished to-day? and the boy answers, 'No, for I have been very careful;' and then comes the question: 'And how about your comrades?' to which the reply is, 'Why do you ask me about that? I do not dare to tell you our secrets. Each one knows whether or not he has been whipped.' Such an answer betrays no servile fear of his superior who asks the question. Yet it is plain that these youths had to walk warily, and to be strictly obedient. When the service bell rang there could be no lingering, but every one must drop whatever he had in hand and hasten to service, but hasten with circumspection, and not heedlessly, nor might he run and get out of breath, and if he were a little late he was not allowed to stand in his own

---

See the Old English *Bened. Rule*; Grein, *Bibliothek der A. S. Prosa*, Part II., p. 62.

place in the choir, but 'last of all, or in that place apart which
the abbot has appointed for such careless ones.' [1]   It was
when Ælfric was at Winchester that St. Swithun's miracles
laid extra duties on the monks, for Æthelwold had commanded 'that as often as any sick one should be healed, the
monks should go in procession to the church and sing the
praises of the great saint.' This they did 'and sang the Te
Deum sometimes three, sometimes four times in one night,
and they began to be very reluctant to rise so often when
they needed to sleep. At last they gave up the singing, for
the bishop was all the time occupied with the king, and did
not know that they were not singing the song of praise as
before.' Then, the story says, the saint appeared in vision
to a good man, and announced that if the monks ceased their
praises the miracles would also cease. The dream was reported to Æthelwold, who 'immediately sent to the monks
from the king's court, and bade that they should sing the
Te Deum, and he that neglected it should atone for it by
seven days fast.' 'Then always after that,' continues Ælfric,
'they observed the custom, as we ourselves have seen very
often, and we have not seldom sung the hymn with them.'

The period that followed the death of King Edgar (975)
was a time of great anxiety for Bishop Æthelwold and his
friends; with the removal of the king came a disputed succession and a period of interregnum. Ælfhere the powerful
ealdorman of Mercia, who advocated the claim of Edward the
elder son of Edgar, headed a party which sought to overthrow
the monks. Florence of Worcester says that 'blinded by
presents of value, Ælfhere and many other nobles, expelled
the monks from the monasteries, and introduced clerks and
their wives.' This was in Ælfhere's territory. But, besides
this, he threatened to do the same in the diocese of Dorchester. On the other hand Æthelwin of East Anglia, the friend
and patron of Oswald at Ramsey, who put forward claims for

---

[1] *Bibliothek der A. S. Prosa*, II., 67-8.

Æthelred the younger prince, was the head of a monastic
party. He, with Brithnoth the ealdorman of Essex, afterwards the brave leader of Maldon, took arms 'and declared that
they would not permit the monks who possessed all the religion of the kingdom to be driven out of it.' [1] Dunstan and
Oswald, the two archbishops, stood by Ælfhere in behalf of
Edward, which shows how completely the question was a political one in its motives, for there can be no question that
these two were friendly to the monasteries. But there was a
strong faction in England in favor of clerical marriage, and
this party, many of whom hated the moral life advocated by
the reformers, was ready to use any opportunity to bring back
the old condition of things. When we remember that that condition was the one which had had sway for a hundred years or
more, the strength of the opposition is not to be wondered
at, and we see why Ælfric, who believed that it was contrary
to Christ's teaching for priests to marry, was forced to say in
his pastoral letter for secular clergy, 'We can not compel you,
but we exhort you to chastity.' Robertson says upon this
subject: 'The Anglian population of the diocese probably
looked upon the monks as "new men;" for the secular canons
were at this period members of the leading provincial fam-
lies, and it had long been customary to fill the sees and min-
sters with bishops and abbots who, in return, leased out the
church lands among their kindred. To support the secular
canons therefore, was to uphold "the time-honored customs
of the past," and in his inroads upon the monks Ælfhere
may have been moved less by any inveterate hostility to the
Benedictine rule, than by a desire to re-establish the old
provincial families of Anglian origin.' Yet whatever of
right the secular clergy had on their side in this struggle,
whether derived from the customs of the past, or from the in-
herent reasonableness of their position in regard to marriage,
its weight as an argument was counteracted by their general

---

1 Florence of Wor., *Chron.* p. 106. Bohn ed. Freeman's *Norman Conquest*, I, 177-9.

disregard for religion and education, and by the shocking coarseness and immorality of their lives. It is probably this determined struggle on the part of professedly Christian men to maintain the existing conditions, instead of trying to reform them, which leads one writer to say that 'the tenth century is perhaps the most repulsive in Christian annals.' [1] The moral earnestness, so far as the records tell us, was all on the side of the reformers who favored monasticism. In this attempt to overthrow the monks, which was partially successful, Æthelwold and his disciples at Winchester must have taken the keenest interest. We can reasonably trace the strength of Ælfric's repeated insistence upon the celibacy of the priests to his life under Æthelwold in those years when party strife outside the monastery was waged upon that question, and when it must have seemed to the bishop and the monks that all the good to which they were devoting their lives was in danger of being destroyed.

Relieved from duties of the state by King Edgar's death, Æthelwold devoted the later years of his life to the interests of his diocese and his abbey. For several years before his death the Danes were plundering and burning along the coasts, coming in 981 as near Winchester as Southampton, where they slew or took prisoners most of the inhabitants. Worn-out by long ill-health, which for years he had borne with fortitude and cheerfulness, he died in 984. His office was given to Alphege, a man chosen by Dunstan in opposition to the clerical party, which attempted to regain control of the cathedral. Alphege had proved his devotion to the cause of the monasteries by a life of self-denial at the abbey of Deerhurst, and later at Bath. His courageous defense of the interests of England and of the church, and his martyr death for their sakes, show his fitness to succeed the resolute monk and bishop, Æthelwold.

---

1 H. C. Lea, *Hist. of Sacerdotal Celibacy*, p. 147.

4

Of Ælfric during these years we know nothing directly,[1] but when it appears that at the request of Æthelmær, a powerful thane of Dorset, Alphege selects Ælfric for a mission to that new abbey, perhaps to organize its life and to establish the Rule there, no doubt can be felt that he had already at Winchester proved his efficiency as a teacher, and his understanding of the methods and aims of the Benedictine life.

---

[1] Dietrich suggests that Ælfric was a dean at Winchester. He draws the idea from a letter in *Cod. Dip. A.-S.* IV, 261. We are not warranted in accepting it unless we can show that Ælfric was an older man than he appears to have been. See Dietrich, pp. 245-6.

CHAPTER III.

AT THE ABBEY OF CERNEL.

An old tradition of Cernel[1] in Dorset relates that Augustine, the first missionary to the English (597-604), converted the people of that neighborhood, gave the place its name, and when it was time to baptize the converts caused the needed water to spring forth from the rock at the very place where the well is pointed out, even at the present day (1898). This story, which is told by William of Malmesbury, is doubtful in all of its details, and Augustine probably never visited that region. A later tradition makes Cernel and St. Augustine's well the scene of the hermitage of Eadwold, brother of Edmund, the king of the East Anglians who was murdered by the Danes (870). This tradition, though somewhat obscure, has perhaps a basis of fact. The third important event connected with this place, the founding of the abbey of Cernel, is well authenticated by the foundation charter of King Æthelred, which is still preserved.[2] This abbey, said to have been begun in Edgar's reign (959-975), and as a memorial of the pious Eadwold, was finished in 987, and dedicated by its founder, Æthelmær, to St. Mary, St. Peter, and St. Benedict.

This Æthelmær, and his father, Æthelweard, are so closely connected with the life of Ælfric that it is worth while to say something here of their character and position in the England of that day. Æthelweard the ealdorman, there is no good reason to doubt, is that ealdorman whose name appears as such in many lists of witnesses attesting charters from 975 to 998.[3]

1 Now Cerne Abbas, five miles north of Dorchester.

2 Dugdale, *Monasticon*. II. 621; Kemble, *Cod. Dip. A.-S.* III. 224.

3 Ælfric's friend Æthelweard was ealdorman in 990 or 991, when the first volume of Catholic Homilies was issued; according to the signatures of charters given by Kemble, but one man of that name was 'dux' from 975-998; hence the identification. This is also emphasized by the fact that Æthelweard signs himself 'Occidentalium Provinciarum dux' (*Cod. Dip. A.-S.* III. 304), showing that he was ealdorman of the province in which were situated Cernel Abbey and several ancestral estates of Ælfric's friend, Æthelmær.

The office of ealdorman dated from an early time in West Saxon history, and in the tenth century it had become of exceptional influence and importance. The man who held it was the king's representative in the district over which he presided, and in case of war he led the king's forces as *'heretoga'* (in the charters he signs as *'dux'*). At the time of which we speak, all of the different ealdormanries were held by kinsmen of the king, by whose influence, as centralization was far from complete, he strengthened his power in the different provinces of his kingdom. When the king was a man of wisdom and ability he controlled the ealdormen, but if he was weak or foolish their power worked for disunion and against the national cause. We have seen how, upon the death of Edgar, the great ealdormen worked against each other, seeking partisan ends.[1]

The district in which Æthelweard was ealdorman included probably Devon, Somerset and Dorset; and the lands in Dorset which Æthelmær gave to Cernel Abbey were a part of the heritage of his family, whose estates lay in that region.[2] Æthelweard is known as the author of a Latin chronicle of Saxon history, which ends with the death of King Edgar. It is written in a pompous style and in very faulty Latin,[3]

---

1 For discussion of the position and power of the ealdorman, see Freeman, *Nor. Conq.* 51-53, 79, 392-394, 420-423; Green, *Conq. of Eng.* Ch. VII.; Robertson, *Hist. Essays, The King's Kin;* Bosworth-Toller, *A.-S. Dic.* p. 229. For map of England under the ealdormen, see Green, *Conq. of Eng.* p. 302.

2 Of the lands given by Æthelmær to the abbeys of Cernel and Eynsham, Dietrich writes as follows: 'I have not spared pains to establish the identity of the places according to their shires, and the labor has been almost entirely successful. Æthelmær's earliest home and his paternal estates at Cernel and Chesselborne were in Dorset. He gave the income of over thirty hides of land there to Cernel Abbey. His whole estate amounted to far above ninety hides.' 'Twelve hides assured the dignity of a great thane.' 'The lands with which he endowed the monastery of Eynsham lay for the most part in Warwickshire.'

3 This identification of the author of the Chronicle is so nearly certain that it is here stated as a fact. Æthelweard the author of the Chronicle was a descendant of King Alfred's brother Æthelred. He calls himself 'Patricius Consul.' 'The title Patricius seems to have been given in the eight century to the leading official in the Northumbrian kingdom, ranking next to the sovereign, and it may have been applied at the period when Æthelweard wrote to the senior ealdorman,' which the Æthelweard of the charters was from 993 till his death, since his signature precedes those of all other ealdormen. (See Robertson's essay, *The King's Kin;* Green, *Conq. of Eng.* p. 49).

and tells little that is not known by other means. But in an age when noblemen left learning to the clergy, such a work testifies to a taste for books, and this agrees well with what we know of Æthelweard in connection with Ælfric.

There are traditions which ascribe the founding of Cernel Abbey to Æthelweard. These, though false by the letter of the foundation charter, have this basis in fact, that Æthelmær had received from his father estates with which he endowed the abbey, and that the father was in accord with the son in this enterprise.[1] Probably this was not the first undertaking of the kind on Æthelweard's part. The restoration of Pershore Abbey in Worcestershire by his means is noted by William of Malmesbury. This points back to the great assembly held by Oswald, probably at Winchester, when King Edgar decreed the establishment of many new monasteries.[2] Æthelweard, not yet an ealdorman, was perhaps present and received at that time the strong impulse which led to the two foundations of Pershore and Cernel.[3]

Æthelmær, the son, is mentioned as Earl of Cornwall and Devon, and by the *Saxon Chronicle* as Æthelmær the Great. In some way he was nearly related to the ealdorman Brithnoth of Essex. Cockayne speaks of Æthelweard as the son-in-law of Brithnoth.[4] Evidences of the connection will be mentioned later.

1 In the foundation charter of Cernel, Æthelmær says: ' Tribui illum locum qui vulgo Cernel nuncupatur, cum possessionibus quas ego ei subjugo cuncticreanti deo ad almi onomatis ejus laudem, et ad honorem Sanctae Marie . . . . , ac sancti Petri . . . . , necnon et sancti Benedicti, pro meo carissimo hero basileo Æðelredo, et pro memetipso, necnon et pro dilecta mihi animula mei genitoris, et redemptione meorum praecedentium patrum, qui propria colla sponte fidei christianae subdiderunt suarum possessionum me haeredem haud ingratum relinquentes.' From the words used here in reference to his father, Mores and some others have inferred that Æthelweard was dead. The word ' animula ' was used as a term of affection or contempt, here with dilecta as the former. Had the father been dead Æthelmær would doubtless have used the term ' redemptione ' in respect to him, as well as in respect to his other ancestors. The Æthelweard who was 'dux' or ealdorman of just that part of England; who was constantly associated with Æthelmær in Ælfric's writings; who describes himself as a descendant of King Æthelwulf; cannot be other than the father of Æthelmær. For the genealogy of this family, see Robertson, *Hist. Essays*, p. 190.

2 See p 32.

3 An Æthelweard, a thane, is a witness of charters at about that time.

4 *Leechdoms, Wortcunning,* etc. III, p. XXIII.

After years of preparation and delay the new monastery was ready for use, and in the year of its dedication, we may believe, Ælfric went thither from Winchester. It has sometimes been said that he was the first abbot of Cernel.[1] This cannot be true, for there are many years after this before he speaks of himself as abbot. The idea is based only upon his statement that he was sent there at Æthelmær's request. It is worthy of notice that the first impulse to his great work of teaching the English laity came to him when he was sent on a special mission of instruction to Benedictine monks. Up to this time, responsible to the bishop and the prior of his abbey, he had lived a student life, teaching in the Old Minster the boys who in their turn were to be monastic or secular clergy. Now, since his aptitude as a teacher, and his breadth of attainment according to the standard of his time, had been well proved, he was sent forth by the bishop, and came into a relation of responsibility with two laymen, the patrons of the abbey, and his position there, there is good reason to believe, was still that of a teacher. Just as Abbo of Fleury was summoned by Oswald to Ramsey to teach, so Ælfric was summoned to Cernel. And now, in these new surroundings, all that he had gained by many years of study assumed a new value in his eyes; he thought of the uses to which it could be put, and he longed to share it with his people. They could not read the Latin books that he read, but it was possible for him to translate them into English. Conscious of his own limitations, and well aware that some were better educated than he, he yet knew of no one who was ready to undertake the task. 'The people,' he said, 'have no books that teach in their own language the truth of God, save those that King Alfred translated. There are indeed many English books that teach error, and the unlearned in their simplicity esteem them great wisdom.' What were the many heretical books to which he referred? It has been suggested that they were the Old English poets, such writings

---

[1] Thus, Dugdale, Monasticon, II. 622.

as those of Cynewulf.[1] Did Ælfric know these poems? We
find no certain proof of it, although he knew metrical writings in English. He would not have called the poems ascribed to Cædmon heresy, nor the Judith, and probably not
those of Cynewulf. He might have disapproved of secular
poems as foolish or trivial, but scarcely as heretical. That
age was not one of fine doctrinal distinctions, nor noted for
theological controversy. The false doctrines probably had to
do with matters of practice. Why should not the common
custom of clerical marriage have called forth writings in its
defense?[2] Ælfric was accustomed to hear arguments in its
favor, for he often quotes them and tries to refute them.
It is not likely that the books of which he speaks, survive to
the present day. The literature of that time has been chiefly
preserved by transcription of the monks, who had no interest
in writing anything contrary to their own teachings, and who
did not think of saving the doctrines of their opponents in
order to furnish historical data for generations to come.

But whatever heresy Ælfric wished to oppose, his object
was not controversial. He saw before him manuscript-writ-
ings esteemed by all the Christian Church, and yet inaccessi-
ble to those who needed them most. Writing of this many
years after, he looked back to the moment in which he first
thought of making his translation as one in which he received
the suggestion of God. He accepted it as such, and in the
intervals of his daily duties began the new task, the preparation of a volume of English sermons from the Latin church-
fathers. Doubtless he consulted his abbot or prior; it appears that Æthelweord and Æthelmær also knew of the
translation, for when the forty homilies were placed together

---

1 By Dietrich. 'What can the misleading books have been for which the unlearned,
the worldlings, cared so much, if not poetry? The abbey of Cernel was under the bishop
of Sherborne, and near Crediton. From this region may have come the precious manuscripts of Old English poems (the *Exeter Codex*) which soon after Leofric, Bishop of Crediton from 1046, afterwards of Exeter and Cornwall, bequeathed to his cathedral of
Exeter.'

2 The words of his preface to Genesis imply that there were some who held that the
Bible taught that a man might have more than one wife. Such belief can hardly have
been common. See Pref. to Gen. p. 22: 'Hwilon . . . . þære niwan.'

in a volume, Æthelweard asked that he might have forty-four in the copy which he had ordered for his own use. As laymen, unhampered by the prejudices of the clergy, these men would take a special interest in the work of translation into English. As kindred of King Alfred, they would be following the traditions of their family when they encouraged it. [1]

Whether Ælfric was acquainted with these noblemen before he came to Cernel is not known. Unquestionably he knew them well by report. In the preface to his first volume of homilies he speaks of Æthelmær as 'the thane whose birth and goodness are known everywhere.' As Æthelweard's official duties had called him often to the king's court, he had certainly been acquainted with Æthelwold, and he had been for many years interested in the good that the monks were doing: all this affords strong presumption that Ælfric had already made his acquaintance in the Old Minster. However this may be, Æthelweard had now recognized Ælfric's ability, and so long as he lived stood always ready to urge him to new undertakings.

It accords with Ælfric's respect for authority that he should desire for his completed volume the amendment or approval of the Archbishop of Canterbury. Sigeric, to whom it was dedicated, assumed that office in 990. We may conclude that the translation was finished by that year or the next, for before Sigeric's death, in October, 994, Ælfric was to complete yet another volume, and to dedicate that also to the archbishop.

The questions must be considered, did Ælfric go back to Winchester? or go elsewhere? or remain at Cernel? The first positive statement as to his place of abode after this comes many years later, when he writes as abbot. We are thus left to conjecture, but not without many indications that enable us to decide what is the probable truth. The probability, so strong as to amount almost to certainty, is that he

---

[1] Ælfric was not the only translator whom Æthelweard incited to such work. See Ælfric's preface to Genesis, *Bibl. A.-S. Prosa*, I. 22.

remained at Cernel. So long as Æthelweard lived, that is, till near the close of the century, Ælfric was in close relations with him, writing for him and for Æthelmær even when his own desires would deter him from it. This agrees with the service of a monk, who, while in a sense independent of laymen, was yet bound by ties of friendship and of obligation to the patrons of the abbey where he lived. Again, we find him some ten years later (probably about 998) commissioned by the bishop of the diocese in which Cernel lies, to write for him a pastoral letter to his clergy. Still further, we shall see that when next we can positively fix upon the place of his abode, he is living in another monastery in another part of England, but this time also in a monastery founded by Æthelmær. Thus there is good reason to believe that he continued quietly teaching and writing at Cernel until another foundation of Æthelmær's called him to follow his friend to that place. The tone in which he writes his life of Æthelwold is a very strong argument against his return to Winchester for anything more than brief visits. Nor does there appear any reason to think that he went elsewhere. The negative argument speaks against it, and it is not to be lost sight of that it was the needs of the Dorset people which first deeply moved him to undertake the work of a translator. Those needs must still have called forth his interest and sympathy; his patrons certainly desired his presence and his services, and their wealth would provide for the library such books as he needed for his literary work. This quiet life in an obscure abbey during the period of his greatest literary activity, and in another abbey equally obscure during his declining years, explains, in part, at least, the mystery which has hidden his identity down to the present day.

We see then our monk living, as at Winchester, according to the Rule of St. Benedict, teaching young boys the elementary studies of a monastic school, instructing the monks in those more advanced, preaching sometimes in the parish church that belonged to the estates of Æthelmær, and full of

interest in the people, and in his work as teacher and translator.

The first volume of homilies was completed and forwarded
to the Archbishop. Its teachings must have pleased Sigeric,
for he praised the work, and Ælfric promised to write a
second. It may have been at this time, between the two volumes of homilies, that he translated the *De Temporibus* from
Bede's scientific writings.[1] The years 991 to 994, the period
in which the second volume of homilies was translated, were
full of distress to the English people. In the first year (991),
Brithnoth the ealdorman was slain at Maldon, and by counsel
of Archbishop Sigeric, and of the ealdormen, Æthelweard and
Ælfric, the first Danegelt of ten thousand pounds bought off
the invaders.[2] The next year (992) died Oswald the archbishop, and Æthelwin of East Anglia. Ælfric the ealdorman of Mercia, the son of Ælfhere, proved a traitor and tried
to thwart the attempts of the English to overcome the Danes
by battle. In 993, great evil was done to the northeast of
England; Bamborough was captured and plundered. 'Then
when a great army was gathered together against the enemy,
the English leaders set the example of flight.' In 994 the
kings of Norway and Denmark besieged London, and when
turned aside by the citizens, 'they went thence,' the Chronicle
says, 'and wrought the utmost evil that ever any army could
do, by burning and plundering, and slaying of the people,
both along the sea-coast and among the East Saxons, and in
Kent, and in Sussex, and in Hampshire. And at last they
took to themselves horses, and rode as far as they would, and
continued doing unspeakable evil. Then the king and his
council decreed that tribute and food should be given them
if they would cease from their plunderings.' 'And all the
(Danish) army came to Southampton and took up winter-

---

[1] He speaks of the *Saints' Lives* as his fourth work. We should expect him to call it
the fifth if the *De Temporibus* were already translated. Possibly at that time he retained
that in the monastery for the use of his monks, and did not consider it as one of his published books.

[2] Florence of Worcester, *Chronicle*, and the *Saxon Chronicle*, 992.

quarters; and there they were victualled from all the realm of the West Saxons, and were paid sixteen thousand pounds of money. And the king sent Bishop Alphege and Æthelweard the ealdorman, to Olave (the Norwegian king) and they brought Olave to the king at Andover,' 'and he made a covenant with the king that he would never again come as an enemy against the English nation.'

These were the circumstances of anxiety under which Ælfric translated the second volume of the *Catholic Homilies,* and in the preface he says to the archbishop: 'With sorrowful mind, distressed by the many evils received from wicked pirates, we have, lest we should be found a false promiser, completed this book' The date of this volume can not be placed later than 994, because of its dedication to Sigeric, nor would the labor necessary for its completion allow the date to be fixed much earlier. The reference just quoted from Ælfric makes it almost certain that it was finished in that terrible year, whose horrors are sufficiently indicated by the words of the *Saxon Chronicle* given above.

Ælfric, like his contemporaries, believed that the end of the world was near at hand But instead of making this an excuse for inaction, he found in it an incentive to labor. Speaking of his first translation, he wrote: 'I undertook this task because men have need of good instruction, especially at this time, which is the ending of this world.' 'There will be many calamities among mankind before the end cometh.' 'Everyone may more easily withstand the future temptation, through God's help, if he is strengthened by book-learning.'

His next work was of a different character, and reminds us that Ælfric was a teacher of children as well as of older people. He was probably not the first, as he is certainly not the last, of the teachers whom practical experience has induced to make a text-book; but, so far as we know, his *Grammar* is the first of book of this kind in English. The prefaces tell us that the book is designed for children, and give the

author's reasons for writing it. He is aware that his book will
be looked upon as a foolish innovation. Men have learned
Latin for hundreds of years without any such book, and why
not now as well? But Ælfric's practical experience as a student and as a teacher taught him the wisdom of adapting
his work to the child's mind; he would answer his objectors,
but he would not be guided by them. 'Whence,' he says, 'are
to come wise teachers among God's people, unless they learn
in youth?' My book is for young children, not for grown
people; I have written in simple language so as not to discourage them. Let any one think as he pleases of my translation, I am satisfied to put in practice the things which I
learned in the school of Æthelwold my teacher, who instilled
good into many minds.[1] The date of this work is about 995,
for according to his English preface it followed the second
volume of the *Catholic Homilies.*

It would be a satisfaction if we could know who were some
of Ælfric's pupils in this school at Cernel. It was his interest in their progress that led him to write his *Grammar,* and
what he says in his prefaces leads us to think that there were
boys of noble promise in that school. There is one whom
we may without very rash conjecture believe to have been
among Ælfric's pupils at this time. Æthelnoth, the son of
Æthelmær, many years later than this was a monk, a dean of
Christ Church at Canterbury, and in 1020 Archbishop of
Canterbury. Thirty years earlier than 1020 he may have
been at Cernel in his father's monastery, near his father's
home. A glimpse into his character is afforded by the *Saxon
Chronicle* of 1038, which records: 'This year died Æthelnoth,
the good archbishop, and Bishop Æthelric in Sussex, who desired of God that he would not let him live long after his beloved father, Æthelnoth; and accordingly, within seven days,
he departed.'

After 998 the name of Æthelweard no longer appears in

---

1 Compare with this what Ælfric says of Æthelwold as a teacher, p. 40.

the charters.[1] The inference is that he had died. As
Ælfric translated two books for the ealdorman after writing
the *Grammar*, their dates must fall between 995 and 998.
Of these, the *Lives of the Saints*, written at the earnest request of Æthelweard and Æthelmær, was the first, for he says
in its Latin preface, that it is the fourth of such translations.
That it was at least as late as 996 is shown by his mention of
Æthelwold as saint,[2] for his name was not placed in the
church calendar until that year. The *Lives of the Saints* is
a long work, filling two hundred and thirty-six folio-pages in
the manuscript, therefore it is reasonable to place the date as
late as 997. Between this time and Æthelweard's death he
translated the Genesis. Both of these works he undertook
with much reluctance, not for lack of interest, but fearful lest
he should weary his readers. It is plain that the judgment
of laymen prevailed over the prejudices of the Roman ecclesiastic, and that the modest reluctance of the author was overcome by many assurances of appreciation, and of desire for
the continuance of his work. By this time his writings were
well known to many in the south of England. Probably
copies of his different works were ordered for individuals and
for monasteries. Among the few books remaining at Pershore Abbey at the time of the dissolution of the monasteries
in the sixteenth century, was a copy of Ælfric's *Grammar*.
It may possibly have been the gift of Æthelweard to that
abbey.[3]

Wulfsige, Bishop of Sherborne (993-1001 or 2), to whose
diocese Cernel belonged, was one of those who knew of

---

1 The difficulty in identifying this Æthelweard with the king's high steward, who, by
the *Saxon Chronicle*, died in 1001, lies in this disappearance of the name from the charters three years earlier, when the name of Ælfric of Mercia which before was second
stands at the head. If the ealdorman were ill or infirm, so as to be no longer able to attend
to his official duties, he would hardly have met his death in battle. As it is uncertain just
what is signified by the term high-steward (heah-gerefa), and there were many men named
Æthelweard, there does not appear now any way to settle the question positively. If it
could be proved that the high-steward was Ælfric's friend it would enable us to set the
dates of the *Grammar*, *Saints' Lives* and his translations from the Bible a little later.

2 *Lives of the Saints*, I. 264.

3 See p. 49; also Dugdale, *Monasticon*, II. 413.

Ælfric's writings, for, about the time of Æthelweard's death, Ælfric wrote at Wulfsige's bidding a pastoral letter addressed to the clergy of the diocese. Wulfsige is said to have introduced Benedictines into his cathedral at Sherborne, which implies a sympathy with the doctrines taught by Ælfric. This letter however is not written for monks, but for the secular clergy. As Ælfric was well acquainted with the habits and needs of Dorset, we can discover in that letter the sins and abuses most common among the clergy there. The prefatory letter which Ælfric addressed to the bishop himself shows that he did not fear to speak with boldness and independence, though he held no higher office in the church than that of priest.

There are no data that enable us to say positively whether Ælfric wrote any other of his works at Cernel. MacLean has called attention to the fact that the *Glossary* shows Ælfric's use of Isidore. This indicates that it may date from the same period as that in which he wrote the *Lives of the Saints,* in which he probably used Isidore, or from that in which he wrote the work *On the Old and New Testament,* of which Isidore is the most important source. It is such a compilation as his actual work of teaching would call forth, and is perhaps to be assigned to the years 998-999.

No book of Ælfric's points more directly to his work in a school than the *Colloquium,* and that may have been written at Cernel sometime before 1005.

These earnest years, filled with good deeds undertaken from patriotic love to the English people, must have brought their due rewards, and have been in many ways successful years. But there are passages scattered through his writings which disclose a keen sensitiveness to the evil condition of England in politics and in morals. He lamented that the English were not brave in defending their land; that the priests did not set a good example to the people; that the Gospel teachings were little known. He saw the country beset by heathen enemies whose power was constantly increasing; and the part of England in which he lived, suffered year after year from such in-roads as those of 994. Yet he does not write as a man dis-couraged, but as one who believed that constant faithfulness to duty would in the end accomplish the high aims which he had set before him.

CHAPTER IV.

AT THE ABBEY OF EYNSHAM.

The year 1000, long anticipated as that of the end of the world,[1] was safely past. In England the year had been preceded not only by a vague fear of unknown ill, but by terrible sufferings realized. Heathen invaders had spared neither seaports nor interior towns; there had been repeated plunder and slaughter; the incompetence and treacherous action of King Æthelred and some of the ealdormen had resulted in divided counsels; treachery again and again in the commanders of the English armies and fleets had betrayed the hopes of the people. All these things answered well to the occurrences which prophecy declared should precede the end of the world. The passing of the dreaded year brought no cessation of ills, and many thought that the looked-for consummation was only delayed for a brief time. But life is so strong a force that men can not cease to believe in its continuance, and so the thought of the uncertain future event did not wholly paralyze their activities.

It must have been at about the beginning of the century that Æthelmær, who had succeeded his father as ealdorman,[2] began to build the new abbey of Eynsham.[3] The foundation charter, of the year 1005,[4] is of interest in connection with Ælfric. It is not improbable that he composed it himself;[5]

---

1 The true strength of this belief is difficult to estimate. Its vagueness and uncertainty must have rendered it inoperative as a motive when compared with the definiteness and reality of the common affairs of life. Yet it must have had some weight if the documents of that time mean anything.

2 Green, *Conq. of Eng.* p. 394; Robertson, *Hist. Essays*, p. 184-5.

3 Eynsham on the Thames (Isis) river, a few miles above Oxford. 'This place is considered to be of great antiquity, and to have formed a royal vill (manor) in the reign of King Æthelred.'

4 *Cod. Dip. A.-S.* p. 339-346; Dugdale's *Monasticon*, III. 11-13.

5 'It is even to be supposed that Ælfric composed the charter. The style is simple, well-considered, and coherent. A healthy tone prevades the whole of this long document, which has nothing of the bombast used by his brethen elsewhere.' Dietrich, p. 240.

certainly it is a document that he read with interest and approval, and one to which, there is every reason to believe, he added his own signature. It is of even more importance as the writing which tells nearly all the little that is known of the circumstances in which Ælfric spent the last period of his life. The first part of it is written in the name of King Æthelred, and confirms to his 'beloved and faithful Æthelmær'[1] the rights and liberties of the abbey of Eynsham. After speaking of the great tribulation of those days, the charter continues: 'It especially behooves us upon whom the ends of the ages are come, to examine with diligent care the needs of our souls, that we may know how and with what merits we may in that world which is soon to appear be victorious with Christ, for here we have no dwelling place, but we seek one to come. Therefore we, with earthly riches, have great need to try with all our powers to obtain that future world.' The charter relates that Æthelmær obtained this monastery from his son-in-law Æthelweard, in exchange for three parcels of land. As there is no record of a monastery there before this time, this may possibly mean that the land upon which the new abbey was built was thus obtained. Of the many lands with which Æthelmær endowed the abbey, two estates, Shipford and Micklantun (Mickleton), had formerly been given by King Edgar to Brihtnoth, the ealdorman of Essex. The first of these, Æthelmær inherited from a relative, Leofwine; the second was bequeathed to him by Brihtnoth, which is easily explained, if, as has been said, his mother was Brihtnoth's daughter.[2]

The family connections and inheritances of Æthelmær, and his relations with the king, probably led him to build

---

1 In *Cod. Dip. A.-S.* VI. 174, Æthelmær is called ' the kinsman of King Æthelred.'

2 ' Villam quoque quae Scipford dicitur, dedit vir praedictus ad monasterium antedictum, quam ei Leofwinus suus consanguineus spiritu in ultimo constitutus donavit, quam Birthnoðus antea dux praeclarus ab Eadgaro patre meo dignis praemium pro meritis accipere laetabatur; Micclantun similiter ad monasterium dedit, quam ille Birthnoðus dux praedictus ultimo commisit dono ab Eadgaro quoque ei antea donatam et in kartula firmiter commendatam.' *Cod. Dip. A.-S.* III. 341.

the new abbey at this place. The charter states that Æthelmær himself was to have his own home in the monastery, living as a father among the brethren. After the account of, the boundaries of the lands which are secured to the abbey, are these words: 'I, Æthelmær, make known to my dear lord, King Æthelred, and to all his counsellors, that I assure this gift to God, and to all his saints, and to St. Benedict.' [1] 'And I desire that he who is now the superior may continue to hold that office so long as he lives, and after his death that the brethren may choose one from their own number according as the rule prescribes, and I myself will live with them, and enjoy the endowment as long as life lasts.' [2] That Ælfric is the superior of whom Æthelmær speaks, is proved by his own words in the preface to his book of extracts from Æthelwold's *De Consuetudine,* addressed to the monks of Eynsham. They are these: 'Abbot Ælfric desires for the brethren of Eynsham salvation in Christ. Dwelling with you, I see that you need to be instructed either by spoken or written words in monastic usages, since recently by Æthelmær's request you have been ordained as monks.' [3] These words by themselves are sufficient proof that Ælfric was the abbot whom Æthelmær had appointed, even as might be expected from the warm friendship which existed between these two men. But further than this, there are two Abbot Ælfrics who witness this charter. The sixteen abbots whose names appear here can all be identified as presiding over monasteries in the neighborhood of Eynsham, except one of these two Ælfrics. It

---

1 See end of Ch. XIII.

2 Ego Æðelredus . . . literarum apicibus insinuare curavi, quod Æðelmaro viro valde fidelissimo mihi quoque dilectissimo impetrante absolutissimum libertatis privilegium constituo monasterio ejus in honore sancti salvatoris, omniumque sanctorum suorum jure dedicato in loco celebri juxta fluvium qui vocatur Tamis constituo, quod ab incolis regionis illius Egenesham nuncupatur vocabulo; quod quidem monasterium Æðelmarus ab Æðelweard genero suo mutuando accepit. . . . Vitae igitur regularis monachos inibi constituens ipse patris vice fungens vivensque communiter inter eos abbatem sanctae monachorum congregatione preferre, se vivente, instituit, ut ita deinceps post ipsum quem constituit abbatem, abbatum electio secundum regulae praeceptum, ex eadem congregatione usu teneat perpetuo.' *Cod. Dip. A.-S.* III. 340.

3 See that preface in Ch. XIII.

was the custom then for an abbot to witness all documents which related to his own monastery. It is therefore to be inferred that Ælfric was the name of the abbot of Eynsham. [1] Of the various other English abbots of that name, it can be shown that none of them would be likely to sign this charter, because either their dates or the location of their abbeys do not allow it. [2]

The words of the charter imply that when it was written, monks were already gathered, and the abbot was established in their midst. Thus it may be that Ælfric came there somewhat earlier than 1005, and perhaps had been active in making all the preparations for opening a new monastery. It was probably so. Some of his pupils from Cernel would have come with him, as those from Glastonbury followed Æthelwold to Abingdon.

The first one of Ælfric's writings which is of this period, is, no doubt, the above-mentioned extract from Æthelwold's *De Consuetudine Monachorum,* and is probably of the year 1005. He was now in Mercia, a region where there was great opposition to his ideas on clerical marriage; and most of his monks, who had come from the ranks of the secular clergy, [3] had little acquaintance with monastic life. Ælfric would not force upon them the long Rule with its many minute details, he would have defeated his own ends if he had done so. Instead of this, he carefully selected from Æthelwold's Eng-

---

1 ' I have little hope that documents relating to the abbey of Eynsham by which the list of its first abbots can be determined, will ever be found in England. The *Codex Diplomaticus* published by Kemble, throws no light upon it. Having noted in Wanley, p. 105, that there was a codex in the library of Christ College, Oxford, which had records of Eynsham, I paid a visit to Oxford. There the dean and librarian of Christ Church kindly gave me the opportunity to inspect the manuscript. I have now convinced myself that the earlier abbots of Eynsham are not there. In the village of Eynsham there are no records, as also no longer an abbey. In order to leave nothing untried, I asked Dr. Bandinell of the Bodleian library if anything in reference to Eynsham had been found since the completion of the *Monasticon,* and received an answer in the negative.' Dietrich, p. 241-2.

2 See Dietrich, p. 237-8, 248, n. 164.

3 Contrast in Kemble's *Cod. Dip. A.-S.* the charters of Oswald with those of the south of England: i. e. note that the former are attested by many clerks; the latter by few or none.

lish translation those parts which were adapted to their need, adding to these those things 'from the book of Amalarius' which he thought would be useful for them to know. It is sometimes said that Ælfric had little imagination; but he had an unusual ability of putting himself in the place of others. He was always feeling his way carefully so as to meet the exact needs of his readers, and not to surfeit them with superfluous teachings. A long list of passages from his homilies could be cited in proof of this. The preface of his *Grammar* shows one instance; that of the *Lives of the Saints* yet another; and to these extracts from the *De Consuetudine* he might fitly have added the words of Paul: 'We were gentle among you, even as a nurse cherisheth her children;' 'I have fed you with milk and not with meat, for hitherto ye were not able to bear it, neither yet now are ye able.'

Up to this time the friends of whom Ælfric speaks have been of the south of England. From now on they are those who can be identified as belonging to Mercia. The new monastery was well known to the king and his counsellors, and Æthelmær's lay friends had probably heard of Ælfric and his books. Those of that region who cared to read would be interested to have such a man and such an author come among them. He can not have been there long before he was solicited to lend his writings, for it was probably before 1006, or early in that year, that Wulfgeat of Ylmandune, [1] a favorite thane of the king's, borrowed some of them. Afterwards he talked with Ælfric about them, told him how

---

1 Fl. of Wor., 1006, ' King Æthelred stripped his chief favorite, Wulfgeat, son of Leof sige, of his estates and honors, on account of his unrighteous judgments and arrogant deeds.' The *Saxon Chronicle* simply states the fact that he was deprived of his possessions. Greene, *Conq. of E.* 382, ' Wulfgeat probably directed the king's policy in the short interval of peace that followed Swein's departure at the end of 1004. But only two years later the new minister was displaced by a revolution which seems to have been accompanied by deeds of violence.' See Freeman, *Nor. Conq.* I. 220, 435-6; *Cod. Dip. A.-S.* III. 224-345; VI. 154, 160, 169. *Leechdoms, Wortcunning, etc.* III. p. XXVII, ' Ylmandun here mentioned may be certainly interpreted as Ilmingdon, on the borders of Warwickshire and Gloucestershire, with the down close to it. Ilmingdon is the next parish to Mickleton where one of the Eynesham-foundation estates lay.'

much he liked them, and obtained from the abbot the promise of more, a promise which was fulfilled by Ælfric's sending
him one of his sermons. Wulfgeat's name is attached to the
charter of Eynsham, and he is to be identified, without doubt,
as that thane of the king's who in 1006 was deprived of his
estates and honors.

In November, 1005, Ælfric, Archbishop of Canterbury,
died, and early in the next year, Alphege, Bishop of Winchester, became archbishop. Kenulph, Abbot of Peterborough, succeeded at Winchester, but died within the year.
As Ælfric dedicated his life of Æthelwold to Bishop Kenulph, there can be no question as to its date. The words of
the preface lead us to think that he may have visited Winchester not long before he wrote it, possibly on his journey
from Cernel to Eynsham. There his own remembrance of
Æthelwold, who had been dead more than twenty years, had
been refreshed, and he had noted down traditions of the
monks and historical data ready for use when the opportunity
to write should come.

As we read the chronicles of these years, we can not help
admiring the courage and constancy with which Ælfric pur-
sued his way, writing and teaching in the midst of national
disasters that would have discouraged every patriotic citizen
who did not look, as he did, far beyond the passing events of
the hour. In this very year in which he wrote Æthelwold's
biography, the Danish army was burning towns and plundering the land not far from Eynsham. The *Saxon Chronicle*
tells how in mid-winter the army passed through Hampshire
into Berkshire, to Reading, which they burned, and to Wallingford, about thirty miles farther down the Thames river
than Eynsham, which they also burned, and, a little farther
on, to Cholsey, which Florence of Worcester says had the
same fate. 'Then were forces assembled at Kennet, and they
there joined battle and put the English to flight.' 'Then the
Winchester people could see an army that feared nothing, as
it passed by their gates going on to the sea, carrying food and

treasure from over fifty miles inland. The dread of the army became so great that no man could think or discover how their foes could be driven out of the land, or how the land could defend itself against them, for they had put their marks upon every shire in Wessex by burning and by plundering.' Then follows the old story of tribute and food unwillingly given. This was not the end; the chronicles tell a similar tale for the years that followed this, and it was only when the Danish victory was complete and Cnut was king, after Æthelred's death (1016), that anything like peace dawned upon England.

Sometime within the few years after 1006 Ælfric wrote his treatise, *On the Old and New Testaments.* In this he refers to many of his writings, so that its date is determined as a late one. In the opening words of this work, and in two other passages, he addresses Sigwerd of Easthealon at whose request he prepared this writing. He speaks of having visited Sigwerd at his house, so that Sigwerd's home must have been not far from Eynsham. As land at East Healle was granted to the abbey of Abingdon in Mercia in 963,[1] it is certain that Sigwerd was a Mercian, and one of Ælfric's neighbors. He is probably the thane Sigwerd who witnessed the foundation charter of Eynsham, and whose name often appears in documents between 995 and 1012. As the name disappears after that, and his death is to be inferred, we may date this work of Ælfric's somewhere between 1005 and 1012. As this work follows in one manuscript the letter to Wulfgeat, it may have been written soon after that. One little incident of Ælfric's visit to Sigwerd, related near the end of this writing, tells something of Ælfric, and also of the spirit of the Benedictine life. Ælfric says: 'When I was at your house you urged me to drink more than I was accustomed. You ought to know, dear friend, that if any one compels another to drink more than is good for him, and any harm result, the

---

1 See *Chronicon Monasterii de Abingdon*, II. 327-8

blame is upon him who caused it. Our Saviour Christ in his gospel has forbidden believers in Him to drink more than is necessary. Let him who will, keep the law of Christ.' Thus Ælfric was not ascetic for the sake of asceticism. This visit is an illustration of his friendly intercourse with the people in the neighborhood of the new abbey, and of the practical efforts that he no doubt was making all of the time to elevate the common life of the people about him. Strict as he was in regard to purity of life, his loving and unselfish spirit won him friends wherever he went.

One other instance of his intercourse with his neighbors is the writing addressed to Sigeferth, who may possibly be the thane of that name whose signature is attached to the charter of Eynsham and to other documents from 1005 to 1024, but the name is a very common one. This Sigeferth had a private chapel on his estate, and his priest was openly teaching that it was quite right for the clergy to marry. Perhaps Sigeferth was acquainted with Ælfric, or it may be that he was known to Æthelmær. In any case, Ælfric knew of the teaching of Sigeferth's priest, and the result was a carefully prepared sermon on chastity addressed to Sigeferth, which no doubt reached the priest, but we do not hear that he abandoned his teachings. Had the times been less confused and troubled, the efforts on the part of the secular clergy and their friends to carry this point, and prove their teaching correct, might, and probably would in time, have resulted in the modification of the teachings of such earnest men as Ælfric. The course of Dunstan and Oswald is an indication of this.

Ælfric's *Life of Æthelwold* which he sent to the brethren at Winchester, can hardly have reached there much before the death of Bishop Kenulph. It may have been this fresh reminder of the Winchester alumnus, that led to a request from the new bishop, Æthelwold II, that Ælfric would write a sermon for him. It was in answer to this that a homily was translated, that on the text: 'Watch, therefore, for ye know neither the day nor the hour when your Lord doth come,' and the date must fall in Æthelwold's term of office, that is, between 1007 and 1012.

It was in this latter year, 1012, that the cruel death of Ælfric's former bishop, Alphege, occurred at Greenwich. The contrast of unrest and terror outside the monastery, with calm steady purpose, and attention to every-day duties of life, is shown in the writings which Ælfric produced at this time, still mindful of the spiritual needs of the people when the outward circumstances were as disheartening as possible.

The pastoral letter which Ælfric wrote for Bishop Wulfsige when in Dorset, suggested to Wulfstan, Archbishop of York and Bishop of Worcester, that such letters would be useful for his numerous clergy. Eynsham, though under the Bishop of London, was not far from the Worcester diocese; Wulfstan was one of the signers of the Eynsham charter, and must have known its abbot and his writings, and among them that pastoral letter. His first request to Ælfric was for letters in Latin, and the next year, for an English translation of the same. The date of these was probably not before 1014, for section 52[1] of the first letter is apparently taken from laws of Æthelred which were issued in that year. It is also probable that the date is not much later than that. Wulfstan's famous *Address to the English* shows how deeply he felt the calamities of the time, the sins of the people, and the pressing need of a remedy; and so his request for these letters would hardly have been delayed until the last years of his life. The connection between these two most important writers of this period of Old English is worth noting here. If we judge by Wulfstan's homilies he would not have hesitated to rebuke the faults of his clergy. Nor did Ælfric hesitate to use plain language when occasion demanded. He was gentle with the ignorant laity and the young, but the secular clergy had no excuse for their conduct. They were bound by their office to be an example to the people. Wulf-

---

[1] Cf. with Section 52 a passage in Wilkins' *Leges Anglo-Saxonicae*, p. 115.

stan's request was not made simply because Ælfric was a scholar and a skillful writer of books. He recognized in him one who was working with his whole heart for the practical ends that he himself was seeking. There are marked differences in the temper and in the literary work of these men, but they were manifestly in sympathy with each other.

Æthelmær was probably an older man than Ælfric. This is indicated by the words of the charter in which he refers to himself as being in the place of a father in the abbey. In the charters from 1006 to 1012 his name occurs but twice, and his life was probably spent in quiet retirement as the words already quoted would lead us to expect.[1] In 1013, the *Saxon Chronicle,* giving the account of Sweyn's conquest of the different parts of England, says, 'Then went King Sweyn to Wallingford, and so over the Thames westward to Bath, and encamped there with all his forces. And Æthelmær the ealdorman came thither, and the western thanes with him, and they all submitted to Sweyn and gave hostages for themselves.' Probably at this time Æthelmær was an old man. The next year we hear of his death. Three years later, in 1017, his son Æthelweard was put to death by Cnut, but unjustly, according to Florence of Worcester. Again in 1020 his son Æthelnoth became archbishop of Canterbury, and his son-in-law Æthelweard was banished by the king.

What do we know of Ælfric in these years?[2] Little that is definite, and yet it is certain that the death of his friend and the fortunes of his family touched him very closely. We have a hint of literary work in the English preface of the first volume of *Catholic Homilies,* in which he speaks of King Æthelred's day as if it were past. It was not far from 1020

---

1 From 983–1005 Æthelmær's name is found more than twenty times among the attendants of the king as witness of documents.

2 'It is impossible to believe that Ælfric became a bishop in these last years of his life. The only one of his name who is chronologically possible is the bishop of East Anglia who died in 1038. But the Mercian abbot would not have been sent to the eastern end of the country, to Elmham. It is yet more improbable that our Ælfric, who wrote his language with purity and force, could have written East Anglian as carelessly as did Bishop Ælfric in the testament handed down from him.' Dietrich, p. 241.

that he revised his homilies and prepared a second edition. He no longer wrote large new volumes of translation, but single sermons as occasion demanded, those writings, perhaps, for which no date can be suggested. His life was not simply that of a student, or a teacher in the cloister-school; as abbot his social rank was high, and social duties must have devolved upon him. His great interest in the secular clergy and the laity points to active efforts on his part outside of the monastery.

There is no record of the year of his death. In 1020 or 1021 an Abbot Ælfric signed a charter of gift to St. Paul's Abbey in London.[1] That abbey, like the Old Minster of Winchester, had no abbot: it stood directly under the Bishop of London. The abbot of Westminster at that time was named Wulnoth, and there is no Abbot Ælfric under the Bishop of London nearer than Eynsham. The probability is that the Ælfric whose name is found here is Ælfric the abbot of that monastery. We may reasonably suppose that he died somewhere between 1020 and 1025, as there is no longer any trace of him

Of the monastery over which he presided few records remain, and no list of its abbots begins earlier than 1115. The obscurity which involved his house concealed the identity of its most famous abbot. As we consider the confusion of the time, and the revolutions in state and church which were to come with the Norman Conquest, the mystery which has surrounded the person of Ælfric is easily explained. After all, we may be thankful that so many facts of his life are certainly known; there are men of greater note than he of whom we know less. Students of this period of history, which has sometimes been called 'the darkest of the dark ages,' will yet gather together more and more facts which will explain the life and the works of Ælfric, and make more clear his services to the English language, and to the higher life of the English people.

---

1 *Cod. Dip. A.-S.* IV. 304.

CHAPTER V.

ÆLFRIC'S EDUCATION AND CHARACTER.

Had the tenth century not been filled with a constant, war-like unrest, which disturbed the peace of the cloister; had there been a love of learning as in the time of Aldhelm and Bede, protected, and incited, by kings like Alfred, and main-tained by more frequent associations with the scholars of other lands, the zeal of an Ælfric would have reached a more many-sided perfection. Under such circumstances, his mind, which was open, clear and firm, desirous of everything good and noble, would have come to a higher degree of in-sight and independence than we see really attained by him. This is evident when we examine closely his writings and teachings, and compare him with the educated men of his century in other lands.

Nevertheless, when judged fairly according to the condi-tions of his time, he stands forth an eminent man among the Old English. But his chief excellence is not to be sought in special learnedness, nor in the distinguished place assigned him in relation to traditional Catholicism. Rather it is to be found in the fidelity with which he devoted whatever learn-ing his opportunities enabled him to acquire to the educa-tion of the people, adapting to their needs his whole thought and activity.

It is not probable that he ever enjoyed a court-training, or travelled in foreign lands. His book education was nar-rowed to the *Trivium* and *Quadrivium* of the cloister-schools. Grammar and rhetoric he must have studied with a keen interest, and all the knowledge of these subjects that he was able to obtain, he transmuted into sap and blood. This is shown by his clear, vigorous, consistent use of language, both

English and Latin, and by the flexibility and force of his rhetorical movement in the homilies. That he may also have been successful in the study of theory we can infer from his translation of Priscian; but classicism is not to be found in his Latin. It is free from the excessive ornamentation and the disjointed constructions of the writings of the preceding century, and from the barbarous importations from Greek and the modern languages of Western Europe which characterized the Latin of his own time; it is simple and correct according to the grammatical standard of that age. At the same time it is always the Latin of the Middle Ages, with its strange constructions and word-forms after the example of the Latin translations of the Bible. Ælfric says, for example, 'interpretavimus,' and uses 'si' in the indirect question, just as Bede does.

It is not probable that he was acquainted with any language except Latin and the mother-tongue. The knowledge of Hebrew was not to be thought of, for since Jerome such learning had been transmitted only in his writings. The representation and explanation of the Hebrew words with which the separate books of the Pentateuch begin, and by which they are named; the interpretation of proper names of sacred history, and of other expressions, for example, of 'Hallelujah,' show only the diligent use of Jerome. If Ælfric had obtained knowledge of Hebrew at first hand, perhaps through rabbis, he would not have explained Nain as 'agitation' (*Hom.* I. 492), or make Ananias signify sheep' (*Hom.* I. 390). He had read the Old Testament only in Latin, and so he is guilty of many little inaccuracies and misunderstandings. Thus he calls the queen who came to Solomon 'Saba,' holding the uninflected genitive in 'in regina Saba' to be a proper name; and he says that the books of Kings and of Chronicles were written by 'Samuel and Malachim.'

He might perhaps have known Greek, since the knowledge of it had never quite been lost in England. It is clear, how-

ever, that he did not, for he nowhere shows any independent
acquaintance with the significance of Greek words. When he
does give them he generally gives them correctly. 'The Holy
Ghost,' he says, following Bede, 'is called in the Greek language "Paraclitus," that is, "Spirit of Comfort."' Once he
writes a word of a Greek stem: the six jars at the marriage at
Cana are called in his text *hydriae,* in which is the Greek
word *hydor,* 'water.' In this etymology he follows Bede. He
explains the name Stephen (*Hom.* I. 50), not by the Greek,
but by the Latin, and not by corona, but by coronatus, which
he translates into the Old English *gewuldorbēagod,* 'crowned.'
He gives as explanation of the name Gregorius, (*Hom.* II.
118) Vigilantius, and translates this again by the neuter of
the comparative, *wacolre,* 'more watchful,' and offends by this
the Latin as well as the Greek. Thus it appears that
there is not the slightest ground for ascribing to him even the
rudiments of Greek. At that time only Latin was deemed
necessary for an understanding of the Bible. He says
'Jerome translated from Hebrew and from Greek into Latin,
the language in which we learn.'

It was the custom to join with the astronomy of that day
teachings on physics, and on the reckoning of the calendar
according to its movable feasts. In this branch Ælfric had
more than the usual knowledge, which appears to have been
limited in the cloister-course to the finding of Easter-day,
including whatever was necessary for that in the courses of
the sun and of the moon. He had read of eclipses of the
sun and moon, and of shooting stars. He knew that the
moon rises daily about four points *(fēower pricum)* later,
and so the tide of the sea comes so much later. What a
favorite subject, and how familiar astronomy was to him, is
shown by the account of the different beginnings of the
year with different nations which is found in a homily for
the first of January, the beginning of the Roman year.

Of general history he knew hardly more than the summary of the Origenistic world-ages, to which he sometimes

refers. It is true that he often quotes historical or geograph-
ical observations with the words: 'historical writers *(wyrd-
wrīteras)* say so and so;' but the contents of such quotations
point only to acquaintance with Josephus, and with the
native history, whose political and ecclesiastical events were
recorded in Bede's oft-named work.

As is to be expected, he was most familiar with church
history, especially with the work begun by Eusebius and continued after his time. He nowhere names Eusebius, nor, in
this connection, Rufinus, the true translator of Eusebius'
work into Latin, for he understands Jerome to be its author,
and ascribes the story of the finding of the cross to him.
This is a confusion of the *Ecclesiastical History* with the
Chronicle of Eusebius, of which Jerome translated the second
part, and carried it forward to 378 A. D. Ælfric had read
many church-legends, but not with the critical spirit, in the
modern sense of the term, that rarest of all spirits in the
Middle Ages. His own lives of saints show knowledge and
graphic talent, but he nowhere distinguishes by any law of
inner probability that which is worthy of belief from that
which is suspicious. His test of reliability was only the goodness of the person from whom the history or tradition was
received. He repeatedly says that he has taken diligent care
for correct belief in his teachings, since he has followed those
fathers whose authority is accepted by all Catholic churches.

His theological education embraced Biblical knowledge
and dogmatics, ecclesiastical history, customs, and statutes,
and liturgical and pastoral theology. In these his education
was extensive, and chiefly of a practical tendency. His homilies sometimes approach dialectical development, yet he goes
little beyond the Christian speculations of Augustine, and
does not from principle allow himself individual, free doctrinal development. Although he chooses his teachings with
tolerable freedom, he is to be classed with divines who are
adherents of tradition. It was his wish to use for the common
people the doctrines which had been developed by the greatest

Christian teachers, those teachings that the whole church preserved and held sacred, and which he himself received with full conviction. In the homilies he usually gives the exposition which is found in the Latin original, considering, first, the literal meaning of the Scripture-passage, and then the moral and typical meanings. Indeed he often makes the lesson of the types more important than the moral lesson. For this reason he sometimes has strange interpretations, for example, when he says that the five shillings which redeemed the first-born (*Hom.* I. 138) signify the five senses which should be dedicated to God; or, that the return of the Magi is to image our return to the true fatherland by another way pointed out by God.[1] Even where he moves freely, and has not old homilies before him, as in the introduction to Genesis, he shows that his thoughts follow easily the typical explanations of the old church-fathers. For the first word of the Old Testament, 'In the beginning,' he postulates a deeper and more spiritual understanding than the obvious one: it means 'in Christ God created the heavens and the earth,' an interpretation drawn from John 8, 25, of which his translation read, 'I who speak to you am the beginning.'[2] Likewise his explanation of the tabernacle and its single component parts, as a type of the church, to which men are to bring faith, virtues, and penitential deeds, is not his own, but that of the ancient church.

In the New Testament, especially in the parables and other addresses of our Lord, he held generally to the simplest literal explanation; he seeks here only the proper, obvious understanding of the words. An example of simple, striking exegesis is his explanation of the parable of the different kinds of seeds, which he drew from Gregory and from Bede.

The text which he comments on is always the Vulgate, though occasionally he mentions variations between different

---

1 In this he treats the subject as Otfried does, because he draws from similar sources.

2 The interpretation is an old one found in Isidore, in the *Hexameron* of Basil, in Tertullian, in Hilarius, in a fragment of Ariston of Pella, and in Bede's Commentary on Genesis.

Latin translations (*Hom.* I. 172; II. 446; cf. I. 436), and he knew and used, besides the Vulgate, the translation by Jerome. He was acquainted with what Isidore's prefaces to the books of the Bible contain about the authors and the history of their times. The collection into a comprehensive whole of such knowledge as is now found in an introduction to the Scriptures, belongs to a time much later than Ælfric, but his complete and hearty appropriation of the whole contents of the Bible itself appears everywhere, and he was able at need to reproduce it independently. He is incontestably a master in the portrayal of Biblical story, understanding well how to weave into the narrative his own practical applications and comments. Here and there he shows the influence of legend upon sacred history, of which he was perhaps unconscious. Thus he tells of the creation of the angels and of the fall of Lucifer, as if they stood in the first book of Moses; and he makes Job the fifth after Abraham, Isaiah to be sawn asunder under Manassah, and Jeremiah to be stoned in Egypt, just as if they all stood in the Bible. His historical and Biblical teachings always have reference to a moral effect, but he has not principles of morals developed by themselves.

His pastoral letters show his comprehensive and accurate acquaintance with the canons of the ecumenical councils.

In making profane and Biblical history accessible to his people, Ælfric sought to adapt his material to the character and customs of the English, in order that it might either accord with that which they had experienced, or become by association with that comprehensible to them. With facile hand he makes plain also those things which could not be so brought home to them: now he suppresses that which is secondary in the foreign narrative, and again he inserts the familiar in so far as the truth is not prejudiced by it. This is seen especially in respect to the social stations of persons of high rank. He seeks to show that the relation of the saints to God is the same as that of thanes to their king: as thanes intercede with the king, so do the saints with God.

Saint Sebastian is represented as a truth-loving, wise inter-
cessor, as a good English thane of God; and the great men
of Egypt are called Pharaoh's thanes, or his *witan,* 'counsellors.' The English prince next below the king was called the
Ætheling. Thus Christ is named by Ælfric, as he had been
by the earlier poets. Moses he calls the mighty duke
(heretoga), and sometimes he gives the judges this title;
Pilate is King Herod's ealdorman; Holofernes and Sisera are
Syrian ealdormen. The Jewish high-priest is always the
elder bishop *(ealdorbisceop),* not exactly archbishop, and not,
as in the gospels, high-priest.

As over the prisons of an English shire there was placed
an official called the high sheriff *(hēahgerēfa),* so Ælfric
gives that title to Valerian in his life of Lawrence, and,
again, to an Agrippa by whose counsel Nero had caused Paul
to be beheaded. The English reeves had to receive rents and
customs for their lords. So Joseph in Egypt is called a reeve
because he filled the king's granaries. The publicans in the
gospels are introduced as reeves, and thus they were much
more intelligible and more alive than if they had been called
tax-gatherers, or publicans as they are in the New Testament.
To the English the Welsh men and women *(wealh* and
wylen) were servants by birth, hence the Egyptians are made
to say 'the Israelites are our *wēalas;'* and it is said that
Abimelech took *'wēlas* and *wylna.'* The free servant as an
assistant is *gingra,* with the judge he is the beadle *(bydel),*
a word which also meant herald, and so John is introduced as
Christ's beadle.

In Old English law, reparations for crime or neglect were
graded according to locality, in short, according to the rank
of the authority which hallowed the place. How living to
the people must have been the passage which shows that
transgressions under the New Covenant are more to be
dreaded than those under the Old, where Ælfric explains:
'One thing is the regulation which the king ordains through
his nobles or officials, but another is the edict issued when

6

he is present' (*Hom.* I. 359). The instigator of murder for-
feited his property even as did the doer. This Ælfric used
in reference to the property which Satan had in mankind,
and especially in reference to Satan's instigation of the Jews
to the killing of Christ (*Hom.* I. 216).

From early times every English province was spoken of in
relation to jurisdiction by the name of shire. By the use of
this term Ælfric transfers that which was foreign to domestic
ground, as when he calls Cæsarea the fortress of the Cappadocian shire. One of the duties accompanying the use of
land in England was the repair of the walled towns: so the
spies under Caleb were required to see whether the walls of
the towns were in repair.

How distinctly the country, the domestic concerns, and the
manner of life of the Old English, come before the eye in
many passages from Ælfric; as in the words: 'Foolish is the
traveller who turns into the level path that leads him astray,
and forsakes the steep path which leads to the walled-town;'
or where tar, honey, frankincense, and also acorns and nuts,
are sent from Palestine to Egypt; and where every fruit-
garden figures as an apple-orchard *(æppeltūn)*. Again, the
Old English dwelling-house had the guest-room under a separate roof, hence we read that Abraham received the three
angels in his guest-house *(on his gest hūse)*. The feasts of
the patriarchs are called beer-drinkings *(gebēorscipas),* and
it is said that John drank neither wine, nor beer, nor ale, but
ate fruit and 'what he could find in the wood;' the locusts,
as strange, are omitted. Thus—and it might be illustrated
much further—the assimilation of that which was foreign
reached from the most important legal relations to the
smallest features of daily life.

This method of Ælfric's, by which he enlivens foreign
material with the native colors and tones, may be less the
artistic impulse, so praiseworthy in the author of the *Heliand,*
than the desire to cherish and enoble the native culture and
manners. Not only the poetical clothing of his thought, but

also such transformations as these, were intentional; they show that he wished to be a man of the people, notwithstanding his monkish education by means of Latin literature, and all his zeal for ecclesiasticism in Roman forms. Perhaps some are inclined to pre-suppose in monks, especially in those who are zealous for celibacy, only a mind for asceticism, or, at least, for repression of the people. To such it must be agreeable and surprising to find Ælfric full of patriotic love for his whole fatherland. The way in which he cites a list of victorious English kings, Alfred, Æthelstan, and Edgar, as examples of leaders of the people conducted by God to greatness and power, makes it easy to see his joy in the welfare of the whole nation. In his time, courage to bear arms against foreign pirates had weakened, was even asleep. He used the Biblical history over and over to arouse that courage. 'There is a righteous war,' he says, 'war against raging pirates, or against other peoples who wish to destroy the fatherland.'

But his love for his nation shows itself most in activity for the spiritual good and education of the laity. He was incited to make several of his translations by men of high rank, who desired religious readings for themselves and their subordinates, but his first undertaking was of his free choice, and arose from sympathy with the people. It was with this spirit that he wrote: 'It is good and right to minister to God's poor, and especially to the servants of God, but it is greater to speak heavenly lore to the unlearned, and to feed their souls' (*Hom.* II. 442).

Besides the translation of the Lord's Prayer and the greater and smaller formulas of belief, Ælfric put before the people other prayers, distinguished by their depth and brevity, and entirely suited to the common need. The whole manner of his exposition and use of Scripture, which he brings so near to the common man that he can, as it were, grasp it with his hands, shows that he never forgot his aim, to give sound nutriment to the untaught, and that he remained always under the control of the inner pressure to help his 'English people' *(Angelcyn)*.

I cannot trace, consistently with Ælfric's character, his teaching upon election, and his use of Gregory's authority upon the same, to a lax conception of church belief; but only to his love for the people and to his desire to win as many as possible. He explains the frightful words, 'Few are chosen,' in the mildest way, referring to the words of Christ in Matt. 8, 11; and that no doubt may remain upon the subject, he brings forward as a church authority for the not small number of those who shall be saved, a passage from Gregory, which scanned more closely, scarcely justifies the conclusion of Ælfric. He says, 'though the chosen of God seem few in the present life, among the carnally-minded, yet they are not few when they are gathered together' (*Hom.* II. 82). Thus he precludes the thought that a whole people which had come into such dire need as the Old English were in, should be represented as rejected of God.

That his love for the people was the true love which is bound up with moral earnestness, is shown sufficiently in his reproofs of their darling sins, foremost, that of drunkenness.

The Old English had great pleasure in alliterative verse; and if so small a thing may be allowed to count as a token of pure love of the people, Ælfric's introduction of the popular metrical discourse into his homilies, which, so far as I know, no other preacher in German lands had done, is an evidence that he wished to penetrate directly to the hearts of his hearers. Though Aldhelm had used his poetical powers for oral delivery of sacred history itself, yet it had not been undertaken for church discourse. Ælfric appropriated the universally favorite form in order that the proclamation of salvation might take hold upon hearts with the power of the song of the old heroes, who had been hitherto the moral exemplars of that which was noblest. The subjects of those selections which he has handled poetically, lead one to believe that this was probably his aim. They were in most cases histories of saintly warriors, either of those of the Old Eng-

lish who had fallen fighting for the everlasting treasure, or
heroes and deeds of sacred story. Even the homily on the
Passion is purely narrative, and aims to impress upon the
soul the glory of the victorious Jesus in his struggle and
death.

Ælfric's humility is to be estimated in accordance with
the time and the monastic condition to which he belonged.
His numerous expressions of humility are not for the
sake of calling attention to himself, but are signs of true
self-knowledge. The English preface of *Catholic Homilies,* I. shows well this trait of his character. If one notes
also how strictly he keeps his own opinions and devices out of
the way when he has to do with the divine word and with
the teaching of correct belief, one cannot deny that he has the
right self-restraint, heart-felt veracity, and the concurrence
of his inmost thinking with his outer expression of thoughts
and motives. Yet even if complete humility was only an
object aimed at, and not yet fully acquired, who could hold
an Egyptian death-trial in the innermostsanctuaryof another
soul? Who would not put up with some self-satisfaction in
a good author?

More questionable are his requests to those who are more
learned than he that they will forgive the simplicity of his
instruction, and not blame his abridgments. What does it
mean, except that they are not to attribute it to ignorance
and a low standpoint of knowledge and of faith on his part.
Similar to this is the declaration which he sometimes makes,
that he will not translate more, and does not wish to be asked
to do it. Yet he allows himself again and again to be determined to the undertaking of new works, which he could not
avoid with true love to the people and the church. Could
he not have known this beforehand?

It should no more be called a fault in Ælfric than in any
other author that he wishes to preserve the meaning and
outward form of his texts pure and unaltered. We know how
carelessly the writings of others of that time were treated,

how much was transcribed only in order to remodel and enlarge. Ælfric makes it a matter of conscience with the scribes to write with care and to correct mistakes. If anyone seeks to find in that a little literary vanity, it will be only the vanity of a man who wishes to appear always in a good and pure garment.

CHAPTER VI.

ÆLFRIC'S SERVICE AND INFLUENCE.

There may be a question in many minds whether the service and influence of Ælfric were of much importance to his people. This doubt may be felt because he took no prominent part in ecclesiastical or doctrinal controversy, and did not rise above the traditional theology of his day; still more, because he did not attain to any position of control in the affairs of the national church.

As an author, considered in the general sense of that term, we cannot rank him with those who have promoted the development of knowledge. He belonged to an age in which there was almost no struggle for the formulation of doctrine, and in which all learning languished. His aim was chiefly a practical one; his writings were to serve the church of his time, and were called forth by pressing needs. Thus the questions may be fairly asked: in what degree was he fortunate in the choice of his material? independent in his treatment of it? and successful in promoting practical ends?

Already, by the ninth century, the Germanic countries of Western Europe had received a store of poetical works: among them the *Heliand*, the works ascribed to Cædmon, and the writings of Cynewulf. The tenth century demanded decidedly more appropriation of knowledge, such as would be furnished by homilies in the mother tongues, and by translations and paraphrases of the books of the Bible. Germany has still some fragments of sermons of the tenth century to show, as well as a German psalter and German gospels. But only the Old English of that time has handed down such a commentary as Ælfric's three collections of doctrinal and historical homilies. Besides these works he provided translations of Genesis and of portions of nearly all of the historical books of the Old Testament, and made accessible to the people a considerable part of the text of the gospels and epistles, in the prescribed readings for Sundays and festival days of the year. These writings, together with his introductory work *On the Old and New Testaments,* gave just the material which was urgently needed. In his use of the homilies and treatises of the most distinguished writers of the ancient church he follows the custom of his own and earlier times. Bede worked almost exclusively in the church fathers. The before-mentioned German homilies were, so far as can be judged by their fragments, translations of old sermons, especially of those of Gregory the Great, whose writings Alfred had found especially practical, and whom Ælfric has often used.

In a very modest way Ælfric has designated himself as a mere translator; but, in fact, even where he has followed the foreign originals, he has not simply translated. He has sometimes extended and more often abridged, and in both cases he has shown great tact. His homilies are freely-adapted revisions in which he has omitted whatever was abstruse, subtle, and wearisome in his originals. He often says, 'this may be sufficient for you, laymen,' or, 'it would be tiresome for you to go more deeply.' Thus his hearers were made to understand the simple, obvious meaning of the truth taught, and at the same time to feel that they had not exhausted its deep treasures.

The literary aspect of our author is attractive in its noble simplicity, clearness and vigor of expression. We see that he has taken Alfred's writings as his pattern. Both of these authors have written religious poetry, and in this Alfred stands higher; but in prose Ælfric is more exact, finished and pleasing.

As a theologian, he was always striving for intelligent and practical apprehension of dogma, and he received with vital freshness and sincerity the mystery of redemption and of the person of the Redeemer.

A true teacher of the people has always to struggle. So

we find Ælfric contending against coarse and subtle superstitions. In the northern and eastern parts of England much heathenism may still have existed openly, and as, especially since Edgar's time, the Scandinavians had found access to the whole land, the old propensity of the Saxons and Angles to the customs of their forefathers was fostered anew. Ælfric included in his *Saints' Lives* a sermon on the false gods. In this he identifies the Roman gods with those of the Scandinavians, but not with those of the heathen English. From this we may conclude that the English themselves were now quite free from coarse idolatry, and that he feared for his people on account of contact with the Danes. But various forms of magic were still practised among the English. Against these he speaks in the *Catholic Homilies* (I. 366, 474, 476), and preaches a special sermon against them in the *Lives of the Saints.*[1] Ælfric, in accordance with the custom of the church, allowed various incantations, if only the Triune God were invoked, and not an idol (*Hom.* I. 150, 218). He rejected the curse as wrong, but allowed that it had power (*Hom.* II. 30-36).

A part of the old popular belief had passed over under changed names into church belief: the veneration of Mary beside God the Father and the Son, had taken the place of that of Friga beside Wodan and Thonar; and the veneration of saints and of the cross, that of heroes and demi-gods and of the tree. In respect to the invocation of Mary and of the saints, Ælfric held by the tradition of the church, but he did not wish such address to be mistaken for worship.[2] Of the cross, he says, 'The sign of the cross is our blessing, and we pray to the cross, yet not to the tree, but to the Almighty One who for us hung upon it' (*Hom.* II. 240).

He had no belief in a mechanical influence of good works, but all his teaching and exhortation aimed to bring men to strive after righteousness of heart (*Hom.* II. 314, 432).

---

[1] *On Auguries*; *Lives of the Saints*, I. 364-382.
[2] See *Hom.* I. 174.

Ælfric labored unweariedly for the culture and elevation of secular clergy and monks. Not only did he rebuke their ignorance and evil example, but he undertook the work of their education, roused them from their careless lives, and overcame all the excuses with which they tried to free themselves from these burdensome demands. His zeal against the marriage of priests has not been regarded by Protestant judges as a merit. But the laws which were directed against the English clergy of that time appear to justify some restraint. In the practical carrying out of the celibacy of the officiating priests, Ælfric was more mild than some of his predecessors. He did not wish that already existing marriages should be severed. He permitted the marriage of the members of the lower orders of the priesthood, and appealed to Gregory in confirmation of this (*Hom.* II. 94); but he demanded that priests who officiated at the holy eucharist, and those who were monks should make up their minds to complete chastity. This was by all evidences the opinion of the best and most distinguished laymen among the Old English: men like Æthelweard and Æthelmær, Æthelwin of East Anglia, Sigwerd of Northumbia, Leofric of Mercia, and Brithnoth who fell at Maldon.

Of Ælfric's pupils, we learn the name of but a single one; but all the clergy of the following period who wished to cultivate themselves were obliged to go to school to him: his books were the most easily accessible means of instruction.

Of direct influence, we hear that in accordance with the regulations prescribed by him, the priests were obliged to possess at least ten books; and to preach in English. It is of more importance that they, following his example, learned to preach independently. To all appearance he had in his own time influenced suggestively the literary activity of Archbishop Wulfstan.

From the time of the Danish wars, far on into the period after the Norman Conquest, Ælfric's sermons were copied again and again, as their altered language betrays; and the manuscripts noted below as *mixed,* contain Old English homilies which originated with other authors, but are modelled after his.

His work does not stand alone; we must remember that such sermons as the *Blickling Homilies* were written a little earlier than his, and that the Old English translations of the gospels were made near the close of the tenth century. But he was the most efficient of the writers of his time; none before him had written such urgent, impressive reproofs to the shepherds of the people; none had attained to such dignity, fullness, and power of discourse. It was reserved for him to establish the reformatory movement among the English, and to gather its fruits. His fame is to be compared with that of an Aldhelm in an earlier time, and with that of a Wyclif in a later riper age.

CHAPTER VII.

EXPLODED THEORIES OF ÆLFRIC'S IDENTITY.

The answers to the questions: Who was Ælfric, the once distinguished ecclesiastical author? What offices did he fill? Where and how long did he live? were so completely forgotten in the twelfth century, that William of Malmesbury, librarian and historian, could claim our author as that abbot of his own monastery who in 979[1] became bishop of Crediton.[2] But, as was shown by Wharton, this was impossible. Ælfric, Bishop of Crediton, died four years before the accession of Sigeric, Archbishop of Canterbury, to whom Ælfric the author dedicated his *Catholic Homilies*, and eighteen years before the accession of Archbishop Wulfstan of York, to whom Ælfric dedicated still another of his undoubted works. The fall of Old English culture, which yielded to that of the Normans soon after Ælfric's time, is probably the chief cause that almost no information has been received from those early centuries concerning his life and works.

In the sixteenth century attention was directed anew to Ælfric. The reformers began to honor him as their first forerunner, and gave themselves to scholarly investigation of his personality, which older writers had left undetermined. These investigations were quickened by the publication of Ælfric's *Sermon on the Paschal Lamb*, first, in 1566, by Parker,[3] the second protestant Archbishop of Canterbury, the father of Old English studies in England; and again by John Fox, in 1571. It seemed most probable that the highly-valued scholar who had written so much had held an important

---

1 Perhaps a year or two earlier.

2 See W. Malmesberiensis, *Gesta Pontificum*. (Rolls Series), p 406.

3 The first edition is attributed to Parker (1504-1575), whose secretary, Joscelin, wrote its preface. In the *Biog. Brit.*, Lond. 1747, fol., in the article *Parker*, this rare book is described, and Ælfric is named as Abbot of St. Albans, about 996.

position in the church. Ælfric the author was a pupil of St. Æthelwold. But Ælfric, Bishop of Wilton (989-995), and afterwards Archbishop of Canterbury, was also a pupil of St. Æthelwold; in him they thought they could find Ælfric the author. This view was brought forward by Bale and by Pits in their works on the authors of Britain, and was strengthened by the opinions of historians like Camden and Bishop Usher. It was introduced by Junius into manuscripts and catalogues,[1] and after the Civil War was accepted by Wanley (1691), Elstob, Lewis, and others. Still later it was defended in a learned treatise by Edward Rowe Mores, *De Ælfrico Doroverniae (Cantuariae) Archiepiscopo Commentarius*, published by Joseph Thorkelin, London, 1789. This opinion was the prevailing one up to the middle of this century, and has been repeated again and again in more recent years. It was that of Henry, the historian, of Watt, the bibliographer, and also of writers who have drawn up more in detail the circumstances of Ælfric's life, such as Norman, and Thomas Wright, the author of the Biographia Britannia Literaria.[2] The larger encyclopædic works of Germany and France allowed themselves to be deceived by it. The *Halle Encyclopædia* based its short article of 1819 only upon Mores' Treatise; and the *Biographie Universelle* in the first supplementary volume of 1834, where Ælfric's writings are treated very inadequately; the *Nouvelle Biographie Generale*, 1855; and Meyer's *Conversations-Lexikon*, 1879, all accepted the same theory.

This identification of Ælfric the author with the Archbishop of Canterbury who died in 1005, is indeed untenable.[3] Wharton in 1691, in his thorough study of the sub-

---

[1] In the catalogue of manuscripts found in the second part of Hickes' *Thesaurus* (1705).

[2] Lingard at first adopted this theory, but writes later: 'A more minute and patient inquiry has convinced me, that there exists no sufficient reason to believe that Ælfric the translator was ever raised to the episcopal bench, much less to either of the archiepiscopal thrones.' *Hist. and Antiqs. of the A.-S.*, *Ch.* II, 453, London, 1845.

[3] Ælfric: monk at Abingdon, and there pupil of Æthelwold; probably Abbot of St. Albans, 969-989 or 990 ; Bishop of Wilton, 989 or 990-995 ; Archbishop of Canterbury, 995-1005 (Nov. 16).

ject, *Dissertatio de Elfrico Archiepiscopo Cantuar, utrum is fuerit Elfricus Grammaticus,*[1] disproved it from the preface to Ælfric's *Life of Æthelwold.* This biography is dedicated to Bishop Kenulph, who in 1006 succeeded Alphege at Winchester, when the latter, on the death of Ælfric, Archbishop of Canterbury, became primate. As Kenulph could not receive a dedication addressed to him as bishop earlier than 1006, the Abbot Ælfric who there addresses him could not be the Ælfric who died in the previous year after ten years' service as archbishop. After Wharton explained this the defenders of the opinion were obliged to deny the *Vita Æthelwoldi* to the author Ælfric, who so often boasted of his education by Æthelwold, and that, too, in spite of the direct testimony of the manuscript and of William of Malmesbury. They were also forced to reject Ælfric's authorship of the *Pastoral Letters for Wulfstan,*[2] which in themselves bear every mark of authenticity. The letters to Archbishop Wulfstan were written by an Abbot Ælfric. But Wulfstan did not become archbishop until Ælfric of Canterbury had been archbishop seven years.

If we compare more closely Ælfric the scholar with Ælfric the Archbishop, their identity is in the highest degree improbable. The noble love which the author felt for the fatherland he expressed by constant efforts for the education of the clergy and the laity, and for their elevation he devoted himself as a scholar to the production of numerous writings in the language of the people. What we know of him with certainty from his own mouth shows him as a humble, conscientious and diffident nature. Ælfric the archbishop, according to the testimony of *Antiquitates Britannicæ,* stood at the head of the citizens of Canterbury against the Danes for the defence of his church and city.[3] His last will, which has

---

1 See Appendix I.
2 Mores and Wright.
3 'Alfricius, ubi plures annos Cantuariensis ecclesiam ab incursu crudeli Dacorum pie fortiterque defendisset.' Matt. Parker, *De Antiq. Brit. Eccles.*, p 136.

fortunately been preserved,[1] helps us to know him better. In this will he bequeaths to the king sixty helmets, sixty hauberks, and his best ship; to the cities of Canterbury and Wilton, each one ship; to the monastery of St. Albans, three estates, his books and his tent. What remains is to be disposed of at the discretion of Bishop Wulfstan and Abbot Leofric, probably his own brother. There follow some smaller bequests of valuables, among which is a psalter which his friend Bishop Wulfstan is to receive. But there is not a word of mention of any of those writings for whose preservation the Grammarian Ælfric was most solicitous. In short, either everything which we learn from Ælfric's works as to his character and education is false, or this rich, warlike archbishop, with his splendid household in Canterbury, is quite another man.

Furthermore, in all else that has come down to us there is not a trace that Ælfric the Archbishop shone in his time as an author, or even as a scholar. Gervasius names him only as a man of distinguished holiness. The sole witness that the friends of this opinion have known how to bring forward is that of the anonymous biographer of Dunstan, a contemporary of both Ælfrics. But what witness does he bear? He dedicates his life of Dunstan to the Archbishop, but only in general terms, 'on account of his very great wisdom, which is known to all, and the extremely great kindness with which he adorned his distinguished office.'[2]

In this there is witness borne to such an education and experience as befitted a pupil of Æthelwold who had risen to the archbishopric, but there is nothing about remarkable scholarship; nothing, in brief, about the services which an

---

[1] Kemble's *Codex Diplomat. Anglo-Saxonum* III, 351: also, in Earle's *Land Charters and Saxonic Documents*, pp. 222–224. In this will the cloisters and cities in which the archbishop had previously lived, are remembered in due succession ; Abingdon, where he was a monk and a pupil of Æthelwold ; St. Albans, where he was Abbot (according to Ranulf de Diceto and Eadmer's *Life of Oswold*); Wilton, where he was bishop ; and Canterbury.

[2] 'Ob enormitatem divulgatae peritiae, perque magnificam placidam privilegii dignitatem.' From Preface to *Life of Dunstan :* Memorials of St. Dunstan. (Rolls Series), p. 3.

author would have been able to extol in Ælfric, the great preacher, biographer, and teacher of the people, not even that which William of Malmesbury knew how to praise in Ælfric the writer. Tradition ascribes no writing to the Archbishop except a liturgy, which was still in use at St. Albans in Leland's time.[1]

But there are besides, authentic data in the life of Ælfric the theologian, which can in no way be reconciled with the known career of the southern archbishop. The author of the *Catholic Homilies* conceived the first idea of them at the Abbey of Cernel, whither he was sent by Alphege II, Bishop of Winchester (984-1006). This must have happened in or after 987, for in that year Cernel was founded anew by Æthelmær, and the same thane had requested that a good Benedictine be sent there to train the monks. At this time the Ælfric who was later archbishop was already Abbot of St. Albans, and by 989 or 990 he was Bishop of Wilton. The monastery of St. Albans in Mercia was under the Bishop of Dorchester. How then came a Mercian abbot to be sent on a mission to Wessex, not by his superior, the Bishop of Dorchester, but by the Wessex bishop? not to mention that, by ecclesiastical law, an abbot was not allowed to be absent a long time from his monastery.

Our Ælfric was at this time, as we have seen, nothing beyond a priest, and lived in Winchester itself, so that his spiritual superior, Alphege, was the one who sent him. Other and more important historical allusions in Ælfric's works, which exclude the southern archbishop, are spoken of elsewhere. Yet what has been brought forward here is quite sufficient to preclude forever the opinion which has been discussed. It has been possible to defend it only by repeated dictatorial statements. Whoever ascribes to the Archbishop of Canterbury the writings of Abbot Ælfric, has to declare two of the least suspicious works, and the homily written for

---

[1] 'Alfricum * * * quem constat D. Albani Liturgiam, qua etiam nunc monachi ibidem utuntur, exarasse.' Leland, *De Script. Brit.* I, 170; but see *Dic. Nat. B.* I. 162.

Bishop Æthelwold II, who became bishop in 1007, not to be genuine; to strike out well-attested facts in the life of the Archbishop, and to bring the strangest inconsistencies into the character of the author Ælfric.

Another current theory, that Ælfric Archbishop of York from 1023 till 1051, was the author, is defended in detail and with great discretion by Wharton in the treatise mentioned above. It commends itself in that the designations 'priest and abbot which Ælfric gives himself in his prefaces remain undisturbed. According to this supposition his archbishopric fell after the completion of all or nearly all of his literary works. Only we must reject, in order not to stretch the life of the author to an improbable length, Wharton's theory that he was the Ælfric born in 952, who worked on the *Saxon Chronicle,* a theory improbable also from internal evidence.

But indeed the historical character of the northern archbishop looks very unlike the gentle mind of the author of the Homilies. Ælfric of York was especially 'detested by the people.' William of Malmesbury[1] says that by his counsel Hardicanute caused the body of his brother Harold to be beheaded and thrown into the Thames; and he says, further, that when vexed against the people of Worcester, who did not receive him to that bishopric, he incited the same king, on the occasion of a resistance to the royal officers, to plunder Worcester and to set it on fire. We have these facts from the mouth of an inhabitant of Worcester, and of a Norman writer who is most to be believed when he says anything unfavorable of the clergy.[2] Such an Ælfric could not

---

[1] 'Ælfricus habetur in hoc detestabilis, quod Hardacnutus ejus consilio fratris sui Haroldi cadavere, etc. Quin et Wigorniensibus pro repulsa episcopatus infensus, auctor Hardacnuto fuit, ut, quia pertinatuis illi exactoribus regiorum vectigalium obstiterant, urbem incenderet, fortunas civium abraderet.' William of Malmesbury, '*Gesta Pontificum,*' III, 115.

See also Matt. Paris, *Chronica Majora* I, 513, Rolls Series.

[2] The first, Florence of Wor.; the second, Wm. of Malmes. 'Rex Ælfricum Eboracensem archiepiscopum, Godwinum comitem, etc. Lundoniam misit, et ipsius Haroldi corpus effodere, et in gronnam projicere jussit.'

'Rex, ira commotus, Thuri, Leofricum, et caeteros, Ælfrico Wigornensem pontificatum tenente, illo misit, mandans ut omnes viros, occiderent, civitatem depraedatam incenderent.' Florence of Worcester's *Chronicle,* Thorpe's edition, I, 194, 195-6.

7

have gone forth from the training of Æthelwold, the noble friend of the people. To such actions that Ælfric could not sink who had dedicated his whole previous life to the culture of the people as no one before him had done. One of the last defenders of Wharton's view, Thorpe, the editor of the *Catholic Homilies,* has therefore placed in contrast with those stories about the archbishop a passage of the *Saxon Chronicle,* where he is called a reverend and wise man. It is indeed possible that tradition has given him a worse character than he deserves, but that any one could invent such stories about him would be sufficient ground for keeping him at a distance from the popular author who was of such a different spirit, and manifestly worthy of praise.

It is a suspicious circumstance that the Archbishop Ælfric of York has the surname Puttoc, while not a single one of all the extant manuscripts of Ælfric's works has any title appended to the author's name save that of abbot.

But if it be allowed that learning and literary activity may have been passed over or forgotten in Ælfric of York, the fact remains that his earlier life does not agree with that of the monk and abbot Ælfric. The succession of bishops in England is now satisfactorily known; their chronology is in most instances in the tenth and eleventh centuries, well ascertained. In 1023, the year that Ælfric became archbishop, no bishop's seat which had been filled by an Ælfric became vacant. Thus he became archbishop immediately after being abbot, or perhaps prior or provost. Relying upon Ralph de Diceto and Florence of Worcester, who say that Ælfric Puttoc, Provost of Winchester, became Archbishop of York, Wharton maintains that this Ælfric may have been abbot at Winchester. This in general would fit the pupil of Æthelwold. But this can be proved false from still existing documents. Ælfric, the writer, as Wharton admits, must have been settled as abbot in 1005. At that time there were but three abbeys in Winchester, and in none of these was there an abbot of the name of Ælfric who could have become archbishop in 1023. By the testimony of the historians he was provost at Winchester when he received the call to York. Thus, without degradation from the abbacy held in 1005, he could not have been provost in 1023. He appears to have been one of those who through the favor of a king have been quickly lifted from a lower ecclesiastical position to the highest, and who then have become either tools without wills of their own, or ambitious incumbents, and he has nothing in common with the teacher of the people, Abbot Ælfric. This last theory, which proceeded, as it appears, from Spelman, has been widely received. It was defended by Wharton in the seventeenth century and accepted by many without further investigation, especially by German scholars. It was repeated in 1830, by Anna Gurney, the author of *A Dissection of the Saxon Chronicle.*[1] Even in 1885, the *Dictionary of National Biography* declared it not to be impossible.[2]

Yet it must be noted that there have always been conservative scholars who have hesitated to accept either theory without more adequate proof. Such are William L'Isle, the editor and publisher of Ælfric's work *On the Old and New Testament;*[3] Cave, the bibliographer; and Lingard, in his later writings.

Ælfric's writings are the chief sources of definite information concerning his person and his position. If we trace in his prefaces his own testimony, we find that he introduces himself in the *Homilies,* his acknowledged first writing, as monk and priest, and *'alumnus Ethelwoldi;'* that he gives himself merely the title of monk in the prefaces to the second part of the *Homilies* and to his *Genesis;* that he calls himself *'humilis frater'* in the introduction to the *Pastoral Letter*

---

1 Miss Gurney attempted to prove that Ælfric was Abbot of Peterborough.

2 Note also from T. D. Hardy, *Cat. of Brit. Hist.* (1862), Vol. I. Pt. II. 587 : 'Mores holds Ælfric the Grammarian to have been Archbishop of Canterbury, and Ælfric, Abbot of Eynsham, afterwards Archbishop of York, to have been the writer of the *Life of Æthewold; and this is probably correct.*'

3 ' Thus as well in his owne Epistles, as in all other books of Sermons in the Saxon tongue that I have seene, I finde him alwais called Abbod and onely so called.' *Sermo Paschalis or Testimony,* etc. Preface by W. L'Isle.

for Wulfsige, and *'humilis servulus Christi'* in the Latin preface to the second volume of *Homilies.* In the *Grammar,* and in the *Saints' Lives,* he gives only his name Ælfric, but his subordinate position shows itself in the latter, where he greets the ealdorman Æthelweard, not 'friendlily' but 'dutifully,' for abbots as well as bishops were the equals of the ealdormen, and indeed sometimes take precedence of them in the documents of the time. In his five other writings which have dedications he gives himself the title of abbot. As such he sends to the Reverend Bishop Kenulph of Winchester, to Archbishop Wulfstan of York, and to the brethren of Eynsham, his greeting in Christ, and greets 'friendlily' the thanes Sigeferth and Wulfgeat. As has been shown, these last five books belong to the eleventh century, the ones before-named to the last decade of the tenth. Thus there is an historical advance in Ælfric's titles; up to a certain time he calls himself monk or mass-priest, after that abbot.

The position of abbot, we must believe, is the highest that he ever occupied, but English scholars have repeatedly asserted that he designates himself as bishop. It is true that a copyist of a manuscript calls him such, but in contradiction of the author's own words. And again, the copy of Ælfric's *Pastoral Letter for Wulfstan,* prepared in the seventeenth century by Junius and now in Oxford, has the rubric, *Insigne fragmentum epistolae ab Ælfrico Episcopo scriptae to gehadedum mannum h. e. ad jam nunc ordinatos.* But this superscription is modern in its whole content. It is plainly nothing but the conclusion of Junius or his scribe from the opening words of the *Pastoral Letter,* 'Ús bisceopum gedafenað' ('It is fitting for us bishops'). It was said by Wharton that a codex of Ælfric's *Pastoral Letter for Wulfstan* in the library of Corpus Christi College, Cambridge, named Ælfric in the superscription as bishop. But Wharton probably confused the original with the copy, the manuscript prepared by Junius from the Cambridge one, and now at Oxford.[1]   The

---

[1] Bodl. Lib. Jun. 45.   cf. Bodl. 4. 12 ;   C. C. C. C.   B. 4.

original has neither superscription nor prologue. All the other old manuscripts which have the prologue, begin, *Prologus venerabilis Ælfrici abbatis. Ælfricus abbas Wulfstano venerabili Archiep. salutem,* etc. The matter is explained very simply by the consideration that the letter was written for and in the name of Wulfstan, who as Archbishop of York and Bishop of Worcester, was to send it forth to his clergy. In the words, 'it is fitting for us bishops,' the spiritual head speaks, not the abbot who had been commisioned by Wulfstan to give in Old English the earlier Latin hortatory letter. Ælfric again clearly designates himself as subordinate in the words with which the preface begins: 'Since I have rendered obedience to the commands of Your Grace and translated the two letters.' That is not the address of one who has the episcopal dignity. If we could decide from this letter that he held that position, we could conclude with equal justice from the sentence in the first pastoral letter, that for Wulfsige: 'We bishops decided when we were convened,' that Ælfric who calls himself monk in the preface was already a bishop. Indeed, the expression 'humilis frater' used in this last connection has been adduced as a proof that he was a bishop addressing a bishop, but this is quite against the sense of this expression and contradicts the testimony of the whole preface, and his plain statement to Wulfsige: 'Nos vero scriptitavimus hanc epistolam, quae anglice sequitur, quasi ex tuo ore dictata sit.' It has even been ascribed to modesty that Ælfric gives himself no higher titles, but Wharton and his followers forbore to make any such preposterous claim for the simple, unaffected sense of Ælfric's words. We confess that we do not understand the modesty which, instead of continuing to remain hidden behind the title of monk, is immodest enough to appear always after a definite time with the title of abbot, which conferred no small honor among the Old English.

The opinion that he held a higher rank after the period of his literary activity is doubtful when viewed in the light of external testimony. At a time when his whole life was manifest, a time not too far removed from his death, when men could not yet have forgotten him, they must necessarily call him by his latest title, both on account of propriety, and to distinguish him from the many clergy of the same name. But to the writers and transcribers of those early centuries he was known only by the title of abbot, there is no dissenting voice. The last ray of possibility of episcopal or archiepiscopal position for Ælfric disappears in the testimony of a man who positively could not have forgotten who Ælfric was, that of Ælfric Bata, the pupil of our much mistaken Ælfric, whose unquestionably reliable witness comes to us in a manuscript from the eleventh century itself. This man says in the enlarged glossed dialogue of his teacher: 'This Latin composition Abbot Ælfric, who was my teacher, wrote some time ago *(olim),* but I, Ælfric Bata, have nevertheless added to it many things.' The use of *olim* does not permit us to suppose that the teacher was still alive, for he would then have been called *venerabilis* or *honorabilis.*

Finally, unlike Dunstan and Æthelwold, there were no kings among Ælfric's patrons. Unusual education and literary influence were not combined in him with a strongly aspiring tendency. Besides, among the Old English the priest had a considerable dignity, he stood in the ranks of the thanes or landed gentry, and abbots were equal to dukes, and were always independent of the bishops and respected at the king's court. Bede, who was more significant as a theologian than Ælfric, and to whom seventy manuscripts are ascribed, never advanced further than the office of mass-priest.

The chief points of refutation of the theories which have been considered, we summarize as follows:

1. Ælfric, Bishop of Crediton, cannot have been Ælfric the scholar, for the following reasons:

    (a) He died in 985, four years before the accession of Archbishop Sigeric, to whom the first writings of Ælfric were dedicated; and

(b)   Seventeen years before the accession of Archbishop Wulfstan, for whom Ælfric wrote a pastoral letter.

2.   Ælfric cannot have been the Archbishop of Canterbury, for these reasons:

(a)   He dedicates his *Life of Æthelwold* to Bishop Kenulph of Winchester, who became bishop after the death of Ælfric of Canterbury.

(b)   As Abbot Ælfric he writes a pastoral letter for Archbishop Wulfstan, who became Archbishop of York in 1002.   It was then at least twelve years since Ælfric of Canterbury left his abbacy at St. Albans, and seven years since he became archbishop.

(c)   The character of Ælfric does not correspond with that of the Archbishop of Canterbury.   The first was a scholar and taught especially that the clergy should not bear arms; the second was warlike, and possessed armor and ships to bequeath to his king and his cities.

(d)   None of the cities mentioned in Archbishop Ælfric's will are those associated with the author Ælfric, nor does the will mention the writings for whose preservation Abbot Ælfric was solicitous.

(e)   Tradition does not ascribe special scholarship to the Archbishop of Canterbury.

3.   Ælfric cannot have been Archbishop of York, for these reasons:

(a)   Ælfric of York died in 1051.   Had the author lived until that time he would have been about ninety-six years old, but no notice of such great age is found in any of the records of the Archbishop of York.

(b)   The Archbishop of York was hated by the people, and was the ready servant of an unpopular king. Ælfric the writer was a friend of the people in all that we know of him, until sixty years of age.   It is inconceivable that when more than eighty years of age he was actively engaged in cruel treatment of the people, or even that such cruel stories could have been invented about him.

(c)   The archbishop's surname, Puttoc, is never joined to the name of Abbot Ælfric.

(d)   There is no evidence whatever that the Archbishop of York ever held an abbacy, but every probability is against it.

CHAPTER VIII.

ÆLFRIC'S HOMILIES.

The
Catholic
Homilies.
'I, Ælfric, monk and priest, although less able than is fitting for such offices, was sent in King Æthelred's day, by Bishop Alphege, Æthelwold's successor, to a monastery called Cernel, at the request of Æthelmær the thane, whose birth and goodness are known everywhere. Then the thought came to me, I trust through God's grace, that I would translate this book from Latin into English; not from confidence of great learning, but because I saw and heard of much error in many English books, which unlearned men in their simplicity esteemed great wisdom; and I was grieved that they neither knew, nor had the gospel teachings in their language, except those who knew Latin, and except the books which King Alfred wisely turned from Latin into English.'

Thus Ælfric relates the origin of his first and most important writing. It was the direct outcome of his practical life as an educator and preacher.

This work, the great collection of homilies for Sundays and the general feast-days of the year, was appropriately named by Wheloc, *Catholic Homilies,* in distinction from those which were written for festivals celebrated only in the monasteries. It is divided by Ælfric into two parts, each one of which has a Latin preface addressed to Archbishop Sigeric, and an English preface on the origin and plan of the work. The volumes are not divided according to the two halves of the church year, but each runs through the whole year. Yet not all the common Sundays are provided with homilies. For example, there are in the two parts only ten for the twenty-seven Sundays after Trinity, here called Sundays after Pentecost. On the other hand, there are nine feast-days doubled, or provided with a separate homily in each book. Except these nine, the second volume takes up Sundays and feast-days which are not considered in the first. Ælfric gives the number of homilies as forty in each part, and eighty in all, although in the preface to the first he says that Æthelweard wished to have forty-four in his copy of that volume. The manuscripts do not show exactly eighty in all. Thorpe in his edition gives forty in the first part, and forty-five in the second.

This last number is made up of thirty-nine of the original collection, with six appended. Following the thirty-ninth is the author's apology, in which he writes: 'Many excellent gospels we omit in this work. These he may translate who will. We dare not lengthen this book much more, lest it be out of due proportion, and repel men by its size. We will nevertheless include in it a few discourses of a general nature, about apostles, and martyrs, confessors, and holy women, to the Saviour's praise.' Then follow six homilies of the kind described.

Ælfric's repeated assertions make it certain that the second part once contained just forty homilies. The fortieth may have been the second discourse on Midlent Sunday, or the one on St. James the apostle included in the numbering with that for Philip and James. The four which Æthelweard wished to have may perhaps be found in the supplement to the second part.

No strict line separates the subjects treated in the second volume from those in the first. Yet it can be said of the first, that it has a larger proportion of scriptural and exegetical content; of the second, that it contains more of legend and of history. Eight homilies of the first are legendary, sixteen of the second. More instruction directly from the Bible is found in the first, which is especially devoted to teaching about God the Creator, the Trinity, the person and work of Christ, and the sin and redemption of man.

The second part especially sets forth ecclesiology and the

means of grace through the church. It is in this that instruction on baptism and on the Lord's Supper are found. Here, too, are the stories of Gregory, and the founding of the English Church; of Cuthbert, one of the great apostles of the English; of Benedict, whose monastic foundations had been strengthened anew in Ælfric's own days. Three of the homilies of the appendix relate to Christ's second coming in judgment, and the final purification of the church.[1]

From the Latin and English prefaces it is clear that Ælfric himself issued at least two editions. The Latin prefaces addressed to Archbishop Sigeric of Canterbury, who assumed that office in 990, with their requests for Sigeric's correction of the manuscripts, must have been written as early as 994, the year in which the Archbishop died. But the English preface to the first volume was probably written or revised in a time long subsequent to 994. Ælfric says in this, that he was sent to Cernel in the day of King Æthelred, as if that day were now past. Æthelred died in 1016. Again, the tone in which he writes is not that of one who speaks of a work just completed, but of one who surveys his own action in past time. In the passage quoted above he says, 'I was grieved that they neither knew nor had the gospel teachings in their language.' Were his work one not yet given to the public, he would have used the present tense. The same can be said of another passage in the preface: 'For this cause I presumed, trusting in God, to undertake this task.' Yet at the same time it is true that several particulars of the preface are especially suitable for the first edition. Such is the emphasis placed upon the expected end of the world; the defense, by a passage in Ezekiel, of his presumption in undertaking so exalted a work; and what is there written of the need of book-learning to strengthen men against temptation. Still further, it is not improbable that the appended sermons of the second

---

1 Many of the homilies are wholly or in part metrical. Such are *Hom.* I, 156 f; *Hom.* II, 132 f, 212 f, 240 f, 298 f, 302 f, 308 f, 314 f, 332 f, 498 f.

volume were added to an edition later than the first, when
Ælfric had on hand sermons not incorporated in any collection.

Ælfric makes no claim to originality in his homilies. In
the Latin preface to Volume I he names six authors as sources
of his work: Augustine, Jerome, Bede, Gregory, Smaragdus
and Haymo. He also gives the original author in the case of
individual homilies. A careful investigation of his sources
has been made by Dr. Max Förster, who reaches the following results:[1]

1. 'The *Catholic Homilies* of Abbot Ælfric are derived in
the largest measure from Gregory's homilies. Next to Gregory in the amount contributed stand Bede, Augustine and a
number of legends, which include, beside single legends, the
Abdias collection. In the third degree of importance as
sources are Smaragdus, Jerome and Haymo. To these should
be added occasional contributions from Alcuin, Amalarius,
Cassian, Ratramnus, Gregory of Tours, Rufinus, and the
Vitae Patrum.

2. Ælfric, in comparison with other translators—for example, King Alfred and the translator of the Blickling Homilies—has preserved a complete independence and freedom,
even where he follows an original. He often derives from his
sources the substance of thought, but clothes it entirely in
his own language.

3. So long as no other sources are pointed out, we must
admit that Ælfric, in additions and in longer explanations
than his originals show, made much use of traditional teachings current in his time.'[2]

It was Ælfric's earnest desire that these two volumes
should be kept intact, not mingled with the writings of
others, and not carelessly transcribed. The only liberty he
allows is that of arranging the sermons of the two volumes
together according to the church year. In the preface of

---

1 *Anglia* 16, 59–60.   2 See Appendix II.

Volume II he says: 'I have placed the translations which I have made in two books, because I thought it would be less tedious to listen if one book were read in one year and the other in the next.' 'Before each homily we have placed the argument in Latin; nevertheless, if any one wishes, he may arrange the chapters each according to its preface.'

The last sermon of the second volume is followed by a prayer of thanksgiving. 'With all my heart I thank the Almighty Creator, that he has granted to me, a sinner, to unfold, for his praise and honor, these two books to the un-learned among the English people. The learned have no need of them, for their own learning will suffice them. I say now, that hereafter I will not translate the gospel or gospel exposi-tions from Latin into English.[1] If any one chooses to trans-late more, I beg him for the love of God, to keep his book separate from the two books which we have translated, as we trust by the guidance of God. To Him be glory to eternity.' These desires of Ælfric in regard to his books were observed by copyists with considerable fidelity. But as the personal tradition of Ælfric faded, his request came to have less weight, and the makers of manuscripts became less careful to keep his homilies apart from those of others. There are ac-cordingly to be distinguished three classes of manuscripts of this work.

I. *Manuscripts which preserve the two volumes of homilies separate from each other.* These must be the oldest, or, if not, copies of the oldest. The best of these is the one upon which Thorpe has based his edition—that of the University Library at Cambridge. It contains both parts, with all of Ælfric's prefaces and some of his later writings. Another manuscript in this class is that in the British Museum, Reg. 7, C.XII. This gives only the first volume and no prefaces. The ser-mons are the same as in the first manuscript, but the thirty-eighth is divided into two, making forty-one in all. The

---

[1] This thanksgiving may have been added to the second edition.

above named manuscripts belong to Ælfric's own time. MS. 188 (earlier No. S. 7), Corpus Christi College, Cambridge, contains Volume I, but without prefaces. Instead of the first sermon on the Creation stands another on the same subject; a few sermons are divided into two parts, and one, *On the Birthday of the Virgin,* is inserted after the one on the beheading of John the Baptist. As an appendix is one *On the Birthday of a Confessor;* not the one in the appendix of the second volume, but that from the text *'Vigilate ergo,'* which is published by Assmann in the third volume of Grein's *Bibliothek der Angelsächsischen Prosa.*[1] These additions appear to justify the claim that Ælfric caused a third edition of his homilies, in which he provided for that feast of Mary which had been before passed over, and added the last homily, of which he expressly states that although it was written at the request of Bishop Æthelwold II of Winchester, yet he was to have a copy for himself.[2]

II. *Manuscripts in which all the sermons of the two volumes are arranged together according to the order of the church year.* The Cotton Codex, Vitell. C. 5, contains a better arrangement than that of any other manuscript of this class. It extends through the whole church year, from Christmas to the Second Advent. It has the first sermon of Ælfric's first volume, *De Init. Creat.,* but that is preceded by a homily on the Trinity and the Feast-days of the Year; it contains a new Christmas sermon, several additional ones for Sundays after Pentecost, and then the usual ones to Second Advent. From there begins an appendix of Lenten sermons for week days, which are probably Ælfric's.

The Bodl. Lib. MSS. NE. F. 4, 10 and 11, contain a rearrangement of the two volumes. The second manuscript, which contains forty-six sermons, is arranged with especial care and accuracy, and from the second edition of the Hom-

---

[1] 'This MS., written before the Conquest, was once Ælfric's own property.' Wanley. Even if this is not the case, it is without doubt copied from one of his own.

[2] See p. 109.

ilies, since it contains its appendix. The first manuscript has but thirty-four sermons.

III. *Mixed manuscripts.* This class, the most numerous of all, places Ælfric's homilies indiscriminately among those of other authors. Here belong Bodl. Lib. Jun. 22; 24, and NE. F. 4. 12; the Cott. MSS., Vesp. D. 14; Vitell. D. 17; Faustina A. 9; Cambridge MSS. C. C. C. 162 (S. 5); (S. 8); 302 (S. 9); and others.

Noteworthy is one of the Cambridge manuscripts, C. C. C. 178 (S. 6). Its scribe explains that he has placed twenty-four sermons in two books; that he has enlarged two of the first twelve from other sermons, but has left the other twenty-two entirely according to their old arrangement. Of the second book, he explains that they are from the books which Abbot Ælfric translated into English, and comparison shows that they are all to be found in Thorpe's edition of the Homilies. The homilies of this second book are arranged together in reference to the life of Christ, from the Annunciation to the day of Pentecost. Some of the sermons in the first book are taken from the *Catholic Homilies,* some from the *Saints' Lives,* and it is most probable that all are Ælfric's work.

From the description of this manuscript by G. E. MacLean (*Anglia* 6. 438-9) we quote the following paragraphs.

'It is quite possible that in this well-compacted and arranged Codex we have a manual edition of selected works, such as the practical Ælfric later in life authorized. The evidence for this theory is not wanting. The older *Benedictine Rules* bound in the Codex show its use as a hand-book.'

'The arrangement of Codex C finely combines an ideal order of thought with the ecclesiastical year. The first sermons of the first Book, (1) De Initio Creaturae, (2) Exameron, (3) Interrogationes, are logically enough placed at the beginning, and in their order set forth (1) creation, (2) its progress, (3) its philosophy and practical trials for man. Then (4) Dom. IIII, post Pen., in which the publicans and sinners draw near to Christ, and the lost are sought by Him, speaks of sympathy and help for man. The course then goes on to prayer, and finally to the field of morals, closing with the immoralities, and the crowning of immorality in *'De Falsis Diis.'* Here the need of the manifestation of the true God leads to the second Book. The *Annunciation,* XVIII (as now numbered), is first, and then the *Birth of Christ.*

'Next, in contrast with the pure One, a New Year's sermon upon the vices is inserted. The regular course of sermons upon the Life of Christ follows, illustrating and pledging the redemption of the world, and culminating upon the day of Pentecost, in the beginning of the new creation.'

When it is remembered that Ælfric lived many years after the *Catholic Homilies* were written, preaching and teaching all his life long, it will not seem strange that single sermons should have been added later to those volumes, or should also be found not placed in any collection, nor will it seem impossible that he may have authorized the arrangement of other volumes. Whether or not the order of this last manuscript is due to Ælfric, it belongs to a time not far removed from him. According to MacLean, the manuscript may be assigned to about 1075.

Thorpe's edition is the only one, but separate homilies are printed in many books.

Homily on the Birth of the Virgin.

In an edition of the first volume of *Catholic Homilies,* that found in MS. C.C.C.C.188 (earlier No. S. 7),Ælfric has inserted a homily for the *Birthday of the Virgin* (see p. 106). He had confessedly omitted this day in his first edition: 'we have not written about it,' he says (Hom. II, 446), 'lest we fall into some error. The gospel of this day is very difficult for laymen to understand.' When at length he decides to provide a homily for this festival, he guards against the aforementioned heresy thus: 'we will not give the false story which heretics have told of Mary's birth, for wise teachers have forbidden it; nor speak of her death, for holy writers do not permit it. Her holy father was named Joachim, and her mother, Anna. They lived in honorable marriage under Moses' law.' 'This day is sacred to the honor of Mary throughout all Christendom.' 'We observe the birthdays of none others in our church, save of Christ, his pure mother, and St. John, who baptized him.'

After the introduction follows the sermon, *'De Sancta Virginitate.'* Its theme is, The Holy Church the Bride of Christ. 'The Church ever imitates the mother of her Lord, who was a virgin and yet bare the Christ.' The sermon is an elaborate plea for celibacy. Its last ninety-two lines consider the rewards of righteous living. They give first an explanation of the penny-reward in the parable of the laborers in the vineyard, and then treat of the eight beatitudes promised by Christ in the Sermon on the Mount. These ninety-two lines are found also as the conclusion of the third edition of the sermon *On Holy Chastity,* in MS. Vitell. C. 5. (see p. 111).

There are three manuscripts of this homily: (1) Corpus Christi College, Camb. 188 (S. 7); (2) C. C. C. C. 303 (S. 17); (3) Bodl. Lib., Oxford, Jun. 24.

This sermon is edited by Assmann in Grein's *Bibliothek der Angelsächsischen Prosa,* Part III.

Homily for the Birthday of a Confessor. A homily from the text, *'Vigilate ergo, etc.,'* bears the rubric, 'We have lately translated this sermon into English at the request of Bishop Æthelwold the Younger (of Winchester, 1007 to 1012), and have had it written in this book, that it may not be lacking to us when he shall have it.' The homily follows the thought of the text closely. It shows the forbearance of God by many instances. 'God punishes those who despise him, sometimes sooner, sometimes later.' 'Sometimes he waits, as we said before, for his great patience, that a man may turn from his sins if he will.' 'Prophets and wise teachers are set to rouse stupid men to action, that if the foolish man does not dread the anger of his Lord, he may perhaps have correc-

8

tion in this world; that thus he may not perish altogether. Everything, even wild beasts, have some terror in this life.' 'The beasts are subject to man, and we should be subject to God.'

Rhythmical form and position in the manuscripts with Ælfric's homilies, render Ælfric's authorship almost certain. The rubric points to the same, and the language and style are Ælfric's.

The manuscripts are the following: (1) C. C. C. C. 188 (S. 7); (2) C. C. C. C. 178 (S. 6); (3 and 4) Bodl. Lib. Jun. 22 and 24; (5) Bodl. Lib. 343=NE. F. 4. 12; (6) Cott. Vitell. D. 17, almost destroyed.

This also is edited by Assmann in Grein's *Bibliothek der Angelsächsischen Prosa,* Part III.

Of Holy Chastity.　　'Ælfric, Abbot, sends friendly greeting to Sigeferth. It was told me that thou saidest of me, that I taught one thing in English writings, and that the anchorite on your manor teaches another; for he says openly that priests are allowed to marry, and my writings deny this. Now I tell thee, dear sir, that I do not like to blame God's own friend if he follows the law of God. But we ought to utter the divine doctrine which the Saviour taught, and we dare not keep silence. His teaching can easily reconcile us.'

With these words of greeting and explanation, Ælfric sends to his friend Sigeferth a homily on chastity, which opens with these words: 'Our Saviour Christ declared plainly that he loved holy chastity in his servants, when he chose a maiden to be his mother.' The writer illustrates his teaching by the lives of Christ and the Apostles, and contrasts it with the permission to marry under the old law.

The line of thought which he pursues further is this: 'There are three orders which are entirely pleasing to God, marriage, widowhood, and chastity.' 'They who live wisely in marriage will have thirty-fold reward from Christ.' 'They who remain widows for Christ's sake will have sixty-fold reward,' and 'they who in the service of Christ live in chastity, and in purity of heart from childhood, shall receive an hundred-fold reward forever with him.' 'We read of countless bishops and monks who lived thus, even as Martin and Gregory, Augustine, Basil and Cuthbert, and many others.' 'And none of them gave permission for any one who was to consecrate the eucharist to have a wife.' Also there were many holy priests like Bede and Jerome, and wise fathers who dwelt in the desert, many thousand, as the *Vitæ Patrum* tells us, who served Christ in purity of heart.

This writing is extant in four manuscripts: (1) Brit. Mus., Cott. Vesp. D. 14; (2) Cott. Faust. A. 9; (3) Cott. Vitell. C. 5; (4) Corpus Christi College, Cambridge, 302 (earlier No. S. 9). The first of these, a MS. of the twelfth century, is the only one which contains the preface. In MSS. 2 and 4 the writing appears simply as a homily; in MS. 3 it is altered and is much longer (see p. 109). Also there is a transcript of the first of these, made before it was injured by fire.

The work as it is found MS. 1 may be a first edition; as in MSS. 2 and 4, a second; and in MS. 3, a third.

The only edition is that of Assmann, in Grein's *Bibliothek der Angelsächsischen Prosa,* Part III.

Homily Addressed to Wulfgeat. Six lines of personal address to Wulfgeat of Ylmandune introduce a discourse in two parts, which is in substance, first, a summary of Christian doctrine, and second, a sermon. In the opening lines Ælfric speaks of English writings which he had formerly lent to Wulfgeat, and of his promise to send him more. From ll. 7-85 he gives an outline of the teachings which Wulfgeat had received already. They treat first of the Trinity; then of the creation and fall of angels; of the creation and fall of man; of redemption through the incarnation, death and resurrection of Christ; of the ascension of Christ; and of the general resurrection and last judgment. The writings thus summarized may be, as Assmann suggests, from the *Homilies*—perhaps *Hom.* I., 8-28, which follows the same line of thought.

The second part is a sermon from the text, 'Agree with thine adversary quickly, whiles thou art with him in the way.' Matt. 5, 25.

The teaching is ascribed to Augustine. The adversary of the text is described as the word of God which we ought to obey. The word will work in us like the healing power of a physician, like the instruction of a good teacher. The adversary is really thy friend. Thou lovest drunkenness. This our Saviour forbids. Deceive not thy neighbor; it were better that each should help the other. God's word forbids all sins in this life. This life is the path in which we are to agree with our adversary, the word. After it there will be no way left us to correct our misdeeds. The word is to be our judge. The Saviour bids us all who labor come to Him. He did not command us to work in another world, nor to work great miracles, but to be gentle in life and meek in heart. We ought to teach the foolish and the careless, else God will require their souls at our hands. God grant to us to tell you often of his holy love, and to you obedience to turn the teaching into works.

This letter is contained in a manuscript in the Bodleian library, Oxford, Laud. Misc. 509, formerly Laud. E. 19. Another manuscript in the Bodleian library, Jun. 121, contains the second part, the sermon. Still a third one at Oxford, Jun. 23, has the whole writing except the seven introductory lines to Wulfgeat.

This writing is found edited by Assmann, in Grein's *Bibliothek der Angelsächsischen Prosa,* Part III.

Homily on John xi, 47-54.   Three manuscripts of the third class, [1] C. C. C. C. 162 (S. 5); 302 (S. 9); Cott. Faust. A. 9, preserve a homily whose style and language are altogether those of Ælfric. Its superscription, and the gospel reading from which the text is taken, assign it to the Friday before Palm Sunday. The theme is

---

1 See p. 107.

the prophecy uttered by Caiaphas, which is explained and applied in the metrical language which Ælfric often uses in his homilies. The sermon shows how the Jews were overtaken by the very evils which Caiaphas described. It tells of their sufferings in the siege of Jerusalem, when the Romans came and destroyed their place and nation, and scattered their people. The second part of the sermon considers, first, the last clause of John XI, 52, and shows how Christ gathered together a people for himself from the heathen nations; secondly, the tenure of office of the Jewish high priest in the older time and in that of Caiaphas, and the establishment of the new priesthood that it might offer the holy eucharist 'as a pledge of the purification of our souls.' The sermon concludes with Christ's departure for the city of Ephraim, by which he gave an example to his disciples, that they might flee from persecutors and yet be sinless.

Assman's edition is printed in Grein's *Bibliothek der Angelsächsischen Prosa,* Part III.

Homily on John xvi, 16-22. An alliterative sermon which is doubtless Ælfric's bears the superscription: '*For the third Sunday after Easter.*' It contains a reference to an earlier writing on 'the great sorrows which came upon the Jews after the slaying of Christ,' and the reference may be to the homily last described, or to any one of several others, or a general reference to all, since the subject was a favorite one with Ælfric.[1]

'For 11. 1-148, the text is John XVI, 16-22; for 11. 149-161, he uses Matt. XXVII, 66, and XXVIII, 11-15. For the conclusion, beginning with 1. 162, the author gives as his source a *cranic* of Jerome.' 'It must have been an apocryphal gospel, apparently related to the Gesta Pilati (cf. Tischendorf: *Evangelia Apoc.* Leipsic, 1876.')[2]

The first part discourses of the sorrows of the disciples

---

[1] 'Many woes and great sorrows befell the Jews, as books tell us, and we have already related in English writings how they perished.'

[2] Assmann, *Bibl. der. A.-S. Prosa* III, 255.

and the joy of Christ's persecutors when he was crucified; then of the church, the bride of Christ, whose martyrs and confessors have suffered, but now dwell with Him.

The second part gives the Biblical narrative from the texts; and the third part tells how Joseph, who buried Jesus, was imprisoned by the Jews and rescued by a miracle.

There is one manuscript of this homily: Trinity College, Camb., B. 15, 34, earlier class, *a dextra ser. suprem.*, 163, 26, fol. 79-90.

This sermon is edited by Assmann, in Grein's *Bibliothek der Angelsächsischen Prosa,* Part III.

Homily on the Sevenfold Gifts of the Spirit. Among the sermons which Ælfric wrote before his work *On the Old and New Testaments,* is one on the *Sevenfold Gifts of the Holy Spirit.* 'Sevenfold gifts he grants mankind, of which I wrote once in another English writing, even as Isaiah the prophet placed it in his prophecy.' This reminiscence of Ælfric's in the treatise *On the Old Testament* is recalled by the opening words of a homily on the gifts of the Spirit found in several manuscripts, and ascribed by Wanley to Archbishop Wulfstan. The words are: 'Isaiah the prophet wrote in his prophecy about the Holy Spirit and his sevenfold gifts.' Wanley's opinion in regard to the authorship of this sermon is derived from the superscription found in several manuscripts: '*Incipiunt sermones Lupi Episcopi.*' It has been shown by Napier that in each of the three manuscripts in which this superscription appears, it is followed by two sermons: the first, an historical summary of Christian teaching; the second, *De Fide Catholica.* The sermons which follow these two in the three different manuscripts do not make three corresponding lists: several of them are the same in all, while others are different, and there is no correspondence in relative position. Some of these are to be ascribed to Wulfstan, some to Ælfric, some to other authors,

---

1 Thus the homily, *De Falsis Diis*, is a paraphrase of a part of Ælfric's homily of the same title.

and still others are mere compilations put together by the
transcriber. Thus the authorship of the sermon in question
is not decided by the rubric.[1]

In Napier's edition of the homilies ascribed to Wulfstan,
the seventh and eighth homilies are on the Sevenfold Gifts
of the Spirit. The second of these is an abridgment of the
first, which it follows sentence by sentence, for the most part
literally. It abbreviates the sentences by omitting everything not necessary for the simplest expression of the
thought; it omits almost all explanatory and amplifying
words and clauses, and leaves out entirely the last two-fifths
of the sermon. Thus the revision is not half as long as the
original. In the attempt to abridge the homily the reviser
has sometimes varied constructions, added new words, and
supplied a closing sentence not found in the first.

The homily first explains the effect of each of the seven
gifts upon the man who receives it, and then tells of the
seven opposite gifts which the devil sends to the hearts of
men. The last part, not contained in the abridgment, shows
the bitter evil of hypocrisy and the deceits of antichrist.

These two forms of the treatise have been studied by D.
Zimmermann. He decides that I. is an independent sermon
of Ælfric's, composed in four-stressed verse, which is to be
regarded as a supplement to his homily for the day of Pentecost, and may have been written between 1000-1008, perhaps in 1005. Zimmermann decides, further, that II. is a
revision of I. by the same man who arranged in their present
form many of the sermons which have been ascribed to Wulfstan.[2]

The first form of the sermon is found complete in MS.
Bodl. Lib. Jun. 99; in part in C. C. C. C. 201 (S. 18); the
second form in Bodl. Lib. NE. F. 4, 12; Jun. 23 and Jun. 24;
Cott. Tib. C. VI; Cambridge, Trinity Coll.

---

1 See Napier's *Über die Werke des Altenglischen Erzbischofs Wulfstan*, pp. 7–9.
2 See *Anglia* 11. 535 f.

On Penitence.

The sermon on penitence which Thorpe has printed at the end of *Catholic Homilies* II., is a free rendering of a part of *Hom.* I. 274-294; it is contained in MSS. which have besides it only works of Ælfric; and its author says that he has written in another place of the Lord's prayer and of the creed. Accordingly Thorpe decided that it belonged among Ælfric's works.

The Hexameron.

A long sermon, called by Wanley the *Hexameron of St. Basil,* was ascribed to Ælfric by Norman, its publisher, and Ælfric is doubtless the author. The style of address to the reader in different parts of this homily is the colloquial one so common with Ælfric. Many passages are almost the same as are found elsewhere in his works, and there are several references to former writings on the same subject. The sermon begins as follows: 'In another discourse we said sometime since that the Almighty God created everything in six days and seven nights; but it is so great and complex a subject that we could not say as much as we wished in the former treatise.' Again, he speaks of the creation of the angels, and says, 'we spoke sometime ago more plainly of them.' Such passages as these remind us of Ælfric's frequent references to his former writings. Other indications of authorship are its alliterative metre, and its presence in manuscripts of the first class.

The *Hexameron* contains an introductory address to the reader; an account of the works of each of the six days of creation; of the fall of the angels before the creation of man; of the seventh day of rest; of the temptation, and sin of man; of his expulsion from Paradise; and of his redemption through Christ.

Of the sources of this homily, Norman says, 'it is by no means a literal translation of the well-known work of that father (Basil), but is partly original, and partly compiled from that work and from the commentaries of Bede upon Genesis.' The arrangement of the material is no doubt Ælfric's; and that the author has drawn from Bede's work which is mentioned above, is seen when the two writings are definitely compared. The scientific passages are indebted to Bede's scientific writings. What Ælfric has taken from Basil's *Hexameron* must be determined by a careful comparison of Bede's *Commentary on Genesis* with the writing by Basil, and then of both with the work in question. Such a comparison has not, so far as we know, been made. It can hardly be correct to call Ælfric's *Hexameron* a 'version' of that of St. Basil.

The reference to a former work on the creation seems to point to the sermon, *De Initio Creaturae,* in the first volume of *Catholic Homilies,* in which also the angels are described 'more plainly' than here. These references, and scientific matter similar to that of the *De Temporibus,* incline us to place the composition at some time between 991 and 998. The following passage which perhaps refers to his writing *On the Old Testament* may point to a much later date. He says, 'All the Old Testament *(gesetnyss)* of which we spoke before (*ǣr*), and the Saviour Himself, in His holy gospel, declare the Holy Trinity in a true unity.'

The manuscripts of the *Hexameron* are these: Cott. Otho B. X, London; Bodl. Lib. Jun. 23 and Jun. 24, Oxford; C. C. C. S 6 and S 7, Cambridge. MS. Jun. 47 is a transcript made after collation of Jun. 23 and Jun. 24. Norman's edition is based on Jun. 23.

Advice to A Spiritual Son. There can be no doubt as to Ælfric's authorship of the Old English version of St. Basil's *Advice to a Spiritual Son.* Its preface, which does not give Ælfric's name, refers to earlier writings on Basil, thus to those found in the first volume of *Catholic Homilies* (p. 448 f) and in the third homily of the *Lives of the Saints;* it gives a brief account of Basil's life, similar in style to the sketch of Alcuin's which opens the *Interrogationes;* it speaks of Basil's *Hexameron* in almost the same words as those with which Ælfric prefaces his account of the six days of creation in the homily called the *Hexameron.* We learn from this preface that the writer was a Benedictine monk who was familiar with the written Rule of St. Benedict. Still further, the two-fold mention of chastity as belonging to the service of God, and the expression: 'We will say it in English; for those who care for it,' are characteristic of Ælfric. All these things, together with the language and the metrical form used by him in other writings assure his authorship.

The work, which is not quite complete, follows the original for the most part closely. Its character and the 'us' of the preface, show that it was written for Benedictine monks.

The preface by Ælfric is followed by a short one by the original author, and by sections on Spiritual Warfare; on the Virtue of the Soul; on the Love of God; on the Love of our Neighbor; on the Desire for Peace; on Chastity; on Avoiding the Love of the World; on Avoiding Avarice.

The date of this writing is probably sometime after 1005, that is, after his preparation of extracts from Æthelwold's *De Consuetudine,* and, like that, it was designed for the monks of Eynsham.

There is one manuscript of this work: Bodl. Lib. Hatton 100. Jun. 68 has a transcript of the same.

The only edition is that of Norman.

CHAPTER IX.

ÆLFRIC'S GRAMMATICAL AND ASTRONOMICAL WRITINGS.

The
Grammar.

The spirit which prompted Ælfric to prepare his Latin grammar, and the practical uses which it was meant to serve, may be learned from the two prefaces of the book. In the second he writes: 'It behooves the servants of God and the monks to take heed lest holy learning grow cold and fail in our days, even as happened among the English only a few years ago, so that before the time of Archbishop Dunstan and Bishop Æthelwold no English priest was able to compose or understand a Latin epistle.' The purpose of the book, which is probably the first Latin grammar in the English language, Ælfric tells in the preface. 'I have endeavored to translate these extracts from Priscian for you, tender youths, in order that, when you have read through Donatus' eight parts[1] in this little book, you may be able to appropriate the Latin and English languages for the sake of attainment in higher studies.' The following extract will illustrate the method of instruction in this grammar of the two languages:

'PARTES ORATIONES SUNT OCTO eahta dǣlas synd lēden-sprǣce: NOMEN, PRONOMEN, VERBUM, ADVERBIUM, PARTICIPIUM, CONJUNCTIO, PRAEPOSITIO, INTERJECTIO. NOMEN is nama, mid ðām wē nemnað ealle ðing ǣgðer ge synderlice ge gemǣne-lice: synderlice be āgenum naman: *Eadgarus, Æthelwol-dus;* gemǣnelice: rex cyning, episcopus bisceop.'

In the author's mind this book was closely connected with

---

1 The grammar of Priscian (ςoo) consists of two parts : Bks. I–XVI (Priscian Major) treat of sounds, word-formation, and inflexion ; Bks. XVII–XVIII (Priscian Minor) of syntax. Among various sources of this work was Donatus' *Ars Grammatica.* Donatus (350) wrote two grammars. The shorter work, *Ars Minor,* which teaches of the eight parts of speech (de octo partibus), was especially used as an elementary text book during the Middle Ages.

the *Catholic Homilies.* He writes: 'I wished to translate this little book into English after I had translated two books consisting of eighty homilies, for grammar is the key which unlocks the sense of those books.' So too, in the minds of Ælfric's readers his *Grammar* has an added importance when considered in connection with his other works. Only then does it appear what it really is, an intrinsic part of a systematic effort to educate the minds and hearts of the English people.

Fifteen extant manuscripts of the *Grammar* show its popularity as a textbook.

The Glossary. Seven of these fifteen manuscripts contain a glossary appended to the *Grammar*. It is introduced by the rubric, *Incipiunt multarum rerum nomina anglice,* and is followed by these words, expressive of its incompleteness, 'we can neither write nor even imagine all names.' This Latin-English dictionary consists of Latin nouns and adjectives with their English equivalents, classified, not alphabetically, but according to subject. It begins with God and the creation, defines parts of the body, names of birds, beasts, fishes, etc., and ends with characteristics of men. Wright suggests that this and similar vocabularies were designed for teachers as well as pupils. He says: 'In the earlier and better period, no doubt the teacher had such lists merely in Latin, or glossed only in cases of difficulty, and he was sufficiently learned in the language to explain them; but now the schoolmaster required to be reminded himself of the meaning of the Latin word.'

Tradition and the nature of the work, as well as its position in the manuscripts render Ælfric's authorship of the *Glossary* probable. It is specially adapted to promote the aims of his *Grammar,* and the words defined belonged to Ælfric's vocabulary.[1]

---

[1] MacLean has called attention to Ælfric's indebtedness in the *Glossary* to Isidore. Cf. e. g. Isidore's *Etymologiarum*, Lib. XII. Cap. II, VI. (Migne. *Patrologia Latina*, 82. ed. 1850).

The glossary entitled *Archbishop Alfric's Vocabulary* printed in *Anglo-Saxon and Old English Vocabularies,* pp. 106-167, is not the one found so often in the manuscripts with Ælfric's *Grammar.* The latter is printed in the above-named book, pp. 306-336. Its presence in the Oxford manuscript which contains Ælfric's *Colloquium* as revised by his pupil, Ælfric Bata, and its use by Ælfric Bata in that revision, strengthen the probability given by its frequent association with the Grammar, that it is the authentic vocabulary of Ælfric. The Oxford manuscript (no. 8 below) is the one which Zupitza has taken as the basis of his edition of the *Grammar* and *Glossary.*

The best edition is that of Zupitza (1880), which gives the text, and variant readings from all of the manuscripts. As enumerated by him they are the following:

1. All Souls' Coll., Oxford; 2. Corpus Christi Coll., Cambridge; 3. Cathedral Lib., Durham; 4. Cotton, Faustina, London; 5-6. Harleiana, London; 7. Cotton, Julius, London; 8. John's Coll., Oxford; 9. Paris; 10-11. MSS. of MSS. Reg., London; 12. Sigmaringen; 13. Trinity Coll., Cambridge; 14. Univ. Lib., Cambridge; 15. Cathedral Lib., Worcester.

Besides the above MSS., three transcripts are mentioned by Wanley: 1. (p. 102) Jun. 7, Oxford; 2. (p. 308) transcript in the possession of Simonds D'Ewes of Stow-Langton, Suffolk; 3. (p. 84) Bodl. Lib., Oxford.[1] MSS. nos. 2, 4, 5, 7, 8, 14, 15 contain the *Glossary.*

The
Colloquium.
Ælfric's Colloquium is a Latin dialogue with English glosses above the lines. Its opening words, '*Nos pueri rogamus te, Magister, ut doceas nos loqui latialiter recte*' ('We boys request thee, Master, to teach us to speak Latin correctly'), indicate its purpose, to serve for practice in Latin in the cloister-schools. Its elementary character and the nature of the conversations show that Ælfric had in mind the same 'tender

---

[1] See Wülcker's *Grundriss der Angelsächsischen Litteratur,* p. 462.

youth' for whom he prepared his *Grammar*. After a pre-
liminary talk with the first speaker, who professes to be a
monk, the Master asks: 'What do these your comrades know?'
The boy replies: 'Some of them are plowmen, some shepherds,
some oxherds, others are hunters, fishers, birdcatchers, mer-
chants, shoemakers, salt-dealers, bakers, and cooks.' There
follows then a conversation of the master with the plowman,
the shepherd, the oxherd, and the rest, in which each tells
something about his daily tasks. The master praises these
worthy companions of the monk, and questions him about
others. Comrades of other crafts come forward, and also a
wise counsellor whom the master addresses thus: 'Wise man,
what calling seems to you the highest among all these?'
Then the counsellor discusses the question with the smith
and the carpenter, and concludes with the sage advice, that
every one should fulfil his own task with diligence, 'for it is
a great disgrace and shame for a man not to be willing to be
that which he both is and ought to be.' The master again
converses with the first youth, who tells of his high aspirations and describes his life in the cloister-school. The agreeable whole is concluded by the master with an exhortation to
his pupils.

This work is found in two manuscripts: (1) Cott. Tib. A.
III, from which it has been printed by Thorpe, who has been
followed by Wright and others; (2) Oxford, St. John's College. In this there is found the following explanation, which
is a sufficient guarantee of authorship: *'Hanc sententiam
latini sermonis olim Ælfricus abbas composuit, qui meus fuit
magister, sed tamen ego Ælfric Bata multas postea huic addidi
appendices.'*[1] As no such words are found in the Cotton

---

[1] This sentence comprises about all that we know of Ælfric Bata. A few words in
Osbern's *Life of St. Dunstan*, written in the time of Lanfranc, say that St. Dunstan
declared in a vision to one who sought his shrine, that Ælfric Bata tried to overthrow the
church of God (*Memorials of St. Dunstan* p. 136). This indicates that Ælfric Bata was
living after the Conquest. It is thus not unlikely that he was a pupil at Eynsham, rather
than earlier at Cernel. It may be, as Schröder suggests, that the above-mentioned Oxford
MS. was wholly prepared by him. It is certainly true that his fame is most of it gratu-
itous.

manuscript, and the form there given is briefer and more concise, the presumption is that we have in that the original work as written by Ælfric. This view is confirmed by the comparison of the two manuscripts made by Zupitza.[1] He finds in the Oxford manuscript most of the matter that is in the other. The only omission is the concluding exhortation, for which a different ending is substituted. But there are, indeed, many additions; additions made in such a way as to spoil the direct, vigorous style of Ælfric the abbot. Even if no other indications were given, it would be clear that some other hand than its author's had revised it. Two passages are here cited, as given by Zupitza from the Oxford manuscript, to show Ælfric Bata's method of adding appendices. The italics show the part common to the two manuscripts; the remainder is Ælfric Bata's addition. '*Quales* autem *feras maxime capis?* *Capio* utique *cervos* et cervas et vulpes et vulpiculos et muricipes et lupos et ursos et simias et fibros et lutrios et feruncos, taxones et lepores atque erinacios et aliquando *apros et damnas et capreos et sepe lepores.*' And again, '*Quid facis de tua venatione? Ego do regi, quicquid capio, quia sum venator ejus. Quid dat ipse tibi?* vel cujus honoris es inter tuos socios? Primum locum teneo in sua aula, vestitum autem et victum satis mihi tribuit et aliquando vero anulum mihi aureum reddit et *vestit me bene et pascit et aliquando dat mihi equum aut armillam, ut libentius artem meam exerceam.*' The work of Ælfric Bata, as compared with that of his teacher, shows useless repetitions, unwise choice of material, and lacks all sense of proportion and literary fitness.

'It is in the highest degree probable that this work was written after the *Grammar* and *Glossary* to serve as an exercise for practice. It is evident that the arrangement of the *Glossary* is pre-supposed in the *Colloquium,* for example in the choice of certain groups of words, such as the names of

---

[1] Zeitschrift für Deutsches Alterthum, 31, 32-45.

animals and fishes.'[1] Schröder, from whom we have just
quoted, shows that the lists of words in the *Colloquium* of the
Cotton manuscript preclude the idea that there is any immediate literary dependence of the latter work upon the
former; but that, on the other hand, Ælfric Bata must have
had the *Glossary* immediately before him when he made his
revision, as is seen by comparison of his additions to the lists
of fishes and of animals, with the lists of the same in the
Glossary.

It is not probable that the Old English gloss of the Cotton
manuscript is by Ælfric. It has been urged by Zupitza that
the author of the glosses showed strange ignorance and shal-
lowness in putting Latin into English; and by Schröder that
many of the Old English words used here are not those which
Ælfric used in his *Glossary* to define the same Latin words;
and further, that the character of the vocabulary makes it
probable that the gloss was not added till two generations
later.

The *Colloquium* in the Oxford manuscript has few glosses,
and the fragment of the *Colloquium* as revised by Ælfric
Bata, found in a recently-discovered manuscript (Brit. Mus.
add. 32246), has none.

The *Colloquium* has been often printed. A good edition
is that of the Wright-Wülcker *Anglo-Saxon and Old English
Vocabularies* (1884). That of the Oxford manuscript has not
yet been printed.

De
Temporibus.
De Temporibus, the Old English compilation from Bede's writings, is in its first part an
astronomical treatise upon the earth, sun,
moon and stars; its second part treats briefly of atmospheric
phenomena. Both its content and its position in the manuscripts lead us to ascribe it without question to Ælfric.
Wright noted the fact that the Ælfrician lament over the ignorance of the priests is found here, and Ælfric's acquaintance with Bede's astronomical writings, shown in one of his

---

[1] *Zeitschrift für Deutsches Alterthum*, 41, 283–290.

homilies, should also be noted. In the homily for the day of
the circumcision of Christ, *Hom.* I, 100 ff., we find a discussion
of the different beginnings of the year among ancient
nations, and an appeal to Bede's authority. The matter here
brought forward corresponds with the second section of the
Old English *De Temporibus.* Moreover, the rest of the contents
of the *De Temporibus* agree with Ælfric's other efforts
for the instruction of the youths of the cloister.

The external evidences are no less clear. In the Cambridge
manuscript, which contains Ælfric's two books of
Catholic Homilies, the treatise which we are considering follows
the last homily of the first book, and is preceded by this
sentence of explanation: 'Here follows a brief writing upon
the times of the year, which is not to be accounted a homily,
but is to be read by whomever it pleases.' All except the
introductory clause is found again in the beginning of the
treatise itself. It would indeed be possible that Ælfric
announced there a translation not his own, which he had in
his keeping, but that idea is rendered improbable by its position
in another manuscript, the very gradually compiled
Codex Cott. Tib. B. V., where it follows a catalogue of
bishops in which Sigeric is the last Archbishop, and immediately
follows an account of the archbishop's stay in Rome,
which can only have taken place in the first year of his office
(990). Ælfric dedicates both volumes of his homilies to
Sigeric.

The preface of the treatise, in which the 'I' of the author
is prominent, the ascription of the work to Bede, the content
of the book, and the reverent postscript, all agree with the
style of Ælfric as we find it in his undoubted works.[1] The
manuscripts of the *De Temporibus* are these: (1) Cott. Tiberius,
A. III; (2) Cott. Tiberius, B. V; (3) Cott. Titus,
XV. (imperfect). It is printed in the third volume of *Leechdoms,
Wortcunning,* etc.

---

[1] See Appendix III.

9

CHAPTER X.

THE LIVES OF THE SAINTS;
CANONS OR PASTORAL LETTERS.

Lives of the Saints. 'Ælfric humbly greeteth Æthelwerd ealdorman. I bring thee word, dear sir, that I have now collected in this book such passions of the saints as I have had leisure to translate into English. I have done this, my friend, at thy request and at that of Æthelmær, who have both earnestly prayed me for such writings. Ye have already received from my hands, for the strengthening of your faith, writings which ye never before had in your language. Thou knowest, friend, that in the two former books we translated the passions and lives of those saints which the English nation honoreth with festival days. Now, however, it hath seemed good to us to write this book about the passions and lives of those saints whom the monks celebrate among themselves.'

Ælfric, in his Latin preface of the *Saints' Lives,* and in the English preface of the same, whose opening words we have given, carefully distinguishes this, his third volume of homilies, from the two preceding. Like each book of *Catholic Homilies,* this is a collection of forty sermons for the church year, beginning with Christmas. A part of the *Catholic Homilies* are written in alliterative form, but nearly all of the *Saints' Lives* are metrical.

Scattered through this book of *Saints' Lives* are many discourses of more general character. The first of these, that for Christmas day, which begins the book, is an abstract treatment of the nature of God, and of the soul of man. This is followed by eight narratives appropriate to eight saints' days—the stories of saints Eugenia, Basil, Julian and Basilissa, Sebastian, Maurus, Agnes, Agatha, and Lucy. The tenth sermon, for February 22d, the day in the calendar on which

St. Peter became bishop of Antioch, according to the Antioch reckoning, is composed chiefly of scriptural incidents of St. Peter's life, and is the second of the general sermons mentioned above. After the legend of the forty Cappadocian soldiers, who 'suffered for Christ in the Emperor Licinius' days,' the third and fourth general discourses follow. These are, one for Ash-Wednesday, which warns and exhorts men to keep Lent and to live a zealous, progressive Christian life; and one for Mid-Lent, on the *Prayer of Moses.* The fourteenth and fifteenth homilies are legends of St. George and of St. Mark, but the second and longer division of St. Mark's homily treats of the four evangelists and is chiefly scriptural in content. Number sixteen, *De Memoria Sanctorum,* 'a sermon for any occasion,' from the text, 'I am Alpha and Omega,' etc., tells how 'we may take good examples, first from the holy patriarchs, how they in their lives pleased God, and also from the saints who followed the Saviour.' The last third of this discourse treats of 'the eight deadly sins, which sorely fight against us,' and 'the eight cardinal virtues, which may overcome these aforesaid devils through the Lord's help.' To this sermon of catholic content succeeds still another, one for Rogation-Sunday, on *Auguries.* The general introduction on Galatians 6, 15, leads to a sermon by St. Augustine, which discourses on auguries, witchcraft, and similar superstitions.

In Ælfric's work, *De Veteri Testamento,* are these words: 'there are many kings in the books of Kings, about whom also I wrote a book in English.' This reference is probably to the eighteenth sermon of the *Saints' Lives.* It tells briefly of Saul and David, more at length of the history of Israel in the days of Elijah and Elisha, then of Hezekiah and several later kings, and ends with Josiah. Numbers nineteen, twenty and twenty-one tell the stories of three English saints: Saint Alban, not of the English race, who perished in the persecution of Diocletian; Saint Ætheldred, wife of King Egfrith, a founder of the monastery of Ely, and a noted one among the cloister saints; and Saint Swithun, Bishop of Winchester, Ælfric's own city, and especially famous in King Edgar's days—that is, when Ælfric himself was living in Swithun's own monastery. The next three are also legends of saints: of Saint Apollinaris, of the Seven Sleepers, and of Abdon and Sennes. Then comes still another referred to by Ælfric in the *De Veteri Testamento,* that about the books of Maccabees, of which he wrote: 'I turned them into English; read them if ye will, for your own admonition.' The *Maccabees* is rather a historical book than a sermon. Its divisions are preceded by references to the chapters from which they are taken in the books of Maccabees, and the whole is very long. At the end a passage set off from the preceding portions treats of three orders of men—laborers, beadsmen and soldiers. 'Laborers are they who obtain with toil our subsistence; Beadsmen are they who intercede with God for us; Soldiers are they who protect our towns, and defend our soil against an invading army.'

The twenty-sixth sermon, for August 5th, is the story from Bede's Ecclesiastical History, of St. Oswald, the English king and martyr. Ten legends follow: those of the Holy Cross, St. Maurice and the Theban Legion, St. Denis, St. Eustace, St. Martin, the English St. Edmund, St. Euphrasia, St. Cecilia, Crisantus and Daria, and St. Thomas the Apostle. Ælfric's translation of Alcuin's *Interrogationes* is the thirty-seventh discourse, and the last two are, *Of False Gods* and *Of the Twelve Abuses.* The placing of St. Euphrasia, whose day is February 11th, among the November saints may be due to a mistake of the transcriber.

The only good manuscript, that which Professor Skeat has taken as the foundation for the text of his edition, is the Cottonian Codex, Julius E. VII, British Museum. But single lives and parts of the collection are found in others. [1] From the description by MacLean of the one good manu-

---

[1] Cf. A. Napier, *A Fragment of Ælfric's Lives of Saints.* Mod. Lang. Notes, 1887, 378-9.

script (*Anglia* 6. 441) is quoted the following: 'The MS. table of contents is printed accurately in Professor Skeat's Edition of *The Lives of the Saints,* pp. 8-10, giving the entire number of articles as XXXIX. Wanley, carefully printing from the titles distributed through the Cod., has XLVIII, without counting the last and missing sermon, which would make XLIX. Subtract Wanley's articles (VIII, XVII, XXII, XXV, XXIX, XXX, XXXII, XXXIV, XXXV = 9) and we have forty remaining. These nine are not mentioned in the MS. index, and are variations of the same narratives, a note, and a sermon inserted with an 'item.' Add Wanley's XXVIII, or, it may be, count some 'Item Alia,' and we have forty in the MS. list and in that of Professor Skeat.' 'We may call forty Ælfric's ideal number for a volume of homilies. And it fits his character to be just so exact.'

Inserted between *The Seven Sleepers* and *Abdon and Sennes* stands a long homily on the *Death of St. Mary of Egypt,* which is not mentioned in the table of contents. This 'may have been bound into this codex many years later.' 'The question cannot be determined until some one makes researches with reference to the portion of the codex involved, and with reference to the origin of the A. S. *Ægyptian St. Mary.*'[1] The language and expressions of this homily seem to be inconsistent with Ælfric's authorship.

Many passages are to be found in the *Saints' Lives* which illustrate the life and times in which Ælfric lived. Such there are worthy of especial note in the homilies on *The Prayer of Moses;* on *Auguries;* on *St. Swithun;* and for Ash-Wednesday.

It is indeed true that saints' lives preponderate in this volume, even as the preface leads us to expect, but written as it was, especially for the laity, at the request of two laymen, Æthelweard and Æthelmær, the teaching of catholic truth was an important part of its purpose. It does not read quite

---

[1] MacLean.

like a book of legends of the saints, but as one of Christian instruction, illustrated largely by those who had exemplified
Christian faith. Its character is not so different from the first
two volumes as its title might indicate. Viewed from this
standpoint, the presence of such chapters as the *Interroga—
tiones,* the *False Gods,* and the *Twelve Abuses,* which have
been sometimes regarded as an appendix, becomes clear and
consistent.

We must believe that not more than three or four years
elapsed from the completion of the second volume of homilies, before Ælfric was ready with the third. As we read his
translations we cannot feel that the work was an uncongenial
one, and its ready acceptance with those whose desires it
satisfied must have made him eager to gratify them yet more.
In the library to which he had access there were still other
Latin books which would be of interest to his friends and to
English Christians. Hence whatever grammatical writings
he had on hand after his second volume was put forth, it is
not likely that he altogether ceased from the sort of translations that he had first undertaken. We can imagine
that one thing after another which was later to find place in
the Saints' Lives, was put into English before the definite
plan of a third volume came to his thought. Then with the
entreaties of his friends who were aware of his work, came the
new idea, that he should make still another book. The
saints' lives already translated suggested the prominent feature of the book, and into the volume he could fit whatever
renderings he now had completed, and also other pieces
which he desired especially to write. The words of the prefaces do not forbid some such origin as this, and the character of the work in detail and as a whole suggests it.

As regards sources, those of particular sermons are often
indicated by Ælfric. The preface, however, mentions only
the *Vitae Patrum,* and leaves it uncertain whether that is
really one of his sources. 'I do not promise to write very many
(passions of saints) in this tongue, because it is not fitting

that many should be translated into our language, lest peradventure the pearls of Christ be had in disrespect. And therefore I hold my peace as to the book called *Vitae Patrum,* wherein are contained many subtle points which ought not be laid open to the laity, nor indeed are we ourselves quite able to fathom them.'[1]

The only complete edition of this work is that by Professor Skeat.[2] Single lives are found in many books.

Queries of Sigewulf the Priest. The Old English translation and revision of Alcuin's treatise on Genesis has been usually ascribed to Ælfric. The slight uncertainty which has been felt because, contrary to his custom in works of importance, he does not name himself as the author, has been more than balanced by the strong internal and external evidences in his favor. Such evidences are the position of this work in the manuscripts with other writings of Ælfric; its style; its subject matter, and its alliterative form. The investigations made by MacLean have settled the question conclusively. The omission of the author's name is now accounted for by the fact that Ælfric did not issue the piece as a separate work, but as one of a series of homilies which is opened by two prefaces in which he writes in his own name. In all of the five manuscripts that contain it, it is found associated with sermons from the *Saints' Lives,* and in the chief manuscript of that work it stands as sermon number thirty-seven.

From MacLean's dissertation we take the following paragraphs descriptive of the purpose and origin of the work:

'Alcuin, the celebrated English scholar, and teacher of Charlemagne, compiled in Latin, at the end of the eighth century, a Handbook upon Genesis. The immediate occasion of the work was the questions upon certain difficulties in Genesis, which his inseparable pupil and friend, the presbyter Sigewulf, had at different times put to him. Therefore

---

1 See Appendix V.

2 Only three parts are yet published, but the fourth is soon to appear.

the little volume, written in cathechetical form, was dedicated, in an affectionate preface, to Sigewulf, whose name it has since borne,—*Interrogationes Sigewulfi Presbyteri.* The aim of Alcuin was, in his words, "to gather from heavy tomes *pretiosas sapientiae margaritas,* which the weary traveller might carry with him, and with which he might recreate himself." The testimony for this work is that it lived.

'Two hundred years later, another Englishman, the A-S. author Ælfric, the teacher, not of a Charlemagne, but of a country, translated Alcuin's work "on Englisc." Ælfric abridged the two hundred and eighty questions and answers of Alcuin to sixty-nine. He added a preface upon the "illustrious teacher," Alcuin, inserted an astronomical page, probably appended a creed and doxology, and in many points impressed the production with his winning personality.

'With great skill he retained the catechetical form, while he adorned the work with a rhetorical, if not poetical, semi-metrical alliteration.

'The *Interrogationes Sigewulfi* retained its old name and was issued as a sermon in a series of homilies entitled *Passiones Sanctorum.*'

The following analysis of the work is that of MacLean:

I. Introduction. The life of Alcuin, and the origin of the Latin work, 11. 1-17.

II. Questions I-XV, inclusive. Difficulties in the Creator's moral government, or in the rational creation.

III. Questions XVI-XXI. The physical creation. This scientific division is crowned by Ælfric's insertion from Bede about the planets.

IV. Questions XXII-XXVI. The Father, Christ, the Spirit, and the Trinity as manifested in creation.

V. Questions XXVII-XXXIV. The Origin of man; his divine image and possible destinies.

Ælfric begins this writing with these words: 'There was in England a remarkable teacher named Albinus (Alcuin), and he had great reputation. He taught many of the English in the sciences contained in books, as he well knew how, and afterwards went across the sea to the wise King Charles, who had great wisdom in divine and worldly matters, and lived wisely. Albinus the noble teacher came to him, and, there a foreigner, he dwelt under his rule, in St. Martin's monastery, and imparted to many the heavenly wisdom which the Saviour gave him. Then at a certain time, a priest, Sigewulf, questioned him repeatedly from a distance about some difficulties which he himself did not understand in the holy book called Genesis. Then Albinus said to him that he would gather together all his questions, and send him answers and their explanations. Sigewulf questioned him first in these words; What is to be understood by this: The Almighty ceased from his works on the seventh day, when he created everything; but Christ said in his gospel, my Father worketh until now and I work? Albinus answered him: God ceased from the new creation, but he renews the same nature every day, and will guide his work until the end of this world.'

The above quotation not only shows something of the methods of Alcuin and of Ælfric, but it is also an example of

Ælfric's practical mind, which always connected the past with the present, and sought if possible to give a reason for each of his new undertakings.[1]

This book, with the Latin original, is printed by MacLean in *Anglia* 7. 1-59.

Life of St. Neot. The Old English life of St. Neot may have originated with Ælfric. In the one manuscript in which it is found complete, Cott. Vesp. D XXI, its language is that of the twelfth century. Different writers have ascribed it to Ælfric. Sharon Turner says: 'It follows an account of Furseus, an East Anglian saint, and some religious essays of Ælfric.' 'As Ælfric wrote the lives of many saints in Saxon, it is most probably his composition.' Wülcker says that the style of narration and the choice of material point to Ælfric as its author.

The homily has been several times printed. The most recent edition is in an article by Wülcker, in *Anglia* 3. 102-114. From that article are taken the few facts here given. Notes on the text published by Wülcker are found in *Englische Studien,* 6, 450-1 (by E. Kölbing).

Life of Saint Guthlae. The Old English prose translation of the *Vita Guthlaci,* found in MS. Cott. Vesp. D. XXI, was ascribed by Wanley to Ælfric. In favor of this claim are the free style of the translation, the discreet abridgment, and the change from the bombast of the original to simple, straightforward language. The language must give the final decision. Since that shows older forms than those of Ælfric's time, it is probably by an earlier writer. From Goodwin who published an edition in 1848, we take the following: 'The *Life of St. Guthlac,* Hermit of Crowland, was originally written in Latin by one Felix, of whom nothing is with certainty known.' 'When and by whom this translation was made is unknown; the style is not that of Ælfric, to whom it has been groundlessly ascribed.' 'The writer often

---

[1] See Appendix IV.

paraphrases rather than translates, and in truth sometimes quite mistakes the sense of the original.'

Besides the manuscript that has been mentioned, the Codex Vercellensis has two chapters of this Old English prose *Life of Guthlac.*

The Latin Life of Guthlac is printed in the Acta Sanctorum under the eleventh of April.

CANONS, OR PASTORAL LETTERS.

Pastoral Letter for Wulfsige of Sherborne. Wulfsige, Bishop of Sherborne (993-1001), requested Ælfric to compose for him a pastoral letter to the clergy of his diocese. Ælfric accordingly writes the letter, not in his own name, but in that of the bishop. He prefaces it with a short personal letter to Wulfsige. 'We have not dared,' he says, 'to write anything about the episcopal office, because it belongs to you to know in what way you should be an example to all by the best practices, even as it is yours to know how to exhort your subordinates with constant admonitions to seek the salvation which is in Christ Jesus. I say, nevertheless, those things which you ought again and again to say to your clergy, and in regard to which you should show their remissness, since through their frowardness the canon laws, and the religion and doctrine of holy church are destroyed. Free your mind, therefore, and tell them what ought to be regarded by the priests and ministers of Christ, lest you yourself perish likewise, if you are accounted a dumb dog. We verily have written this letter which follows in English, as if it were dictated by your own mouth, and you had spoken to your subordinate clergy.'

The pastoral letter is divided into two parts. The first consists of thirty-five sections.

Sections 1-9 inculcate celibacy.

Sec. 1 begins with a peremptory address: 'I say to you, priests, that I will not endure the carelessness of your service, but I will tell you truly what the laws are concerning priests. Christ himself established Christianity and chastity.'

Sec. 2. Persecutions after the days of the apostles prevented any synod of the church until Constantine convened one at Nicea.

Sec. 3. The Nicene Council was assembled for the confirmation of the faith. (Note the superscription of this letter: 'Be synoðe prēosta').

Sec. 4. 'At this synod were appointed the holy church services, the mass-creed, and many other things, respecting God's worship and servants.'

Sec. 5. This synod unanimously decreed that no bishop, priest, deacon, or regular canon, should have in his house any woman save his mother, sister, or aunt.

Sec. 6. 'This will seem strange to you, because ye have brought your wretchedness into a custom.' 'Priests often say that Peter had a wife, but he forsook his wife and all worldly things.'

Sec. 7. The old law allowed bishops to marry. But that was before Christ appointed the eucharist and the mass.

Sec. 8. The same synod determined that no man might enter the priesthood or any order who had been married to a widow or a divorced woman.

Sec. 9. No priest may countenance or bless any second marriage, although a layman may marry a second time if his wife desert him.

Sec. 10. Seven degrees are established in the church: ostiarius, lector, exorcista, acoluthus, subdiaconus, diaconus, presbyter or priest.

Sec. 11-16 define the duties of six orders.

Sec. 17-32 define the duties of the priests.

Sec. 17. The priest must hallow the eucharist. He must instruct the people, and give an example to Christians. There is no difference between a priest and a bishop—although the bishop takes precedence—save that a bishop is appointed for

the ordination of priests, confirmation of children and conse-
cration of churches, and to take care of God's dues.

Sec. 18. Monkhood and abbothood are not reckoned with
these orders, but are also holy orders 'and bring to heaven the
souls of those priests who observe them.'

Sec. 19. The priest should officiate in his church, and
sing there the seven canonical hours.

Sec. 20. He should fervently pray for the king, his bishop,
his benefactors, and all Christians.

Sec. 21. He should also, before he is ordained, possess as
instruments for spiritual work the following holy books: a
psalter, a book of epistles, a book of gospels, a missal, a
hymnary, a manual, a ritual book, a pastoralis (i. e., of St.
Gregory), a penitential, and a lectionary.

Sec. 22. The priest's vestments must not be soiled or torn,
and the altar cloths and vessels of the service must be good,
and in good condition, as befits Christ's service.

Sec. 23. 'The priest ought on Sundays and mass-days to
tell the people the sense of the gospel in English, and about
the Pater Noster and the creed as often as he can, as a stimulus to men, that they may know the faith and hold fast their
Christianity.' 'Blind is the teacher if he know not book-
learning.' 'Therefore take heed against this, as ye have
need.'

Sec. 24-26 speak briefly of tithes, mass and baptism of children.

Sec. 27. No priest shall perform God's service for money;
nor,

Sec. 28, for covetousness go from one minster to another;
nor,

Sec. 29, drink immoderately; nor,

Sec. 30, live as men of the world live.

Sec. 31. He shall shrive sinners and administer the
eucharist to the sick; and,

Sec. 32, he shall anoint the sick according to St. James'
command.

Sec. 33. There were four synods for the true faith against heretics. Their decrees are to be observed, even as the four books of Christ.

Sec. 34. 'How dare ye despise all their ordinances, while monks hold the ordinances of one man, the holy Benedict? Ye also have a rule, if ye would read it. But ye love worldly conversations, and wish to be reeves, and neglect your churches, and the ordinances altogether.'

Sec. 35. 'We will, however, recite the ordinances to you, lest we ourselves also perish. Rejoice not at the death of men, nor attend the corpse unless invited. When so invited, forbid the heathen songs of the laymen, and their loud cachinnations; nor eat nor drink there lest ye be imitators of the heathenism which is there committed.' Dress well, not proudly, but suitably to your order. This section closes with the doxology.

Sec. 36. The second part of the letter, which is of about one-third the length of the first, is devoted for the most part to instructions about the eucharist: first, in reference to the services on Good Friday, when the elements are not allowed to be consecrated, and on the following days; secondly, against the long keeping of the consecrated bread; thirdly, of the significance of the consecrated bread, which 'is Christ's body, not bodily, but spiritually; it is not the body in which he suffered, but that about which he spoke when he blessed bread and wine for the eucharist on the night before his passion.' 'Understand now that the same Lord who could, in a spiritual sense, change the bread into his body before his passion, and the wine to his blood, daily blesses through the hands of his priests the bread and wine to his spiritual body and blood.' Fourthly, instruction is given as to correct rites in the celebration of the eucharist, and as to the observance of the Easter festival; and finally, new ordinances of the assembly of bishops are stated.

Sec. 37. 'Now ye have heard positively what ye have to do, and what to forego.' 'God grant you to take such resolution as shall be for your good.'

The whole of this letter is alliterative. Thorpe in his edition, prints as a footnote a metrical passage, which is found in the second of the two manuscripts named below, inserted near the beginning of Sec. 35. It treats of conduct in the House of God. Its authenticity is uncertain.

Ælfric's authorship of this letter is undoubted. The style, the subjects, and Ælfric's introductory letter, show the writer of the *Homilies* and the disciple of Dunstan and Æthelwold. The secular clergy, not bound by Benedictine rules, are bidden to remember that they are not free from the laws of the church. The strong insistence upon celibacy aims to thwart the persistent effort of the secular clergy to establish their right to marry.

There are two manuscripts of this work:

(a) A MS. which is believed to be the *Scriftbōc on Englisc* mentioned among the books which Bishop Leofric (1046-71) gave to his cathedral of Exeter. It is Corpus Christi College, Cambridge, 190 (L. 12). Besides the letter to Wulfsige, the manuscript contains Ælfric's pastoral letters for Wulfstan, various penitentials, and the Old English Confessional of Egbert, Archbishop of York (735-766).

(b) The other manuscript is the Oxford Bodl. Lib. Jun. 121, called also, because it came from Worcester, the Wigorner Codex. It is a very large collection of canonical writings and some homilies. According to Thorpe, it belongs to the tenth century.

The best edition is that of Thorpe, *Ancient Laws and Institutes of England.*

Pastoral Letters for Wulfstan of York. A second series of canons was prepared by Ælfric for Wulfstan, Archbishop of York and Bishop of Worcester, near whose diocese Ælfric's abbey of Eynsham was situated. He wrote first, two pastoral letters in Latin for Wulfstan's use among his secular clergy, and a year later, at Wulfstan's request translated them into English, 'not always following the same order, and not word for word, but sense for sense.' This he tells us in the Latin preface to the English translation, which he closes with the characteristic sentence, 'if the herald keep silence, who shall announce that the judge is about to come?'[1]

The subjects of the first of these letters are, in general and in particular, almost the same as those of the letter for Wulfsige, but they are treated more in detail, and the arrangement is different. The line of thought is as follows: 'We bishops dare not be silent, but must teach you priests in English the divine doctrine which our canon prescribes, for ye cannot all understand Latin. Yet I know that this admonition will displease many of you.' After a general exhortation to worthy administration of the priest's office, the three periods of the world—before the Law, under the Law, and under Christ's grace—are described.

Of the last he says: 'Christ came and established Christianity in chastity, both by his example and that of his disciples. The Old Law is different from the New.' 'In old days, before Christ's advent, men lived too much after their own lusts, but He said that we should live more rigorously.' There is express admonition to chastity in his words, 'Let your loins be girded.' 'So was Christ seen in vision by John and by Daniel the prophet.' 'God will have in his spiritual service holy ministers, who with chastity of body and mind may offer to him the holy eucharist.'

After the outpouring of the Holy Ghost the church was increased, and the disciples had all things in common, monastic life was established, and the gospel was carried to distant places. Then arose a very great persecution, but the faith increased. There were four great synods, and 'they appointed all the services which we have in God's ministry, at mass, and at matins, and at all the canonical hours; and they forbade all marriages forever to ministers of the altar, and especially to priests.' The great office of the priest is to

---

1 See Hom. II, 536, 374, and prefaces of the Homilies.

celebrate the mass, 'a memorial of Christ's great passion.' To that belongs purity, which by the canons allows no women, save mother, sister or aunt, in the house of a priest. 'This seems grievous to you, priests, because your customs are evil.' 'We cannot now compel you, but we exhort you to chastity.' There are seven orders in Christ's ministry. The highest order includes both priest and bishop; but the bishop is appointed for greater benediction than is the priest, whose duties would be too multifarious if he had the bishop's also. The priest is to be subject to the bishop.

The bishops in the old law must marry, because descent from Aaron was a necessary qualification for the priesthood, but now the bishop may be of any race.

The letter gives, lastly, rules for the service and the life, about marriages, books, vestments, the cup at the Lord's Supper, preaching and visitation of the sick, and funeral feasts. The priest must not be given to drink, nor be too boastful, nor be showy in dress. He must be a man of peace, he cannot lawfully bear arms. It is not true that because Peter had a sword, therefore Christ's servants may do the same.

The original text of the second letter is not yet printed in full, and the question of its authenticity and original form can only be decided later by a study of its language and style in comparison with Ælfric's other works. Nevertheless we are not in ignorance of its content. A short selection from the Latin original was published by the early editors of the Easter sermon, and has been repeatedly reprinted. Again, the first part of the Old English text, about one-eighth of the whole, was published in 1721, by Wilkins, and in 1840, by Thorpe, the first accompanied by a Latin translation, the second by an English. Again, in 1856, an English translation of the whole letter was printed in the appendix of Soames' *Anglo-Saxon Church.*

The letter begins: 'O ye priests, my brothers, we will now say to you what we have not said before, because to-day we are to divide our oil, hallowed in three ways, holy oil, chrism, and sick men's oil.'

10

Then follow directions for the use of oil, for the administration of the Lord's Supper to the sick and to children, and a few metrical lines which forbid ill conduct in a church.

In the editions of Wilkins and Thorpe the letter ends abruptly at this point. But the custom of Ælfric and others of his time makes us sure that there must have been some more formal ending than this, a doxology or a prayer. Even of this brief portion Thorpe says that the latter half 'has apparently been added to the tract about chrism by mistake, having no connection with it.' But the superscription does not exclude it more than does that of the letter for Wulfsige, *Of the Synod of Priests*; nor is there wanting a close connection in the subject matter, in that the priest who anoints the sick also administers the eucharist to the same. Thorpe's view of the letter seems to have been derived from the manuscript (C. C. C. C. 190) from which he took the text. In Wanley's catalogue of that manuscript a little note added to this writing says: 'this letter, which appears to be one in the other codexes, in this is divided into two.' Accordingly, here we find, first, the tract printed by Thorpe; and second, what purports to be a sermon, under the superscription, *Sermo Coena Domini et Feria et Sabbato Sancto.* In the two manuscripts of the Bodleian Library where the letter is found, the above named tract and sermon are found together, with no break in text,[1] and the whole ends with the customary doxology. This, there is good reason to believe, is the second of the letters of which our author speaks in his prefatory address to the archbishop.

The subject matter of the part not found in Thorpe consists, first, of minute directions for the ceremonial observances of Passion Week, and for the celebration of the mass at other seasons, together with instructions on the spiritual

---

[1] 'Neither in the Bodleian MS. (Jun. 121), from which the transcript now published was made, nor in another in that library, is there any break, even after the metrical lines. The whole epistle, as it is called, is perfectly suited to one single occasion, that of giving useful advice and information to a body of clergymen brought together for receiving the annual supplies of consecrated oil and chrism.' Soames, *Anglo-Saxon Church*, p. 263.

significance of the eucharist. Then the priests are bidden to explain the Ten Commandments to the people, even .as, for example, the writer of the letter explains them, one by one, in this letter, with special reference to their spiritual meaning. The writer expounds, too, the eight deadly sins, which 'undo unwary people.' Then follow directions for Ash Wednesday, and Palm Sunday, and exhortations to truth, love, and the keeping of the two great commandments, and the letter closes with the words: 'May the Saviour aid us for his holy commandments, He that liveth with his beloved Father and the Holy Ghost, in one Divinity, the Triune God ever reigning. Amen.'

The Latin originals of these two letters to Wulfstan, not yet published (the Latin translation in Wilkins' edition is not the original), are preserved in two Cambridge manuscripts: C. C. C. 190 (L. 12); and C. C. C. 265 (K. 2).

Of the Old English text there are the following: (1) C. C. C. 201 (S. 18), which contains only the first letter without its preface, and is apparently of the middle of the eleventh century;[1] (2) Bodl. Lib. NE. F. 4, 12, contains both letters and the preface, and is of the twelfth century; (3) C. C. C. C. 190 (L. 12) also contains all; (4) London, Cott. Tib. A. 3, contains the second letter; (5) Bodl. Lib. Jun. 121, has only the second letter.

MS. 1 is the foundation for the text in Wilkins' and in Thorpe's edition. Thorpe gives the Latin preface and the second letter from MS. 3. MS. 5, according to Wanley, does not contain nearly all of the second letter, but ends with the words, *Vespere autem Sabbati.*[2]

These letters for Wulfstan have been denied to Ælfric by those who have ascribed our author's writings to Ælfric of Canterbury, and Ælfric Bata has been brought forward to fill the vacant place; not because there is any positive argument in his favor to balance the positive arguments against

---

1 According to Thorpe. MS. Jun. 45 is a copy of this.
2 See Soames' *Anglo-Saxon Church*, p. 267.

him, but because the work must have been by some Ælfric, and the pupil must have taught the same doctrines as his master. But the correct theory of Ælfric's identity leaves no room for doubt of his authorship (of the first letter at least), when this writing is examined in the light of his other works. Its relation to the earlier letter for Wulfsige is such as we find elsewhere in Ælfric's writings. It is that of a free revision of the earlier letter, with such additions and rearrangement as a new demand for an old work would suggest to an author, and there are many instances in Ælfric's works of similar revisions. It is one of his most prominent traits to view the subjects that he treats from a new standpoint, not chiefly of doctrine, but of application. He tells the same story over and over, as in *St. Martin, The Seven Sleepers, The Life of Stephen*; but when he revises a former work he always sees something to add or to change, or some new way to make it applicable to his hearers. If he writes a new Christmas sermon, the lessons appropriate to the day are taught in a new way. If he issues a new volume of homilies, he carries into it a new central idea, and thus differentiates the work from those which have preceded it, while yet keeping the body of Christian truth consistent and complete. This is made real to us when in the study of his works we try to detach ourselves from our modern thinking and reproduce in thought as far as possible the life and circumstances of our author.

This re-working of the first compilation of canons is that of a skilful writer, but Ælfric Bata has given no evidence of skill in the one work which can be fairly ascribed to him. Also he speaks of Abbot Ælfric as his teacher, but does not call himself abbot. The preface announces this work as that of Abbot Ælfric, not Abbot Ælfric Bata, as, if we judge by the note affixed to the Glossary, we should expect to find in any works of his if he held the position of abbot. This theory has really no importance, save as an historical feature of Ælfrician criticism.

The author speaks as one who is well-known by his writings; he says that he has given offence by such instruction in the past. The offensive teachings are no doubt those of his first pastoral letter. This is not the only instance in which Ælfric says that he has been blamed, but that his good intentions make him above caring for it.

Let any one study the preface, the language of the letters, the subject matter, the treatment of details, the spirit and the emphasis of the teachings; let him compare these with the prefaces of the *Homilies*, of the *Grammar*, and of *Genesis*, and with the language, tone, matter, and method of Ælfric's writings, and no doubt of his authorship of the first letter can longer remain.

The best edition of the Old English text is that of Thorpe, *Ancient Laws and Institutes of England*.

CHAPTER XI.

TRANSLATIONS FROM THE BIBLE; ON THE OLD AND NEW TESTAMENTS.

The Heptateuch. The so-called *Heptateuch* was not intended by its author to be a strict translation. Rather it is translation interchanging with epitomes of the history found in the Pentateuch, Joshua, and Judges. The principle of omission with Ælfric is here unmistakable. He wishes to furnish a practical, easily-understood rendering of the parts which are most important for the laity to know. All else he passes over.

He omits, first, almost all catalogues of names: for example, the descendents of Noah, Genesis 10; the genealogies, Genesis 11; the list of kings, Genesis 36; the numbering of the tribes, Numbers 1, 2, and 26; the names of camping-places, Numbers 33; and of the boundaries, Numbers 34, Joshua 13-22. In the last-named passage ten chapters are compressed into a few lines.

Again, the abstruse passages in the practical portions are omitted; the blessing of Jacob, Genesis 49; the speeches of Balaam, Numbers 23-24; the blessing of Moses, Deuteronomy 33, — the preceding easier song of praise is included,—and the song of Deborah, Judges 5. The other omissions are either short passages which repeat what is given elsewhere, or parts less essential for carrying forward the history: thus Genesis 7, 13-16; 24, 12-14, 16-60. Also the circumstantial description of the Tabernacle, and of the clothing of the priests, and most of the single Levitical laws, are omitted, and the book of Judges, except the life of Samson, is given only in brief abstracts.

With no manuscript authority for the name, Thwaites, the first publisher, called the work the *Heptateuch.* Ælfric himself did not, we believe, join with the six books, the *Book of*

Judges which Thwaites published with them. But Wanley noted that it was added by the scribe of the Bodleian manuscript. In one codex it is contained among many homilies, and the author calls it a sermon. Still another fact speaks for the propriety of placing it among the historical homilies, rather than among the translations of the Old Testament: namely, that, like other tracts and homilies of Ælfric, it is written in metrical form. It is also to be noticed that its author placed among the *Saints' Lives* an alliterating homily similar to the *Judges* in form and matter, drawn from the Book of Kings. Still further, to the *Book of Judges* is added an appendix, in which are brought together Roman, Byzantine, and Old English brave war-leaders and princes, who were victorious through God's help. To the famous judges of Israel Ælfric parallels the last victorious kings of England, Alfred, Æthelstan, and Edgar.

It was always a shock to the mediæval Roman ecclesiastic to render the divine Scripture into the language of the people. In his first work, the *Catholic Homilies*, Ælfric translated the scripture passages for the Sunday or Saint's day to which each homily belonged, and of these passages the homily is an exposition. If this was a bold act, it was nevertheless easier to justify than the translation of the books of the Bible. The latter task would hardly have been undertaken by a beginner.

There is reason to question whether Ælfric wrote the whole of the *Heptateuch.* A long introductory address to Æthelweard prefaces the whole, and begins as follows: ' Ælfric, monk, greeteth humbly Æthelweard, Ealdorman. Thou didst request me, dear friend, to translate the Book of Genesis from Latin into English. Then it seemed to me irksome to grant it to thee, and thou saidest that I needed only to translate to Isaac, the son of Abraham, for another had translated from Isaac to the end of the book.' Now two manuscripts contain only that part of Genesis that Æthelweard requested: one, twenty-three chapters; the other, twenty-four. Add to this, that from the end of the twenty-fifth chapter of Genesis to the end of the Pentateuch, except the book of Numbers, the language shows a marked difference from that which precedes. Words and constructions which are strange to Ælfric elsewhere appear here, and his favorite expressions are not found. But the language of Joshua and Judges is his own.

Nevertheless it is certain that Ælfric added the remaining books of the Pentateuch to his translation, that he translated Joshua for Æthelweard, and that he wrote about the Judges. For in his work *On the Old and New Testaments*, he mentions the three facts separately, and his summary of Joshua is not separated from the Pentateuch by even a superscription. The preface itself treats of the typical explanation of Genesis, but it also extends to the contents of Exodus and Leviticus, and speaks in detail of the typical meanings of the Tabernacle and of sacrifice.

The following may be presumed as to the gradual formation of the work. At first Ælfric received command from the ealdorman only in respect to Genesis, which was to furnish good material for instruction in the history of creation, and of the patriarchs. But he saw difficulties in the way of granting even this; the people might take offence at the marriages of the patriarchs; they might see in the book only a bare history of events. To overcome this reluctance his friend limits the commission to the first half of Genesis. In its preface Ælfric takes pains to guard against false inferences, he insists upon the deep spiritual meaning of the book, and emphasizes the difference between the Old Law and the New. It was not his custom to mix the works of others with his own, but here, where it was mere translation, he took that which had been completed by some one else, perhaps by the one whose translation Æthelweard refers to, and annexed it to his own, to the end of Leviticus, and perhaps to the end of Deuteronomy. First, however, he revised the translation, improved it, and struck out whatever appeared to be unnecessary for his purpose, yet did not at the same time, alter the language so as to make it completely his own. The fourth book, if indeed it existed before his work, he revised more strenuously, because he wished to give the alliterative form to its historical portion. He decided later to extend the work through the book of Joshua. With this whole extension, the preface received those additions which relate to Exodus. The Cotton Codex composed as early as the first half of the eleventh century contains this second authentic edition, which consists of the Pentateuch and Joshua. It seems improbable that Ælfric caused a third edition provided with the book of Judges. The translation is made from the Vulgate of Jerome.

The following are the manuscripts of the *Heptateuch:* 1. Oxford, Laud, E. 19; 2. Cott. Claudius B. IV.; 3. Cambridge, Univ. Lib., a MS. written long after 1066; 4. Cott., Otho B. X.; 5. Lincoln.

Thwaites' edition is from MS. 1; this alone contains the seven books. In MS. 2 the Book of Judges is wanting. A copy of MS. 3 is found in Camb. C. C. C. (Wanley, 151).

Esther. 'Queen Esther, who saved her people, has also a book among these; . . . I translated it into English.' Ælfric writes this in his work *On the Old Testament.* A copy of such a translation is contained in a manuscript of the seventeenth century, which was prepared by William L'Isle (Bodl. Lib. Laud. E 381, earlier, Laud. E 33). Assmann, who has edited this, says, 'Its method and style, with its additions and omissions, its rhythmical form, and its whole phraseology, show it to be the translation which Ælfric made.'

In Assman's dissertation upon this book, the following subjects are discussed: I. Dialect: 1. Phonology; 2. Inflection ; the conclusion is drawn that 'the dialect is late West Saxon, such as is found especially in the works of Ælfric;' II. L'Isle's manuscript; still further, in treating of the question of authorship, A. Method and style of the work; B. Rhythmical form; C. Vocabulary and phraseology.

The text is printed in the *Bibliothek der Angelsächsischen Prosa*, Part III, and in *Anglia* 9, 25-38.

Job. In the brief account of Job found in Ælfric's work *On the Old Testament,* there are these words: 'Be þām ic āwende on Englisc cwide iū:, 'concerning whom I once translated a sermon.' The work to which this quotation refers has been supposed by some to be the writing on Job published with Thwaites' edition of the *Heptateuch* and *Judges.* But there stands among the *Catholic Homilies* one on the same subject (*Hom.* II. 446–460)[1] which is identical with the first, except that that contains a few additional sentences. As a translation, the *Job* is more free than Ælfric's other translations from the Bible, and was evidently meant to be what its author calls it, a sermon, 'cwide.'

We know of no writings of Ælfric earlier than the *Catholic Homilies.* It is most probable that the scripture reading for the first Sunday in September suggested this work to Ælfric, and that later, on account of its large proportion of scripture translation, it was issued as a separate work.

Dr. Förster, who has investigated the sources of the CATHOLIC HOMILIES, says of the *Job:* 'The homily is almost entirely taken from the Bible. I know no source for the explanatory additions.'

Thwaites' edition is made from a copy by William L'Isle, of Bodl. Laud. E. 381 (earlier no. E. 33). Other MSS. are: Bodl. NE. F. 4. 12; two MSS. of the University Library, Cambridge, (Wanley, 159, 164); Cott. Cleopatra B. 13.

Judith. 'Judith, the widow who overcame Holofernes the Syrian Prince, has a book of her own among the books which tell of their victories : it also has been translated into English in our fashion, as an example for you men, that ye may defend your land with weapons against a contending army.' Thus in the work *On the Old Testament* does Ælfric mention a translation of Judith, but leaves his claim to authorship unsettled. What presumption is there in favor of such a claim for him? Several points in the passage above quoted make

---

[1] 'Ælfricus * * * scribat se de Joba homiliam olim transtulisse: quam quidem homiliam in secundo sermonum catholicorum libro, etc.'—Mores, *De Ælfrico Commentarius.*

it probable that Ælfric is referring to a translation of his own. The sentence which precedes this passage says in respect to the book of Esther 'this I translated briefly into English in our fashion.' The '*also* into English in our fashion' of the Judith suggests that he is consciously speaking of another work of his own. Again, Ælfric's metrical homilies were his own invention. He could reasonably say of such an one 'on ūre wīsan,' 'in our fashion.' Still more, this passage is to be noted in comparison with the following passage of the same work, in which Ælfric describes the book of Judges. He says, 'The book tells us plainly that they lived in peace as long as they worshipped the heavenly God, and as often as they forsook the living God they were harried and abased by the heathen nations who dwelt about them. When again they called earnestly on God with true repentance, then he sent them help through some judge, who overcame their enemies and freed them from their misery, and they long dwelt thus in their land. Men who care to hear this can read it in the English book which I translated concerning this. I thought that through the wonderful story ye would turn your mind in earnest to the will of God.' When we remember that England was repeatedly devastated by the Danes during the years of Ælfric's chief literary activity, and that he says in substance 'I wrote the book of Judges to make you patriotic citizens of your country,' we must surely find in his expressed knowledge of the motive which led to the translation of the Judith, and in that motive itself, strong arguments in favor of his authorship of the same.

Such a Judith exists in two manuscripts, and bears every internal evidence of Ælfric's writing. It tells its story in metrical form; it has Ælfric's forcible style; it extols chastity in his characteristic manner; and its allegorical explanations are like those found in many places in his writings.[1]

---

1 See Appendix VI.

On the Old and New Testaments. The Old English work *On the Old and New Testaments* was written at request of one Sigwerd at Easthealon. It has the colloquial style of an epistle, even when the address is not directly made to Sigwerd. At the head stand these words: 'This writing was composed for one man, but nevertheless it may benefit many.' At the beginning of each of the two divisions indicated by the title, and near the end of the second, there is a personal address to Sigwerd, and at the close, Ælfric's usual warning to the scribe. Notwithstanding the variety of matter treated, the work might be called a sermon on the text, 'Be ye doers of the word, and not hearers only.' Its first words are, 'Ælfric Abbot sends friendly greeting to Sigwerd at Easthealon. I say to thee in truth that he is very wise who speaks by works.' This is the key-note of the whole. The occasion of the writing is given in the following words addressed to his friend: 'Thou didst very often ask me for English writings, and I did not consent quickly, until thou didst strive for it with works, when thou besoughtest me earnestly, for the love of God, that I would speak with thee at home, at thine house, and then when I was with thee, thou lamentdst much because thou couldst not obtain my writings.'

The work as a whole is a practical, historical introduction to the Holy Scriptures. It treats of the books and their authors, and inasmuch as it is designed for laymen, is popular in its character, and considers neither the history of the canon, nor the fundamental principles of exposition. As the author takes up the different books of the Bible, he designates himself successively as the translator of the Pentateuch, of Joshua, and of Judges; as a writer on the Kings, and on Daniel; and as a translator from Job, Esther and the Maccabees; and refers incidentally to other writings of his on Old Testament subjects. He speaks, too, of an English translation of Judith, but does not say that it is his. Thus Ælfric's work is evidently intended to direct his readers to the Old English translations of books of the Bible, that each may read for himself.

In the introduction, he tells of the creation of the world by the Triune God; of the traditional creation and fall of the angels with their mighty leader, Lucifer; and of the creation and fall of man. Then are given in brief outline the contents of the Pentateuch, Joshua, Judges, and Ruth; of the four books of the Kings, and of Chronicles regarded as the fifth. Something is told of the individual kings: Saul, David, Solomon, Hezekiah and Josiah, of the capture of Zedekiah and the Babylonian captivity, and of the return to Palestine.

The Psalter, 'placed in the Bible by David,' the three books which bear Solomon's name, and the Books of Wisdom and Ecclesiasticus, whose contents resemble Solomon's writings, 'but were written by Jesus the Son of Sirach,' all are mentioned in their proper connection with their authors, or with their position in the Bible. Then follows discourse about the prophets: of Isaiah, who prophesied 'very wisely about Christ;' of Jeremiah, who lived a celibate, was persecuted, wrote with spiritual understanding about the Saviour, and was, according to Augustine, visited by Plato, 'the wisest man among the heathen;' of Ezekiel, and Daniel carried to Babylon, who, also, were prophets of the Christ. Lastly follow in order accounts of the minor prophets, of the Sibyls 'who prophesied of the Saviour Christ, but their books are not in the Bible,' and of Esdras, Job, Tobias, Esther, Judith and the Maccabees.

Ælfric explains the object of the second part of the work in these words: 'I will now tell thee briefly of the new covenant after Christ's coming, that thou be not deprived of any understanding of it, although thou canst not receive fully all the record of the true writing. Nevertheless, thou wilt be helped by this little example.'

The story begins with John the Baptist, 'the end of the Old Law,' and the forerunner of Christ. 'As the day-star at dawn rises before the sun, so shone John before the Saviour.' The first of the four books of Christ was written by Matthew in the Hebrew tongue in Judea; the second by Mark from the teachings of Peter. Luke learned his gospel from Paul. John wrote at request of the bishops in Asia. After an explanation of the animal symbols of the evangelists, Ælfric gives a short narrative of Christ's life. 'I tell this briefly,' he says, 'for I have written indeed about these four books, forty homilies in the English language, and an addition thereto. Thou canst read this story more fully in those than I tell it here.

The letters of the apostles are enumerated as follows : Peter, two; James the Just, one; John, three; Paul, fifteen, among which are not only the letter to the Hebrews, but also the not-accepted letter to the Laodiceans. Last are considered the Acts of the Apostles, and the Revelation of St. John. With the account of the former are incorporated the traditional stories of the fates of the Apostles. To that of the latter is appended a long episode from Eusebius' Church history, the account of a young man who was saved by John.

After this historical record there is a three-fold appendix. The first contains a comparison of the two covenants with the two Seraphim whom Isaiah saw in vision; a warning to teachers who do not draw their instructions from 'these holy books;' a comparison of the seventy-two books of the Bible with the seventy-two nations after the flood and the seventy-two disciples who ended the fifth age of the world; something about the sixth, seventh and eighth ages of the world; and finally, exhortations to all men: workmen, warriors, and men of prayer, to fulfill their duties. The second appendix tells of the judgment which fell upon the unbelieving Jews in the destruction of Jerusalem. The third, brief appendix is a personal address to Sigwerd upon excessive drinking.

There is no reason to believe that this work is a translation. It moves freely in the epistolary style, and works out an original line of thought in the material. One may ask, what were the sources used? Appparently Ælfric had before him Augustine's *De Doctrina Christiana*, Bk. II. Ch. 13, and drew from this some general information about the books of the Bible; but the details so far as they have to do with the contents of the books are his own. Besides this, the chief source seems to be a writing of Isidore's, in which the latter also is indebted to Augustine. This work is entitled *In Libros Veteris ac Novi Testamenti Prooemia.*[1] With the order of books found there, Ælfric agrees almost entirely. His comparison of the two testaments with the two Seraphim of Isaiah; the explanation of the animal symbols. of the evangelists, and what he says of the wise steward who brings forth things new and old out of his treasure, correspond with this work of Isidore's. Still other correspondences between the two works could be named. Ælfric's comparison of the seventy-two books of the Bible with the seventy-two languages of the earth is found in another short writing of Isidore's: *De Veteri et Novo Testamento Quæstiones.*[2]

There have been three complete editions of this writing: two issued by L'Isle (1623 and 1638); and one by Grein, (1872). Of these, Professor Sweet says, 'The text given by De L'Isle, on which that of Grein is based, is full of omissions and wanton alterations, which I have carefully supplied and corrected,' (that is, in Professor Sweet's *Æelfric on the Old Testament,* in his *Anglo-Saxon Reader*). Parts of this work have been printed several times.

There is one manuscript, Bodl. Laud, E 19, Oxford.

---

[1] Migne, *Patrologia Latina*, 83. 155 ff.
[2] Migne, *Patrologia Latina*, 83. 200 ff.

CHAPTER XII.

THE LIFE OF ST. ÆTHELWOLD; ÆLFRIC'S DE CONSUETUDINE MONACHORUM.

The Life of St. Æthelwold. The authenticity of the Latin life of St. Æthelwold which bears Ælfric's name is hardly questioned at the present day. The doubt which once existed was due to mistaken ideas of Ælfric's identity. The only circumstance which could now lead any one to question his authorship is that the writer says so little of his own acquaintance with Æthelwold, and yet Ælfric must have known him personally.

It may perhaps be accounted for in this way: more than twenty years had passed since Æthelwold's death, and meanwhile he had in a measure been set apart from ordinary men by his canonization, and by the reverence in which he was held. Ælfric when he knew him was a young man, Æthelwold a venerable bishop. The acquaintance need hardly have been one of very much personal familiarity. But this objection to Ælfric's authorship has little weight in comparison with the external and internal evidence on the other side.

The prologue of the work is as follows: 'Ælfric abbot, an alumnus of Winchester, desires for the honorable Bishop Kenulph and the brethren of Winchester salvation in Christ. It seems to me worthy now at last to call to mind some of the deeds of our father and great teacher, Æthelwold, for twenty years have passed since his departure. With my narrative, brief indeed and unadorned, I gather into this writing those things which I have learned either from you or from other faithful ones, lest perchance they pass into utter oblivion for want of writers.' This dedication, addressed to Bishop Kenulph who became bishop of Winchester in 1006, and died in the same year, is by an Ælfric who was an alumnus of Winchester; who was acquainted with the Winchester brethren;

and who had already become an abbot: conditions which suit our author. William of Malmesbury ascribes the work, apparently in agreement with the unquestioned traditions of his time, to Ælfric the well-known writer.[1]

Even more assuring are the style and the tone of this life. It is rare to find among the writers of that day any one who wrote with Ælfric's simplicity and directness. He knew what he wished to say, and when to stop, and could write without bombast. All this is true of the author of this life of Æthelwold. He writes with the historical spirit of one who has tried to find out what the truth is, and to tell it in clear, simple language so that others may understand it also, but he does not expand it for the sake of expansion. The work contains several references to the author's personal acquaintance with Æthelwold, and shows sympathy for the work in which Æthelwold spent his life. Yet it is not written in a partisan spirit, and the author keeps himself well in the background. The Æthelwold whose life and character are described here is the same man who appears in chronicles and other writings of that day, 'terrible as a lion to the disobedient, but gentler than a dove with the meek and humble,' the great founder of monasteries, the trusted friend of Dunstan and King Edgar.

A second life of Æthelwold bears the name of Wulfstan, a monk and precentor of Winchester, who is mentioned as such by Ælfric in Æthelwold's life. This book, which is longer than the first, is not an original production, but Ælfric's work re-written, with expansions and additions, so that it is more than twice as long. Wulfstan claims to write from personal knowledge of his subject ('ea quae praesentes ipsi vidimus'), but makes no acknowledgment of his debt to Ælfric. In some cases he has added interesting details not found in Ælfric: for example, where he tells of Æthelwold's work in the garden at Glastonbury, and of his preparing fruit and vegetables for the table; and again, when he speaks of Eadred's special love for the Old Monastery at Winchester, and of his gifts to Winchester Church. In many places he does little more than ex-

---

1 *Gesta Pontificum*, 406. Rolls Series.

11

pand Ælfric's ideas. Thus Ælfric says of Æthelwold at Glas
tonbury: 'Didicit namque inibi grammaticam artem et me-
tricam,' but Wulfstan: 'Didicit namque inibi liberalem
grammaticae artis peritiam, atque mellifluam metricae rationis
dulcedinem.' The last chapter of Wulfstan's book gives a description of the dedication of Æthelwold's new church at
Winchester, which is not found in Ælfric's, and into this chapter he introduces a poetical passage of his own on the subject
just named. He also relates two miracles not told in the first
life.

That Ælfric's work is not simply an abridgment of Wulfstan's is certain. He says distinctly that he writes lest the
matter should be utterly forgotten. This he could not have
done if the brethren at Winchester were already in possession
of a life written by one of their own number. The deceit
would be quickly found out in such a case. But, aside from
the straightforward tone of Ælfric's life, such dishonesty does
not belong to him; he was always careful to give his sources.
Wulfstan seems to have been of a different mind, for not only
does he fail in the preface of this work to say anything of a
former writing, but in the story of St. Swithun written by him
he makes no acknowledgment of Landferth from whom he
copies.

Wulfstan's additions to Ælfric's life are such as might be
expected from a later writer in a bombastic age who had
something of his own to add, but who did not undertake to
write an independent work. He follows Ælfric's order, often
uses his language, though with variations, and keeps close to
the original in the substance of the story. His work is nevertheless of value, for it adds something to the original life; his
facts are in part derived from his own knowledge, and most or
all of them are doubtless from reliable sources.

It is unnecessary to speak here of the claims that have been
put forward for Ælfric Bata.[1]

Ælfric's life is printed by Stevenson in the appendix of the

---

[1] Cf. pp, 90, 143-4, App. I.

second volume of *Chronicon Monasterii de Abingdon*, from MS. Lat. 5362, of the Imperial Library at Paris. The Codex Fiscannensis is named by Mabillon as the source of Ælfric's preface, which he prints in *Acta Sanct. Bened. Saec. V.* p. 606.

Wulfstan's life is printed by Mabillon in the above-named book, and also in the *Acta Sanctorum* (edited by J. Bollandus), Vol. 35.

Excerpts from
Æthelwold's
De Consuetudine.
Every newly-organized monastery in the tenth century needed instruction in the Rule of the Benedictine order. For this reason Æthelwold, first of all, sent Osgar to Fleury to learn to teach it to the brethren at Abingdon; and Oswald sent thither for Germanus to come and teach those at Worcester. Ælfric was sent to Cernel for a similar purpose; and Bishop Æthelwold himself went from abbey to abbey giving instruction in the same Rule. For a like reason Ælfric when he had become Abbot of Eynsham arranged for the use of his monks an abridgment of the compilation, *De Consuetudine Monachorum*, which had been prepared by Æthelwold. He says in his introduction: ' I give in writing these few things from the book of monastic usage which, in the time of Edgar, most happy king of the English, St. Æthelwold, Bishop of Winchester, with his fellow-bishops and abbots, collected from all quarters, and instituted to be observed by monks.' Ælfric speaks here from personal knowledge of the antecedents of Æthelwold's writing; and that writing which he mentions, is apparently not a translation into English, but a compilation in Latin.[1] What do we know of Æthelwold in connection with the Rule of St. Benedict ?

A passage in the anonymous *Historia Ecclesiae Eliensis* (Bk. I. ch. 49)[2] says that King Edgar and Ælfthryth gave the manor of Southborne to Æthelwold for the abbey of Ely,

---

[1] I thus correct the statement made on pp. 63-4, that Ælfric's excerpts were from the English translation.

[2] 1691. *Historiae Britannicae, Saxonicae*, etc., ex vetustis Codd. MSS. editi opera Thomae Gale.

on condition that he would translate the Benedictine Rule into English, and that ' he did it.'[1]

From what has been said it is to be inferred that Æthelwold made both a translation into English and a compilation in Latin. We will speak first of the translation.

No manuscripts, so far as we know, have come down from ancient times with Æthelwold's name attached. But as there are several anonymous English versions of about his date, there is no reason to suppose that his work has been lost. On the contrary, his position as the king's chief minister in reestablishing monasteries, must have led to the spread of his work, and all of the different English versions of this period are undoubtedly, directly or indirectly, indebted to him. It has long been a matter of much interest to ascertain the authorship of the Old English Benedictine Rule, which has been ascribed to Dunstan as well as to Æthelwold.

A translation which follows the Latin Rule of St. Benedict chapter by chapter, is found in the following manuscripts: MS. A: C. C. C. C. 178 (S. 6), End of 10th or begin. of 11th Cent. MS. O: C. C. C. C. 197, End of 10th or begin. of 11th Cent. MS. T: Brit. Mus. Cott. Tit. A. IV, 2d half of 11th Cent. MS. F: Brit. Mus. Cott. Faust. A. X, End of 11th or begin. of 12th Cent. MS. W: Wells Fragment.

This work, which has been edited by Professor Schröer, is ascribed by him to Æthelwold.[2] One strong evidence in favor of this claim is the following: MS. F contains an historical postcript which by internal evidence is of Æthelwold's composition.[3] Its beginning is wanting. The writing tells of the refounding of Abingdon by Edgar, and of his zeal in purifying the holy places and establishing right life in the monasteries. It speaks also of his commanding a translation of the Rule from Latin into English. Up to this point the

---

1 As Æthelwold refounded Ely in 970, and Edgar died in 975, this translation was probably made between those years.

2 Printed in Grein's *Bibl. der A.-S. Prosa*, Pt. II.

3 Printed, with English translation, in Cockayne's *Leechdoms, Wortcunning*, etc. III. 432-445.

text is written in the third person; but now, with no change of subject, it passes into the first person in a way that indicates that the writer of the tract is the author of the translation. The passage: ' We also teach abbesses, etc.,' suggests an author who was in a position of authority in respect to nunneries, such an one as Æthelwold held and exercised conspicuously when bishop. Moreover, the modest but independent way in which the author in the last part of this tract speaks of the translation, would be appropriate in a preface or postscript by Æthelwold.

To Æthelwold is also ascribed the compilation, *Concordia Regularis*, found (with Old English glosses) in MS. Cott. Tib. A. III, fol. 3–27.[1] From its Preface we learn that it was prepared at the king's desire, as expressed at the Council of Winchester, in order that the monasteries of his kingdom might have a correct and uniform Rule.[2] There is a manifest connection between this Preface and the tract mentioned as found in MS. F, above. It treats, though more fully, some of the same subjects, and so nearly in the same order that the likeness cannot have happened by chance. Yet it is not the same writing. As the Preface belongs to the compilation, so the tract may well be a preface by the same author to the translation of St. Benedict's Rule, which would easily get separated from that, since it was not the important part to be transcribed for actual use.

From the investigation of the subject by Mr. F. Tupper: *History and Texts of the Benedictine Reform of the Tenth Century*,[3] we take the following in reference to the *Concordia Regularis*. He says: ' I paraphrase portions of the "Preface." In his opening address to the churchmen assembled at Winchester, the King advised them to observe the same customs

---

1 Printed by W. S. Logeman in *Anglia* 13. 365–454, with an introduction in *Anglia* 15. 20–40; also (without the glosses) in Dugdale's *Monasticon*, I. xxvii, ff., and in Migne's *Patrologia Latina* 137. 475 ff.

2 The date of this Council of Winchester is not certain. It has been variously given as 967, 968, and 969. See *Mod. Lang. Notes* 1893, 351.

3 *Mod. Lang. Notes*, 1893, 344–367.

in order that an unequal and diverse observance of one rule
might be avoided.

'Written constitutions were, however, necessary to produce
such a concord, and their drafting is described at some length.
The sources of the *Concordia* seem to have been three:

1. The teachings of the Benedictine Rule.
2. The monastic customs of Continental Monasteries.
3. Native monastic customs.'

'It should be stated that the *Concordia* Preface and the
evidence of Ælfric prove that many hands were concerned in
the compilation of these Constitutions. One figure, however,
stands out distinctly from among the drafters; one man, I
believe, brought cosmos into the chaotic mass of collected
materials. My object will be to sustain the view that the
prelate who held the pen and stamped the document with
some of his own personality, was not Dunstan, Archbishop of
Canterbury, but Æthelwold, Bishop of Winchester.'

Tupper then quotes Ælfric's Eynsham Letter (see ch. XIII),
and continues as follows:

'Upon this, two arguments can be based to show that
Æthelwold was the Author of the *Concordia*.

I. The description of Æthelwold's *Liber Consuetudinum*,
given here by Ælfric, proves beyond question that it was the
Concordia.

II. Ælfric's "Abridgment" which follows the "Eynsham
Letter" in the MS. was clearly compiled from the *Concordia*,
cf. Breck, p. 8.'

Tupper supports his view by 'internal evidence,' ' tradition,'
and ' historical and documentary evidence.'

We can hardly agree with him in the contrast that he draws
between Æthelwold and Dunstan. He says: 'I might add
that the careless way in which the *Concordia* writer alludes
to the lax morals of Edgar, is certainly not what we should
expect from the purist Dunstan who had dragged Edwy from
the embraces of his mistress, and condemned Edgar to seven
years' penance for a carnal offence.' But neither should we

expect it from Æthelwold. This passage viewed by itself
alone is, we think, an argument against the authorship of
Æthelwold. It is probably to be explained thus: the relation
between the bishop and the king was about like that of a
father and a favorite son, and in this case the father yielded
to the natural impulse to make excuses for the faults of the son
in consideration of his winning qualities and actions, especially
when the son showed by word and deed sincere interest in the
welfare of the nation, which was the father's dearest interest.
To us the 'high-handed policy of the Bishop of Winchester'
does not indicate 'mildness' 'associated with zeal,' even though
we accept fully Ælfric's statement that he was 'gentler than
a dove with the meek and obedient'; what is told of him shows
that with all his winning traits, and his unusually attractive
personality, he could be, and often was, 'terrible as a lion to
the disobedient.' Contrast his treatment of the secular clergy
with that of Dunstan or Oswald.

We come now to the question of Ælfric's excerpts. His
Eynsham letter, found only in MS. C. C. C. C. 265, fol. 237, is
followed by thirty-one pages of rules of monastic life. These
have not yet been printed, except one page in Dr. Breck's dissertation. From the preface we must conclude that what
was to follow was not an abridgment of Æthelwold's translation, but of the *Concordia Regularis.* Position in the manuscript, closely connected with the unquestionably genuine
letter of Ælfric, is the strongest possible external evidence
that we have here Ælfric's work for the Eynsham brethren, and
Dr. Breck accepts it as such. He says that his personal examination of this Cambridge manuscript 'showed this to be a Latin
letter of Ælfric's.' 'My next step was to discover Æthelwold's work *De Consuetudine Monachorum,* the book from
which Ælfric's Abridgment was compiled. That this searched-
for work could not be the Benedictine Monastic Rule published by Schröer was evident from a mere examination of
Ælfric's letter, the subject-matter being so different in nature
and arrangement as to make this impossible. In the MS.,

however, which occupies the *first* place in the volume Tib. **A.**
III. of the Cottonian Library, I am convinced that I have discovered the *De Consuetudine Monachorum* of Æthelwold
from which Ælfric's epistle was compiled.'

From Ælfric's preface (see ch. XIII.) two points are clear
in reference to his work: first, that it was relatively a short
one (' haec pauca de *Libro Consuetudinum*'), and, secondly,
that to excerpts from the *De Consuetudine* he added ' some
things which the Rule does not touch,' and ' *also* some things
from the book of Amalarius."[1] Therefore the work found in
MS. C. C. C. C. 265, will approve itself as Ælfric's work if it
answers to the following tests: first, it must show additions
from Amalarius, and also from other sources besides the
Concordia Regularis; secondly, it must show Ælfric's manner
of making abridgments or compends; and, thirdly, the language
must be his.

Fragments of the *Concordia Regularis* translated into the
Old English of this period are still extant.   Is there reason to
think that any of these are Ælfric's work?   Dr. Breck has
endeavored to show that the one found in MS. Tib. A. III. fol.
174a ff., is by our author.[2] He writes: ' The fragment is plainly
in the Ælfrician dialect and manner with the exception of a
few phrases seemingly foreign to the Abbot's style; but these
are amply accounted for when one remembers that the Fragment is a *literal translation.*'   ' It is either a product of his
own hand, or that of some one of his contemporaries, or perhaps pupils.'   On the other hand, Zupitza writes of this same
' Fragment': ' Its author's gross misunderstandings of the
original forbid us to ascribe it to the author of the Latin
Grammar and the *Colloquium.*'[3]

---

[1] Amalarius' *De Ecclesiasticis Officiis*, in Migne's *Patrologia Latina*, Vol. 105.

[2] A version of ll. 170–257 of *C. R.*, printed by Professor Schröer in *Englische Studien*,
9, 294-296, and by Dr. Breck in his dissertation (see Bibl. 1887).

[3] Herrig's *Archiv für Neuere Sprachen*, 84. 24. Zupitza printed in this article an
Old English translation of ll. 612–753 of the *C. R.*, found in MS. C. C. C. C. 201 (S. 18).
This is not ascribed to Ælfric.

CHAPTER XIII.

PREFACES OF ÆLFRIC'S WORKS.

LATIN PREFACE OF THE CATHOLIC HOMILIES I.

IN NOMINE DOMINI.

Ego Ælfricus, alumnus Aðelwoldi, benevoli et venerabilis Presulis, salutem exopto Domno Archiepiscopo Sigerico in Domino. Licet temere vel presumptuose, tamen transtulimus hunc codicem ex libris Latinorum, scilicet Sancte Scripture in nostram consuetam sermocinationem, ob ædificationem simplicium, qui hanc norunt tantummodo locutionem, sive legendo sive audiendo; ideoque nec obscura posuimus verba, sed simplicem Anglicam, quo facilius possit ad cor pervenire legentium vel audientium, ad utilitatem animarum suarum, quia alia lingua nesciunt erudiri, quam in qua nati sunt. Nec ubique transtulimus verbum ex verbo, sed sensum ex sensu, cavendo tamen diligentissime deceptivos errores, ne inveniremur aliqua hæresi seducti seu fallacia fuscati. Hos namque auctores in hac explanatione sumus sequuti, videlicet Augustinum Hipponensem, Hieronimum, Bedam, Gregorium, Smaragdum, et aliquando Haymonem; horum denique auctoritas ab omnibus catholicis libentissime suscipitur. Nec solum Evangeliorum tractatus in isto libello exposuimus, verum etiam Sanctorum passiones vel vitas, ad utilitatem idiotarum istius gentis. Quadraginta sententias in isto libro posuimus, credentes hoc sufficere posse per annum fidelibus, si integre eis a ministris Dei recitentur in ecclesia. Alterum vero librum modo dictando habemus in manibus, qui illos tractatus vel passiones continet quos iste omisit; nec tamen omnia Evangelia tangimus per circulum anni, sed illa tantummodo quibus speramus sufficere posse simplicibus ad animarum emendationem, quia seculares omnia nequeunt capere, quamvis ex ore doctorum audiant. Duos libros

in ista translatione facimus, persuadentes ut legatur unus
per annum in ecclesia Dei, et alter anno sequenti, ut non
fiat tedium auscultantibus; tamen damus licentiam, si alicui
melius placet, ad unum librum ambos ordinare. Ergo si
alicui displicit, primum in interpretatione, quod non semper
verbum ex verbo, aut quod breviorem explicationem quam
tractatus auctorum habent, sive quod non per ordinem ecclesiastici ritus omnia Evangelia tractando percurrimus; condat
sibi altiore interpretatione librum, quomodo intellectui ejus
placet: tantum obsecro, ne pervertat nostram interpretationem, quam speramus ex Dei gratia, non causa jactantiae,
nos studiose secuti valuimus interpretari. Precor modo obnixe almitatem tuam, mitissime Pater Sigerice, ut digneris
corrigere per tuam industriam, si aliquos nevos malignae
haeresis, aut nebulosae fallaciae in nostra interpretatione repperies: te adscribatur dehinc hic codicillus tuae auctoritati,
non utilitati nostrae despicabilis personae.

Vale in Deo Omnipotenti jugiter.   Amen.

ENGLISH PREFACE OF CATHOLIC HOMILIES I.

Ic Ælfric munuc and mæssepreost, swaþeah waccre þonne
swilcum hādum gebyrige, wearð āsend on Æthelredes dæge
cyninges fram Ælfeage biscope, Aðelwoldes æftergengan, tō
sumum mynstre þe is Cernel gehāten, þurh Æðelmæres bēne
ðæs þegenes, his gebyrd and gōdnys sind gehwǣr cūþe. þā
bearn mē on mōde, ic trūwige þurh Godes gife, þæt ic ðæs
bōc of Lēdenum gereorde tō Engliscre sprǣce āwende; nā
þurh gebylde mycelre lāre, ac forþan þe ic geseah and gehȳrde
mycel gedwyld on manegum Engliscum bōcum, þe ungelǣrede
menn þurh heora bilewitnysse tō micclum wīsdōme tealdon;
and mē ofhrēow þæt hī ne cūþon ne næfdon þā godspellican
lāre on heora gewritum, būton þām mannum ānum ðe þæt
Lēden cūðon, and būton þām bōcum ðe Ælfred cyning snoter-
lice āwende of Lēdene on Englisc, þā synd tō hæbbenne. For
þisum antimbre ic gedyrstlǣhte, on Gode trūwiende, þæt ic
ðās gesetnysse undergann, and ēac forðām þe menn behōfiað

gōdre lāre swīðost on þisum tīman þe is geenduug þyssere
worulde, and bēoð fela frēcednyssa on mancynne ǣrðan þe se
ende becume, swā swā ūre Drihten on his godspelle cwæð tō
his leorning-cnihtum, 'Ðonne bēoð swilce gedreccednyssa
swilce nǣron nǣfre ǣr fram frymðe middangeardes. Manega
lēase Crīstas cumað on mīnum naman, cweðende, "ic ēom
Crīst," and wyrcað fela tācna and wundra, to bepǣcenne
mancynn, and ēac swylce þā gecorenan men, gif hit gewurþan
mæg: and būtan se Ælmihtiga God ðā dagas gescyrte, eall
mennisc forwurde; ac for his gecorenum hē gescyrte þā dagas.'
Gehwā mæg þe ēaðelicor ðā tōweardan costnunge ācuman,
ðurh Godes fultum, gif hē bið þurh bōclice lāre getrymmed;
forðan ðe þā bēoþ gehealdene þe oð ende on gelēafan purh-
wuniað. Fela gedreccednyssa and earfoðnysse becumað on
þissere worulde ǣr hire geendunge, and þā synd ðā bydelas
þæs ēcan forwyrdes on yfelum mannum, þe for heora mān-
dǣdum siððan ēcelice þrōwiað on ðǣre sweartan helle. . . .

Ūre Drihten bebēad his discipulum þæt hī sceoldon lǣran and
tǣcan eallum þēodum ðā ðing þe hē sylf him tǣhte; ac
þǣra is nū tō lȳt ðe wile wel tǣcan and wel bȳsnian. Se ylca
Drihten clypode þurh his wītegan Ezechiel, 'Gif þū ne ge-
stentst þone unrihtwīsan, and hine ne manast, þæt hē fram his
ārlēasnysse gecyrre and lybbe, þonne swelt se ārlēasa on his unrihtwīsnysse, and ic wille ofgān æt ðē his blōd', þæt is his
lyre. 'Gif ðū ðonne þone ārlēasan gewarnast, and hē nele
fram his ārlēasnysse gecyrran, þū ālȳsdest þīne sawle mid þǣre
mynegunge, and se ārlēasa swylt on his unrihtwīsnysse.' Eft
cwæð se Ælmihtiga tō þām wītegan Isāīam, 'Clypa and ne
geswīc ðū, āhefe þīne stemne swā swā bȳme, and cȳð mīnum
folce heora leahtras, and Jacobes hīrede heora synna.' For
swylcum bebēodum wearð mē geðuht þæt ic nǣre unscyldig
wið God, gif ic nolde ōðrum mannum cȳðan, oððe þurh,
tungan oððe þurh gewritu, þa godspellican sōfæstnysse þe hē
sylf gecwæð, and eft hālgum lārēowum onwrēah. For wel fela
ic wāt on þisum earde gelǣredran þonne ic sȳ, ac God geswu-
telað his wundra þurh ðone þe hē wile. Swā swā ælmihtig

wyrhta, hē wyrcð his weorc þurh his gecorenan, nā swylce hē
behōfige ūres fultumes, ac þæt wē geearnion þæt ēce līf þurh
his weorces fremminge. Paulus se apostol cwæð, 'Wē sind
Godes gefylstan,' and swā ðēah ne dō wē nān þing tō Gode,
būton Godes fultume. Nū bidde ic and halsige on Godes
naman, gif hwā þās bōc āwrītan wylle, þæt hē hī geornlice
gerihte be þǣre bȳsene, þȳlǣs þe wē þurh gȳmelēase wrīteras
geleahtrode bēon. Mycel yfel dēð sēðe lēas wrīt, būton hē
hit gerihte, swylce hē gebringe þā sōðan lāre tō lēasum gedwylde: forþī sceal gehwā gerihtlǣcan þæt þæt hē ǣr tō wōge
gebīgde, gif hē on Godes dōme unscyldig bēon wile. Quid
necesse est in hoc codice capitula ordinare, cum prediximus
quod xl. sententias in se contineat? excepto quod Æþelwerdus
dux vellet habere xl. quattuor in suo libro.

LATIN PREFACE OF THE CATHOLIC HOMILIES II.

IN NOMINE CHRISTI OMNIPOTENTIS.

Ælfricus, humilis servulus Christi, honorabili et amando
Archiepiscopo Sigerico perpetuam sospitatem optat in Domino.
Fateor Almitati tuæ, Domne venerabilis, omnimodis me in-
dignum, et quasi superstitiosum, quod presumpsi tibi alloqui
divinis sermocinationibus, videlicet per codicellum quem
nuper tuæ auctoritati direximus: sed quia nostrum studium
nimium laudasti, gratanter illam interpretationem suscipiens,
festinavimus hunc sequentem librum, sicuti Omnipotentis Dei
gratia nobis dictavit, interpretare, non garrula verbositate, aut
ignotis sermonibus, sed puris et apertis verbis linguæ hujus
gentis, cupientes plus prodesse auditoribus simplici locutione
quam laudari artificiosi sermonis compositione, quam nequaquam didicit nostra simplicitas; et licet multis injuriis infes-
tium piratarum concutiebamur, postquam præfatum libellum
tuæ Sanctitati transmisimus, tamen nolentes repperiri falsidici
promisores, dolente animo hoc opus perfecimus. Igitur in
anteriore opere ordinavimus xl. sermones, in isto vero non
minor numerus sententiarum invenitur, quamvis aliquæ illarum
brevitate angustentur. Hoc quoque opus commendamus tuæ

auctoritati corrigendum, quemadmodum et precedens, precantes obnixe ne parcas oblitterare, si aliquas malignæ hæresis maculas in eo repperies, quia malo apud Benignitatem tuam reprehendi quam incauta seductione apud inscios laudari. Perlegat queso Benignitas vestra hanc nostram interpretationem, quemadmodum et priorem, et dijudicet si fidelibus catholicis habenda est, an abicienda. Nequaquam nos invidorum reprehensio movet, si hoc munus tuæ benigne auctoritati non displicuerit. Vale in Christo jugiter. Amen.

ENGLISH PREFACE OF THE CATHOLIC HOMILIES II.

Ic Ælfric munuc āwende þās bōc of Lēdenum bōcum to Engliscum gereorde, þām mannum tō rædenne þe þæt Lēden ne cunnon. Ic hī genām of hālgum godspellum, and æfter geðungenra lārēowa trahtnungum hī āsmēade, þæra lārēowa naman ic āwrāt on ðære ærran bēc, on ðære Lēdenan foresprǣce. Ic gesette on twām bōcum þā gereccednysse ðe ic āwende, forðan ðe ic ðōhte þæt hit wære lǣsse æðrȳt to gehȳrenne, gif man ðā āne bōc rǣt on ānes gēares ymbryne, and ðā ōðre on ðām æftran gēare. On ægðer þæra bōca sind fēowertig cwyda, būton ðære foresprǣce, ac hī ne sind nā ealle of godspellum genumene, ac sind forwel fela of Godes hālgena līfe oððe þrōwunge gegaderode, þæra ānra þe Angelcynn mid frēols-dagum wurðað. Ætforan ælcum cwyde wē setton ðā swutelunge on Lēden, mæg swā-ðēah se ðe wile þā cāpītulas æfter ðære foresprǣce geendebyrdian. Nū bidde ic and hālsige, on Godes naman, gif hwā ðās bōc āwrītan wylle, þæt hē hī geornlice gerihte be ðære bȳsne, þe-lǣs ðe wē, þurh gȳmelēasum wrīterum, geleahtrode bēon. Micel yfel dēð sē ðe lēas wrīt, būton hē hit gerihte, swilce hē gebringe ðā sōðan lāre to lēasum gedwylde: forðī sceal gehwā gerihtlǣcan þæt þæt hē ær tō wōge gebīgde, gif hē on Godes dōme unscyldig bēon wile.

ADMONITION WHICH FOLLOWS THE ENGLISH PREFACE IN THE CATHOLIC HOMILIES II.

Unum adhuc vellem preponere huic libello, non quasi prefationem, sed quasi ammonitionem: scilicet, cavende ebrie-

tatis, sicut Dominus in Levitico and Aaron his verbis locutus
est, 'Dixit Dominus ad Aaron, Vinum et omne quod inebri-
ari potest non bibes tu et filii tui, quando intratis taberna-
culum testimonii, ne moriamini, quia preceptum est sempi-
ternum in generationes vestras, et ut habeatis scientiam dis-
cernendi inter sanctum et prophanum, inter pollutum et
mundum.' In Novo Testamento quoque Dominus ammo-
nivit discipulos suos, his verbis, dicens, 'Adtendite autem
vobis, ne forte graventur corda vestra in crapula et ebrietate
et curis hujus vitæ, et superveniat in vos repentina dies illa.''
Tantum vitium est ebrietas, ut Paulus apostolus et doctor
gentium adtestetur, "Ebriosos regnum Dei possidere non
posse.' O quam beati sunt qui Deo vivunt, et non seculo,
virtutibus, et non vitiis; et quamvis sanctorum patrum jejunia
vel abstinentiam non valeamus imitari, nequaquam tamen
debemus enerviter succumbere nefandis crapulis et æbrie-
tatibus, Domini nostri et Dei terribilibus commoniti com-
minationibus.   Sufficiunt hæc monita docibilibus, nam in-
docibilibus et duris corde nulla sufficiunt hortamenta.   Iterum
rogo et opto ut valeas, venerabilis Archiepiscope Sigerice,
jugiter in Christo. Amen.

LATIN PREFACE OF THE GRAMMAR.

Ego Ælfricus, ut minus sapiens, has excerptiones de Pris-
ciano minore vel maiore uobis puerulis tenellis ad uestram
linguam transferre studui, quatinus perlectis octo partibus
Donati in isto libello potestis utramque linguam, uidelicet
Latinam et Anglicam, uestrae teneritudini inserere interim,
usque quo ad perfectiora perueniatis studia. noui namque
multos me reprehensuros, quod talibus studiis meum ingenium
occupare uoluissem, scilicet grammaticam artem ad Anglicam
linguam uertendo. sed ego deputo hanc lectionem inscientibus
puerulis, non senibus, aptandam fore.   scio multimodis uerba
posse interpretari, sed ego simplicem interpretationem sequor
fastidii uitandi causa. si alicui tamen displicuerit, nostram interpretationem dicat, quomodo uult: nos contenti sumus, sicut

didicimus in scola Aðelwoldi, uenerabilis praesulis, qui multos
ad bonum imbuit. sciendum tamen, quod ars grammatica
multis in locis non facile Anglicae linguae capit interpretationem, sicut de pedibus uel metris, de quibus hic reticemus,
sed aestimamus ad inchoationem tamen hanc interpretationem
paruulis prodesse posse, sicut iam diximus. miror ualde, quare
multi corripiunt sillabas in prosa, quae in metro breues sunt,
cum prosa absoluta sit a lege metri; sicut pronuntiant *pater*
Brittonice et *malus* et similia, quae in metro habentur breues.
mihi tamen uidetur melius inuocare Deum patrem honorifice
producta sillaba, quam Brittonice corripere, quia nec Deus arti
grammaticae subiciendus est. Ualete, o pueruli, in Domino.

ENGLISH PREFACE OF THE GRAMMAR.

Ic Ælfric wolde þās lȳtlan bōc āwendan tō engliscum
gereorde of ðām stæfcræfte, þe is gehāten GRAMMATICA,
syððan ic ðā twā bēc āwende on hundeahtatigum spellum,
forðan ðe stæfcræft is sēo cǣg, ðe ðǣra bōca andgit unlīcð;
and ic þōhte, þæt ðēos bōc mihte fremian jungum cildum tō
anginne þæs cræftes, ōððæt hī tō māran andgyte becumon.
ǣlcum men gebyra ð, þe ǣnigne gōdne cræft hæfð, þæt hē ðone
dō nytne ōðrum mannum and befæste þæt pund, þe him god
befæste, sumum ōðrum men, þæt godes feoh ne ætlicge and hē
bēo lȳðra þēowa gehāten and bēo gebunden and geworpen intō
ðēostrum, swāswā þæt hālige godspel segð. jungum mannum
gedafenað, þæt hī leornion sumne wīsdōm and ðām ealdum
gedafenað, þæt hī tǣcon sum gerād heora junglingum, forðan
ðe ðurh lāre byð se gelēafa gehealden. and ǣlc man, ðe wīsdōm
lufað, byð gesǣlig, and sē ðe nāðor nele ne leornian ne
tǣcan, gif hē mæg, þonne ācōlað his andgyt fram ðǣre hālgan
lāre, and hē gewīt swā lȳtlum and lȳtlum fram gode. hwanon
sceolon cuman wīse lārēowas on godes folce, būton hī on
jugoðe leornion? and hū mæg se gelēafa bēon forðgenge, gif
sēo lār and ðā lārēowas āteoriað? is nū for ðī godes þēowum
and mynstermannum georne tō warnigenne, þæt sēo hālige lār
on ūrum dagum ne ācōlige oððe āteorige, swāswā hit wæs

gedōn on Angelcynne nū for ānum fēawum gēarum, swā þæt
nān Englisc prēost ne cūðe dihtan oððe āsmēagean ānne pistol
on Lēden, ōðþæt Dūnstān arcebisceop and Aðelwold bisceop
eft þā lāre on munuclīfum ārǣrdon. ne cweðe ic nā for ðī, þæt
ðēos bōc mæge micclum tō lāre fremian, ac hēo byð swā ðēah
sum angyn tō ǣgðrum gereorde, gif hēo hwām līcað.

Ic bidde nū on Godes naman, gyf hwā ðās bōc āwrītan
wylle, þæt hē hī gerihte wel be ðǣre bȳsne; forðan ðe ic nāh
geweald, þēah hī hwā tō wōge gebringe þurh lēase wrīteras,
and hit bið ðonne his pleoh, nā mīn. micel yfel deð se
unwrītere, gyf hē nele his wōh gerihtan.

INTRODUCTORY SENTENCES OF DE TEMPORIBUS.

Ic wolde ēac, gyf ic dorste, gadrian sum ghewǣde andgyt of
ðǣre bēc þe Beda se snotera lārēow gesette and gaderode of
manegra wīsra lārēowa bōcum be ðæs gēares ymbrenum fram
annginne middan eardes. þæt nis tō spelle ac elles tō rǣdenne
þām þe hit līcað.

Postscript of the same.

Sȳ þēos gesetnys þus her geendod. God helpe mīnum handum.

LATIN PREFACE OF THE LIVES OF THE SAINTS.

HUNC QUOQUE CODICEM TRANSTULIMUS DE LATINITATE AD
usitatam Anglicam sermocinationem, studentes aliis prodesse
edificando ad fidem lectione huius narrationis quibus-cumque
placuerit huic operi operam dare, siue legendo, seu Audiendo;
quia estimo non esse ingratum fidelibus.   Nam memini me in
duobus anterioribus libris posuisse passiones uel uitas sanctorum ipsorum, quos gens ista caelebre colit cum ueneratione
festi diei, et placuit nobis in isto codicello ordinare passiones
etiam uel uitas sanctorum illorum quos non uulgus sed coeno-
bite officiis uenerantur.   Nec tamen plura promitto me scrip-
turum hac lingua, quia nec conuenit huic sermocinationi plura
inseri; ne forte despectui habeantur margarite christi.   Ideoque reticemus de libro uitae patrum, in quo multa subtilia
habentur quae non conueniunt aperiri laicis, nec nos ipsi ea

quimus implere. Illa uero que scripturus sum suspicor non offendere audientes, sed magis fide torpentes recreare hortationibus, quia martyrum passiones nimium fidem erigant languentem. Unum cupio sciri hoc uolumen legentibus, quod nollem alicubi ponere duos imperatores siue cesares in hac narratione simul, sicut in latinitate legimus; sed unum imperatorem in persecutione marytrum ponimus ubique; Sicut gens nostra uni regi subditur, et usitata est de uno rege non de duobus loqui. Nec potuimus in ista translatione semper uerbum ex uerbo transferre, sed tamen sensum ex sensu, sicut inuenimus in sancta scriptura, diligenter curauimus uertere Simplici et aperta locutione quatinus proficiat Audientibus. Hoc sciendum etiam quod prolixiores passiones breuiamus uerbis, non adeo sensu, ne fastidiosis ingeratur tedium si tanta prolixitas erit in propria lingua quanta est in latina; et non semper breuitas sermonem deturpat sed multotiens honestiorem reddit. Non mihi imputetur quod diuinam scripturam nostrae lingue infero, quia arguet me praecatus multorum fidelium et maxime Æpelwerdi ducis et Æðelmeri nostri, qui ardentissime nostras interpretationes Amplectuntur lectitando; sed decreui modo quiescere post quartum librum A tali studio, ne superfluus iudicer.

ENGLISH PREFACE OF THE LIVES OF THE SAINTS.

Ælfric grēt ēadmōdlice Æþelwerd ealdorman, and ic secge þē, lēof, þæt ic hæbbe nū gegaderod on þyssere bēc þæra hālgena þrōwunga þe mē tō onhagode on englisc tō āwendene, for þan þe ðū, lēof, swīðost, and Æðelmær, swylcera gewrita mē bǣdon, and of handum gelǣhton ēowerne gelēafan tō getrymmenne mid]ǣre gerecednysse þe gē on ēowrum gereorde næfdon ǣr. Ðū wāst, lēof, þæt wē āwendon on þām twām ǣrrum bōcum þæra hālgena þrōwunga and līf þe angelcynn mid frēols-dagum wurþað. Nū ge-wearð ūs þæt wē þās bōc be þæra hālgena ðrōwungum and līfe gedihton þe mynster-menn mid heora þēnungum betwux him wurðiað.

12

Ne secge wē nān þincg nīwes on þissere gesetnysse.
forþan ðe hit stōd gefyrn āwriten
on lēdenbōcum þēah þe þā lǣwedan men þæt nyston.
Nelle wē ēac mid lēasungum þyllic līccetan.
forþan þe gelēaffulle fæderas and hālige lārēowas
hit āwriton on lēden-sprǣce. tō langum gemynde.
and tō trymmincge þām tōwerdum mannum.

Sum wītega clypode þurh þone hālgan gāst and cwæð.
Mirabilis Deus in sanctis suis. et cet. Wundorlic is God on his
hālgum. hē sylf forgifð mihte and strengðe his folce. gebletsod is hē God. Wē āwrīteð fela wundra on þissere bēc. forþan þe God is wundorlic on his hālgum swā swā wē ǣr sǣdon.
and his hālgena wundra wurðiað hine. forþan þe hē worhte þā
wundra þurh hī.

Ān woruld-cynincg hæfð fela þegna
and mislice wīcneras. hē ne mæg bēon wurðful cynincg
būton hē hæbbe þā geþincðe þe him gebyriað.
and swylce þēning-men. þe þēawfæstnysse him gebēodon.
Swā is ēac þām ælmihtigan Gode þe ealle þincg gescēop.
him gerīsð þæt hē hæbbe hālige þēnas
þe his willan gefyllað. and þǣra is fela
on mannum ānum þe hē of middan-eard gecēas.
þæt nān bōcere ne mæg þēah hē mycel cunne.
heora naman āwrīten. forþan þe hī nāt nān man.
Hī synd ungerȳme swā swā hit gerīsð Gode.
ac wē woldon gesettan be sumum þās bōc.
mannum tō getrymminge. aņd tō munde ūs sylfum
þæt hī ūs þingion tō þām ælmihtigan gode.
swā swā wē on worulde heora wundra cȳðað.
Ic bidde nū on Godes naman gif hwā þās bōc āwrītan wille.
þæt hē hī wel gerihte be þǣre bȳsne. and þǣr
nāmāre betwux ne sette þonne wē āwendon.

UALE IN DOMINO.

RUBRIC OF HOMILY, *In Natale Unius Confessoris.*

Hunc sermonem nuper rogatu venerandi
    episcopi Athelwoldi, scilicet

Junioris, Anglice transtulimus, quem huius
   libelli calci inscribi fecimus,
     ne nobis desit, cum ipse habeat.—

PREFACE OF HOMILY ON CHASTITY.

Ælfric abbod grēt	Sigefyrð frēondlice!
Mē is gesǣd,	þæt þū sǣdest be mē,
þæt ic ōðer tǣhte	on Engliscum gewritum,
ōðer ēower āncor	æt hām mid ēow tǣhð,
forðan þe hē swutelice sægð,	þæt hit sȳ ālȳfed,
þæt mæsseprēostas	wel mōtan wīfian,
and mīne gewritu	wiðcweðað þysum.
Nū secge ic þē, lēof man,	þæt mē is lāð to tǣlenne
āgenne Godes frēond,	gyf hē Godes riht drīfð,
ac wē sceolon secgan	and forswīgian ne durron
þā hālgan lāre,	þe se hǣlend tǣhte:
Sēo lāre mæg ēaðe	unc emlice sēman.

PREFACE OF ÆLFRIC'S HOMILY ADDRESSED TO WULFGEAT.

Ic Ælfric abbod	on ðisum Engliscum gewrite
frēondlice grēte	mid Godes grētinge
Wulfget æt Ylmandune!	Beþām þe wit nū hēr sprǣcon
be ðām Engliscum gewritum,	ðe ic þē ālǣnde,
þæt þē wel līcode	þǣra gewrita andgit,
and ic sǣde, þæt ic wolde	þē sum āsendan gīt.

INTRODUCTION TO THE HEXAMERON.

On sumum ōðrum spelle wē sǣdon hwīlon ǣr. hū se
Ælmihtiga God ealle ðing gescēop binnon six dagum. and
seofon nihtum. ac hit is swā menigfeald and swā mycel on
andgite ðæt wē ne mihton secgan swā swīðe embe ðæt swā
swā wē woldon on ðām ǣrran cwyde. Ne wē gȳt ne magon
swā micclum ēow secgan on ðām dēopan andgite swā swā hit
gedafenlic wǣre. Wē willað ðēah ēow secgan sum ðing
dēoplicor be Godes weorcum on ðysum sōðum gewrite. ðæt gē
wīslicor magon witan ēowerne Scyppend mid sōðum gelēafan.
and ēow sylfe oncnāwan.

PROLOGUE OF THE TRANSLATION OF ST. BASIL'S ADVICE TO A
SPIRITUAL SON.

Basilius se ēadiga be ðām wē ǣr āwriton. wæs swīðe hālig
bisceop on Cessarean byrig, on Greciscre ðēode, God lufigende
swīðe, on clǣnnesse wunigende on Crīstes ðēowdōme,
manegra munuca fæder, munuchādes him sylf.   Hē wæs
swȳðe gelǣred and swȳðe mihtig lārēow, and hē munuc regol
gesette mid swȳðlicre drohtnunge, swā swā ðā Ēasternan and
ðā Greciscean munecas libbað hyra līf, Gode to lofe wīde.
He wæs ǣr Benedictus ðe ūs bōc āwrāt on Lēdenre sprǣce,
lēohtre be dǣle ðonne Basilius, ac hē tȳmde swā ðēah tō
Basilies tǣcinge for his trumnysse.   Basilius āwrāt āne wun-
dorlice bōe be eallum Godes weorcum ðe hē geworhte on six
dagum, "Exameron" gehāten, swīðe dēopum andgite.   And
hē āwrāt ðā lāre ðe wē nū willað on Englisceum gereorde
secgean ðām hē his reccеað.   Hēo gebyrað tō munecum. and
ēac tō mynecenum ðe regollice libbað for hyra drihtnes lufe
under gāstlicum ealdrum, Gode ðēowiende, gehealdenre
clǣnnysse, swā swā Crīstes ðegenas campiende wið dēoflu
dæges and nihtes.

FROM PREFACE OF GENESIS.

Ælfric munuc grēt Æðelweard ealdormann ēadmōdlice. Ðū
bæde mē, lēof ꝥæt ic sceolde āwendan of Lēdene on Englisc
ꝥā bōc Genesis: ꝥā ꝥuhte mē hefigtīme ꝥē tō tīdienne ꝥæs and
ꝥū cwǣde ꝥā, ꝥæt ic ne ꝥorfte nā māre āwendan ꝥǣre bēc
būton to Isaace Abrahames suna, forꝥām ꝥe sum ōðer man ꝥē
hæfde āwend fram Isaace ꝥā bōc oð ende.   Nū ꝥincð mē, lēof,
ꝥæt ꝥæt weorc is swīðe plēolic mē oððe ænigum men tō
underbeginnenne, forꝥan ꝥe ic ondrǣde, gif sum dysig man
ꝥās bōc rǣt oððe rǣdan gehȳrð ꝥæt hē wille wēnan, ꝥæt hē
mōte lybban nū on ꝥǣre nīwan ǣ swā swā ꝥā ealdan fæderas
leofodon ꝥā on ꝥǣre tīde, ǣr ꝥan ꝥe sēo ealde ǣ gesett wǣre,
oððe swā swā men leofodon under Moyses ǣ.   Hwīlon ic wiste
ꝥæt sum mæsseprēost, se ꝥe mīn magister wæs on ꝥām tīman,
hæfde ꝥā bōc Genesis and hē cūðe be dǣle Lȳden understandan;

þā cwæð hē be þām hēahfædere Jacobe, þæt hē hæfde fēower wīf, twā geswustra and heora twā þīnena. Ful sōð hē sǽde, ac hē nyste ne ic þā gīt, hū micel tōdāl ys betweohx þǣre ealdan ǣ and þǣre nīwan. . . .

Wē durron nā māre āwrītan on Englisc, þonne þæt Līden hæfð, ne þā endebirdnisse āwendan būton þām ānum, þæt þæt Lēden and þæt Englisc nabbað nā āne wīsan on þǣre sprǣce fandunge. Ǽfre sē þe āwent oððe sē þe tǣcð of Lēdene on Englisc, ǽfre hē sceal gefadian hit swā, þæt þæt Englisc hæbbe his āgene wīsan: elles hit bið swīðe gedwolsum tō rǣdenne þām þe þæs Lēdenes wīsan ne can. . . .

Ic cweðe nū, þæt ic ne dearr ne ic nelle nāne bōc æfter þis-sere bēc of Lēdene on Englisc āwendan, and ic bidde þē, lēof ealdorman, þæt þū mē þæs nā leng ne bidde, þī lǽs þe ic bēo þē ungehīrsum oððe lēas gif ic dō. God þē sig milde ā on ēcnisse! Ic bidde nū on Godes naman, gif hwā þās bōc āwrītan wylle, þæt hē hīg gerihte wel be þǣre bȳsne, for þan þe ic nāh geweald, þēah þe hīg hwā tō wōge bringe þurh lēase wrīteras, and hit byð þonne his pleoh nā mīn: mycel yfel dēð se unwrītere, gif hē nele hys wōh gerihtan.

EXTRACTS FROM ON THE OLD AND NEW TESTAMENTS.

I. ON THE OLD TESTAMENT.

Ælfric abbod grētt frēondlice Sigwerd æt Ēastheolon.   Ic secge þē tō sōðan þæt sē bið swīþe wīs, sē þe mid weorcum spricð, and sē hæfð forþgang for Gode and for worulde, sē þe mid gōdum weorcum hine sylfne geglengð, and þæt is swīðe geswutelod on hālgum gesetnissum þæt þā hālgan weras, þe gōde weorc beēodon, þæt hī wurðfulle wǣron on þissere worulde, and nū hālige sindon on heofenan rīces mirhþe, and heora gemynd þurhwunað nū ā tō worulde for heora ānrǣdnisse and heora trȳwðe wið God.   Đā gīmelēasan menn þe heora līf ādrugon on ealre īdelnisse, and swā geendodon, heora gemynd is forgiten on hālgum gewritum, būton þæt secgað þā ealdan gesetnissa heora yfelan dǣda, and þæt þæt hīg fordēmde sin-don.   Đū bǣde mē for oft Engliscra gewrita, and ic þē ne

getīðode ealles swā tīmlice, ær þām þe þū mid weorcum þæs
gewilnodest æt mē, þā ðā þū mē bæde for Godes lufan georne
þæt ic þē æt hām æt þīnum hūse gespræce, and þū þā swīðe
mændest, þā þā ic mid þē wæs, þæt þū mīne gewrita begitan
ne mihtest. Nū wille ic þæt þū hæbbe hūru þis lītle, nū þē
wīsdōm gelīcað and þū hine habban wilt, þæt þū ealles ne bēo
mīnra bōca bedæled. . . .

  Se Hālga Gāst . . . spræc þurh wītegan, þe wītegodon
ymbe Crīst, for þan þe hē ys se willa and witodlice lufu þæs
Fæder and þæs Suna, swā swā wē sædon ær. Seofonfealde
gife hē gifð mancynne git, be þām ic āwrāt ær on sumum
ōðrum gewrite on Engliscre spræce, swā swā Isāīas se wītega
hit on bēc sette on his wītegunge.

  Fīf bēc hē (Moises) āwrāt mid wundorlicum dihte. Sēo forme
ys Genesis. . . . Wē secgað nū mid ōfste þās endebirdnisse, for þan ðe wē oft habbað ymbe þis āwriten mid māran
andgite, þā þū miht scēawian, and ēac ðā getācnunge þæt
Adām getācnude. . . .

  On þære ylcan ylde mann ārærde hæðengild wīde geond þās
woruld, swā swā wē āwriton æror on ōðrum lārspellum tō
gelēafan trymminge. . . .

  On þām fif bōcum þe Moyses āwrāt. . Dā twā bēc wē nem-
nodon: Leviticus is sēo þridde, Numerus fēorðe, sēo fīfte ys
gehāten Deuteronomium. . . . On ealre þāre race, þe wē
habbað āwend witodlice on Englisc, on þām mann mæg gehī-
ran hū se heofonlica God spræc mid weorcum and mid wun-
drum him tō. . . .

  Liber Josue. . . . Ðis ic āwende ēac on Englisc hwīlon
Æðelwerde ealdormennn. . . .

  Liber Judicum. . . . Ðis man mæg rædon, sē þe his rēcð
tō gehīrenne, on þære Engliscan bēc þe ic āwende be þisum.
Ic þōhte þæt gē woldon þurh ðā wundorlican race ēower mōd
āwendan tō Godes willan on eornost. . . .

  Nū standað manega cyningas on þæra cininga bōcum, be
þām ic gesette ēac sume bōc on Englisc. . . .

  Daniēl se wītega. . . . His bōc is swīðe micel on

manegum getācnungum, langsum hēr tō secgenne be hire
gesettnyssum and hū hē wæs āworpen þām wildum lēonum,
be þām wē āwriton on Englisc on sumum spelle hwīlon. . . . .
Jōb wæs gehāten sum hēah Godes þegen on þām lande
Chus, swīþe gelēafful wer, welig on æhtum; sē wearð āfandod
þurh þone swicolan dēofol, swā swā his bōc ūs segð, þe hē sylf
gesette siþþan hē āfandod wæs: be þām ic āwende on Englisc
sumne cwide iū. . . . . .

Hester sēo cwēn, þe hire kynn āhredde, hæfð ēac āne bōc on
þisum getele, for ðan þe Godes lof ys gelōgod þæron; ðā ic
āwende on Englisc on ūre wīsan sceortlice.

Judith sēo wuduwe, þe oferwann Holofernem þone Siriscan
ealdormann, hæfð hire āgene bōc betwux þisum bōcum be hire
āgenum sige; sēo ys ēac on Englisc on ūre wīsan gesett ēow
mannum tō bȳsne, þæt gē ēowerne eard mid wæmnum bewe-
rian wið onwinnende here.

Twā bēc synd gesette æfter cyrclicum þēawum betwux
þisum bōcum, þe gebiriað tō Godes lofe, Machabeorum
gehātene, for heora micclum gewinne, for ðan þe hīg
wunnon mid wæmnum þā swīðe wið þone hæðenan
here þe him on wann swīðe. . . . Hīg noldon nā
feohtan mid fægerum wordum ānum, swā þæt hī wel sprǣcon,
and āwendon þæt eft. . . . 'Ac uton wyrcean mihte
on þone mihtigan God, and hē tō nāhte gedēð ūre deriendli-
canfȳnd.' Machabēus þā gefylde ðās foresǣdan word mid
stranglicum weorcum, and oferwann his fȳnd, and sint for ðī
gesette his sigefæstan dǣda on þām twām bōcum on bibliothe-
can Gode tō wurðmynte; and ic āwende hīg on Englisc, and
rǣdon, gif gē wyllað, ēow sylfum tō rǣde!

II. ON THE NEW TESTAMENT.

Ic secge þē nū Sīferð, þæt ic hēr gesett hæbbe þās fēawa
bȳsna of þān ealdan bōcum on þǣre ealdan gecȳðnysse under
Moyses ǣ and hū, gif þū wiltest ealne þone wīsdōm, þe on
þām bōcum stynt, þonne woldest þū gelȳfan, þæt ic nā ne
wæge on þisum gewrite.

Ic wille nū secgan eft sceortlice þē be þǣre nīwan gecȳðnisse
æfter Crīstes tōcyme, þæt ðū mid ealle ne bēo þæs andgites
bedǣled þēah þe þū be fullan underfōn ne mǣge ealle þā
gesetnissa þæs sōðan gewrites: bist swā þēah gebēt þurh þās
lītlan bȳsne. . . .

Ðās fēower bēc kȳðað, hū Crīst cōm tō mannum. . .
Ic secge þis sceortlice, for þan þe ic gesett hæbbe of þisum
fēower bōcum wel fēowertig lārspella on Engliscum gereorde
and sumne ēacan þǣr tō, þā þū miht rǣdan be þissere race on
māran andgite, þonne ic hēr secge. . . .

Ðū woldest me laðian, þā þā ic wæs mid þē, þæt ic swīðor
drunce swilce for blisse ofer mīnum gewunan: ac wite þū,
lēof man, þæt sē þe ōðerne nēadað ofer his mihte tō drincenne,
þæt sē mōt āberan heora bēgra gilt, gif him ænig hearm of
þām drence becymð. Ūre hǣlend Crīst on his hālgan godspelle forbēad þone oferdrenc eallum gelȳfedum mannum:
healde, se þe wille, his gesetnysse! and þā hālgan lārēowas
æfter þām hǣlende ālēdon þone unþēaw þurh heora lārēowdōm
and tǣhton, þæt man drince, swā swā him ne derede, for þan
þe se oferdrenc fordēð untwīlice þæs mannes sāwle and his
gesundfulnysse and unhǣl becymð of þām drence.

Lōca, hwā þās bōc āwrīte, wrīte hīg be þǣre bȳsne and for
Godes lufon hī gerihte, þæt hēo tō lēas ne bēo þām wrītere tō
plihte and mē tō tāle!

PREFACE OF PASTORAL LETTER FOR BISHOP WULFSIGE.

Ælfricus humilis frater venerabili episcopo Wulfsino salutem in Domino. Obtemperavimus jussioni tuae libenti animo,
sed non ausi fuimus aliquid scribere de episcopali gradu, quia
vestrum est scire, quomodo vos oporteat optimis moribus
exemplum omnibus fieri, et continuis admonitionibus subditos
exhortari ad salutem, quae est in Christo Jesu. Dico tamen,
quod saepius deberetis vestris clericis alloqui, et illorum
negligentiam arguere, quia pene statuta canonum, et sanctae
ecclesiae religio vel doctrina, eorum perversitate deleta sunt:
ideoque libera animam tuam, et dic eis quae tenenda sunt

sacerdotibus et ministris Christi, ne tu pereas pariter, si mutus habearis canis. Nos vero scriptitamus hanc epistolam, quae Anglice sequitur, quasi ex tuo ore dictata sit, et locutus esses ad clericos tibi subditos, hoc modo incipiens.

PREFACE OF PASTORAL LETTER FOR ARCHBISHOP WULFSTAN.

Ælfricus Abbas Wulstano venerabili Archiepiscopo salutem in Christo. Ecce paruimus vestrae Almitatis jussionibus transferentes Anglice duas Epistolas quas, Latino eloquio descriptas, ante annum vobis destinavimus; non tamen semper ordinem sequentes, nec verbum ex verbo, sed sensum ex sensu proferentes, quibus speramus nos quibusdam prodesse ad correctionem, quamvis sciamus aliis minime placuisse: sed non est nobis consultum semper silere, et non aperire subjectis eloquia divina; quia si praeco tacet, quis judicem venturum nuntiet? Vale feliciter in Christo.

PROLOGUE OF THE LIFE OF SAINT ÆTHELWOLD.

Alfricus abbas, Wintoniensis alumnus, honorabili episcopo Kenulfo, et fratribus Wintoniensibus, salutem in Christo.

Dignum ducens denique aliqua de gestis patris nostri et magnifici doctoris Athelwoldi memoriae modo commendare, transactis videlicet viginti annis post ejus migrationem, brevi quidem narratione mea, tum sed et rustica, quae apud vos vel alios a fidelibus didici huic stylo ingero, ne forte penitus propter inopiam scriptorum oblivioni tradentur. Valete.

PREFACE OF EXCERPTS FROM ÆTHELWOLD'S DE CONSUETUDINE.

Ælfricus Abbas Egneshamensibus Fratribus salutem in Christo. Ecce video vobiscum degens, vos necesse habere quia nuper rogatu Æthelmeri ad Monachicum habitum ordinati estis, instrui ad mores Monachiles dictis aut scriptis. Ideoque haec pauca de libro Consuetudinum, quem Scs. Æthelwoldus Wintoniensis episcopus cum Coepiscopis et Abbatibus tempore Eadgari felicissimi Regis Anglorum undique collegit, ac monachis instituit observandum scriptitando demonstro. Eo quod hactenus praedictus libellus ūrae fraternitati incognitus habetur. Fateor me valde timide idipsum sumere, sed nec audeo omnia vobis intimare quae in Scola ejus degens multis annis, de moribus seu consuetudinibus didici, ne forte fastidientes districtionem tantae observantiae nec saltem velitis praebere narranti, tamen ne expertis tam salubris doctrinae remaneatis aliqua quae Regula nostra non tangit huic cartulae insero vobis quae legenda committo, addens etiam aliqua de libro Amalarii Presbiteri. Valete feliciter in Christo.

FROM THE FOUNDATION CHARTER OF EYNSHAM.

' Ic Æðelmær cȳðe mīnan lēofan hlāforde Æðelrede cynge, and eallon his witon, ðæt ic an ðysse āre Gode and sancta Marian, and eallon his hālgon, and sancte Benedicte intō Egneshām, ofer mīne dæg æfre tō brice, ðām ðe Benedictus regol æfre rihtlice healdað. And ic wille ðēre bēon ofer hī ealdor ðe ðær nū is, ðā hwīle ðe his līf bēo, and siððan gif hit hwæt getȳmað, ðæt hī cēosan heom ealdor of heora geferædne eal swā hæra regol him tæcð.' 'And ic mē sylfe wylle mid ðære geferrærdne gemænelice libban, and ðære āre mid him notian ðā hwīle ðe mīn līf bið.' *Cod. Dip.* III. 344.

APPENDIXES.

I.

The work of Mores, *De Ælfrico Commentarius,* written 'some years' before 1760, was published by Thorkelin in 1789. Mores treats the subject as follows:

CHAPTER I.

The views held by Leland, Bale, Parker, Foxe, Pits, Spelman, Usher, Cave, and Wharton, are successively considered. Three points of Wharton's argument are answered:

1. Wharton asserts that Ælfric could not have been at Abingdon with Æthelwold, for by the *Saxon Chronicle* he was not eleven years old when Æthelwold left Abingdon for Winchester.

In reply, Mores argues that we know nothing of Ælfric's age from the *Saxon Chronicle,* for the passage in question refers, not to an Ælfric, but to King Alfred.

2. Wharton urges that Ælfric was probably Abbot of Winchester in 1005, when he dedicated his *Life of Æthelwold* to Bishop Kenulph, for he calls himself 'Wintoniensis alumnus' and 'abbot,' but is silent about the seat of the abbacy. In reliance upon Florence of Worcester and others, who say that Ælfric Puttoc, Provost (or Prior) of Winchester, was promoted to the Archbishopric of York, Wharton concludes that the author of the *Life of Æthelwold,* Abbot Ælfric, was Ælfric Puttoc.

Mores replies, that the monastery at Winchester had only priors, not abbots.

3. By a poem which celebrates a bishop, and by a letter addressed to a high official in the church, both joined to the manuscript of Ælfric's *Glossary,* Wharton tries to show that Ælfric the Grammarian was the Bishop of York.

Mores shows that the letter in question does not suit Ælfric of York, and that the poem applies only to Ælfric of Canterbury.

To this chapter are appended items collected by Ballard, an Oxford friend of Mores, to prove the opposite of Wharton's essay.

CHAPTER II.

Ælfric, monk at Abingdon and pupil of Æthelwold, accompanies Æthelwold to Winchester.

CHAPTER III.

Ælfric devotes himself to studies at Winchester, and translates the Pentateuch and other books of the Old Testament, and writes a *Pastoral Letter* for Wulfsige.

CHAPTER IV.

Ælfric is sent to Cernel, and writes one volume of homilies.

CHAPTER V.

Ælfric is made Abbot of St. Albans, and there writes *On the Old and New Testaments,* and in it he refers to the *Job,* which he publishes later among other homilies. He writes also the letter on chastity addressed to Sigeferth.

CHAPTER VI.

Ælfric is made Bishop of Wilton. There he writes a second volume of homilies. He does not call himself bishop, but in explanation 'many parallel examples of such humility can be adduced.' Here probably he wrote the *Grammar,* and possibly the *Saints' Lives,* but the latter may have a later date.

CHAPTER VII.

Ælfric is made Archbishop of Canterbury. Several writers are quoted, to show the high esteem in which the Archbishop was held.

CHAPTER VIII.

Ælfric Bata was Abbot of Eynsham, and wrote *Excerpts from Æthelwold's De Consuetudine;* the *Life of Æthelwold;* and *Pastoral Letters* for Wulfstan. This Ælfric Bata was probably the later Archbishop of York, although some question it.

CHAPTER IX.

Of Ælfric of Malmesbury.

CHAPTER X.

Of other Ælfrics.

There is an appendix, consisting of charters, Ælfric of Canterbury's will, and other legal documents.

Mores' method of proof, if such it can be called, is the following: he states known facts in the life of Ælfric of Canterbury, and weaves in with these such known facts in the life of the scholar Ælfric as can be consistently placed there. To these he adds other more uncertain data, such as the order of the production of Ælfric's most important works. Facts which cannot possibly be reconciled with the theory are assigned to Ælfric Bata, namely: the authorship of the *Life of Æthelwold;* the *Extracts from the De Consuetudine;* and the *Canons* written for Wulfstan of York. We fail to see that he establishes any connection between Ælfric the scholar and Ælfric of Canterbury. The certainty which he felt in his own mind was to him a proof, and made a connection between the two men which fails to appear in his dissertation.

It is, however, of special significance that he places the author of three of Ælfric's important works in the monastery of Eynsham.

II.

The results here given are from Dr. Förster's investigation of the exegetical homilies.[1]

I. By far the chief source of Ælfric's exegetical homilies is Gregory the Great's collection of homilies. In *Hom.* I, fifteen, perhaps sixteen, in *Hom.* II, twelve, perhaps thirteen homilies are derived from twenty-seven of Gregory's forty

---

[1] See Bibliography, 1892.

homilies. Ælfric often takes one homily from two of Gregory's: thus are derived I. 15, 22, 23, 28; II. 5, 42. Of Gregory's homilies, Nos. 10, 12, 16, 26, 34, 39, 40, have each given material for two of Ælfric's, and No. 34 for three.

II. Next to Gregory in the amount of material furnished stands Bede. Indeed, it may be a question whether Bede is not the author most often referred to by Ælfric, although the actual translations from his works occupy less room than those from Gregory. We find everywhere in our homilies single sentences which more or less closely correspond with passages in Bede. Often the agreement is so slight, or the thought so obvious, that it is difficult to decide whether Ælfric has the original before him or quotes from memory. In general his treatment of Bede's writings is freer than of Gregory's.

A. From Bede's *Homilies* Ælfric has taken material for *Hom.* I. 6, 9, 12, 13, 14, 22, 25, 27, 32; *Hom.* II. 4; but only in two cases: I. 12 and 13, are Bede's *Homilies* the only source.

B. From Bede's *Scripture Commentary* is derived *Hom.* I. 33; II. (12), 29, 30, 33, 36.

C. From Bede's three *Mathematical-Scientific* writings are taken the chronological and astronomical parts of *Hom.* I. 6 and 40.

D. From the *Historical* works of Bede are taken parts of of *Hom.* II. 9, 10, 23, 24.

III. Augustine stands third in importance. Ælfric's homilies betray acquaintance with only Augustine's *Sermons, Commentary on John, De Sermone Domini in Monte, De Civitate Dei,* and *De Trinitate.*

A. From the *Sermons* Ælfric derives five whole homilies: I. 3, 18, 19; II. 28, 34; the chief part of I. 18; probably part of I. 19; II. 28, 34, 44; and perhaps of II. 7, 9, and 27. From the pseudo-Augustinian sermon No. 42, *Hom.* I. 3, is taken.

B. From the *Commentary on John* is derived *Hom.* II. 3, 25; part of II. 13, (28).

C. From the *De Sermone Domini in Monte* is derived *Hom.* I. 36, second part.

D. From the *De Trinitate* is derived *Hom.* I. 20.

E. From the *De Civitate Dei* is derived *Hom.* II. 2.

IV. Smaragdus is next in importance of Ælfric's sources. Of his works Ælfric has used only his *Commentarius sive Collectio Evangelia et Epistolas.* Smaragdus' chief sources were Gregory, Bede, Jerome and Augustine. Hence it is difficult in some cases to tell whether Ælfric quotes Smaragdus or his originals, and this is the more the case as there are not critical editions of either.

From Smaragdus are probably taken in part *Hom.* I. 5, 27, 39; II. 8, 14.

V. Jerome is mentioned by Ælfric in the second place among his sources, but his actual contribution is relatively small. To Ælfric, however, he seemed to contribute more than he really did, because the authorship of Rufin's *Church History* was ascribed to him.

From Jerome's *Commentary on Matthew* are probably derived parts of *Hom.* I. 13, 26, 36.

VI. From the homilies of the Halberstadt bishop, Haymo, is derived material for *Hom.* I. 8, 34, second part.

Smaragdus, Jerome and Haymo may be called sources of the second class; the remaining sources are those of the third class.

VII. From Alcuin is derived part of *Hom.* II. 12, p. 219 ff.

VIII. From Cassian comes part of *Hom.* II. 12, p 219 ff., but his share cannot be wholly distinguished from that of Alcuin; also II. 7, p. 106, ll. 116-132.

IX. From Amalarius' *De Ecclesiasticis Officiis* are taken some liturgical remarks in *Hom.* I. 18, 22; II. 5.

X. A writer Hilarius is once cited, *Hom.* I. 21, p. 168 ff. Of the many bishops, etc., of this name, the one mentioned must be either the Bishop of Arles († 449) or the more famous Bishop of Poitiers; it is uncertain which.

XI. Ratramnus, a monk of Corbie, furnished the material for the famous Easter sermon, *Hom.* II. 15. Ælfric follows Ratramnus very closely. Lingard says: 'There is scarcely a sentence in the homily which may not be traced to the work of Bertram' (i. e., Ratramnus).'

XII. In the illustration of Biblical narrative by profane history, Ælfric has confined himself mostly to what others had used before him, as he found it in the commentaries at hand. He has drawn directly from Rufin's translation of Eusebius of Caesarea's *Ecclesiastical History* in *Hom.* I. 5, 28, 32; II. 28. (Two of the legendary homilies are wholly taken from Rufin: *Hom.* II. 18, 19).

XIII. The *Vitae Patrum,* an anonymous collection of pious narratives, had great popularity in the Middle Ages. In *Hom.* I. 36, and II. 15, Ælfric mentions it as the source of some remarks found in those homilies. Of *Hom.* I. 1; II. 1, 25, 45; no sources have been found.

Finally, it is uncertain whether Ælfric chose his material himself, or used a collection of homilies already in use.' Since there were many such collections at that time, and some must have been accessible to Ælfric, he may have taken one as a model. But that he simply translated appears to be improbable. His great self-dependence in translating from the books of the Bible and from legends speaks against it. The fact also that the greater number of his homilies are derived from more than one source, and that among the sources are books like *Vitae Patrum,* the church histories of Rufin and Bede, Bede's scientific writings, etc., renders it yet more improbable.

III.

A. Reum, in *De Temporibus Ein Echtes Werk des Abtes Ælfric,* makes a more extended study of the question.[3] Start-

---

1 *Hist. and Antiq. of A-S. Ch.* II, 460.

2 'It is plain that there is a common source behind both sets of sermons; the well established series of topics for each occasion seems clearly to point to some standard collection of Latin homilies now lost.' Earle, *Anglo-Saxon Lit.*, p. 215.

2 See Bibliography, 1888.

ing with the probability established by Dietrich, that Ælfric is the author, Reum compares this work in its details with the undoubted works of Ælfric.

I. There are three peculiarities characteristic of Ælfric's treatment of his sources; first, he lays stress upon the authors whom he uses and puts himself in the background; secondly, while he gives the thoughts of his authors with conscientious accuracy, he is independent and free in his method of conveying thought; thirdly, he separates the important from the unimportant, and produces a new whole.

These three characteristics belong to the author of the *De Temporibus.* His modest acknowledgment of his source appears in the introduction. On comparison of the *De Temporibus* with Bede's three books, *De Temporibus, De Temporum Ratione,* and *De Natura Rerum,* it is found that the author of the Old English *De Temporibus* has studied carefully all three of Bede's works, and has selected from them all, those things which were of most interest and importance for the laity, and has omitted what would confuse them; he has made a new whole according to his own arrangement.

II. Characteristics of Ælfric's language in his known works are compared with those of the *De Temporibus.*

A. His language as a translator :

1. He took pains to translate Latin terms and quotations into correct Old English, and proved by this the verbal richness and flexibility of his language.

2. He united the short, disconnected sentences characteristic of· Alfred's style, into longer sentences by relative constructions, parentheses, adverbs and conjunctions.

3. He arranged his words with reference to rhythm and alliteration.

B. His language as a teacher:

1. Even as Ælfric selected the most important matters from great compends to form his books, so the

13

weightiest matters of all he enforces and makes prominent by the use of very emphatic adverbs.

2. He enlivens his discourse by rhetorical questions and apostrophes.

3. He imparts to his language the freshness of nature by pictorial expression, and enlivens his discourse by excellent illustrations. The beauty of Old English poetry rests in part upon its pictorial character. But Ælfric borrows his images from quite another range, for they are to serve a different end. They gave spirit and power to heroic song, but with him their first purpose was to enlighten, and their second to enliven and adorn. Hence he took them from every-day life, so that they could always influence the language in its common use.

C. His language as a preacher:

1. Formal announcements of the subjects which he is about to treat, show Ælfric's desire to be clear and to be understood by the many.

2. Formal concluding sentences close the separate sections of his work.

3. He brings Bible words and discourse into scientific treatises.

A, B and C are illustrated by detailed comparisons of the *De Temporibus* with Ælfric's works, and the result is a strong confirmation of Ælfric's authorship of the former.

III. There are other striking agreements between the *De Temporibus* and other works of Ælfric's:

1. The Glossary made by Ælfric, and completed by his pupil, Ælfric Bata, contains many words from the *De Temporibus,* some of which may not have been found elsewhere in Old English.

2. Marked coincidences in phrases, sentences, and material introduced, appear in the *De Temporibus* and Ælfric's books.

3. Ælfric's interest in the subjects treated of in the

De Temporibus is seen in many places in his other writings.

4. In *Inter. Sig.* 68, 114, Ælfric refers to a former writing on the planets, which must be accounted for by such a work as this.

IV. The appendix to the *De Temporibus* printed in Cockayne's edition is examined, and is decided to be an imitation of Ælfric's writing in the *De Temporibus* by some other monk, perhaps Ælfric Bata. The decision rests on these grounds:

a. While the colloquial language resembles Ælfric's, its tone differs from his.

b. The material differs from that which he chooses.

c. Ælfric's favorite words are not found.

d. The author's use of Latin words does not correspond with Ælfric's.

V. The date of the work.

It cannot be Ælfric's first writing, because he designates the first volume of *Catholic Homilies* as the first, and also because the *De Temporibus* refers in its opening words to a former writing.

The following points make it probable that it was written just after the first volume of homilies:

1. Its position in the Cambridge manuscript, where it is joined to the last homily by an announcement of what is to follow, and is closely connected with the preceding by its introductory sentence.

2. There is far more discourse on astronomical and scientific matters in the first volume of homilies than in the second. Therefore Ælfric must have thought it worth while, after sending out the first volume, to give the contents of the *De Temporibus* to the laity.

3. In the second volume of homilies, Ælfric, when he refers to astronomical questions, expresses himself briefly, in the manner of one who is referring to that which is well-known.

4. The unusual brevity used by Ælfric in his *Grammar* in referring to the signs of the Zodiac indicates that he considers the subject a familiar one.

5. The connection of this writing with the words 'on gēares ymbryne' in *Hom.* I, 98. If Ælfric had allowed a long time to pass between this sermon and the *De Temporibus,* he would have followed Bede's order and arrangement of chapters; but he still remembered the chief matters which were referred to in the sermons and joined to the first volume a new work, the *De Temporibus.*

Hence the *De Temporibus* grew immediately out of the first volume of homilies, gave it scientific completeness, and was joined to it. He probably finished it while the scribe of the Cambridge manuscript was doing his work, and was able to deliver it to him when the last homily was transcribed.

According to Dietrich, Ælfric wrote the first volume of homilies in 990-991, and this latter year is probably the date of the *De Temporibus.*

IV.

We extract from MacLean's dissertation[1] the following:

I. *The manuscripts* in which the Old English *Inter. Sige. in Gen.* is contained are described in detail. They are these:

1. MS., originally a part of Cod. 178 (S. 6), Corpus Christi College, Cambridge, but removed from that, probably in the sixteenth century, and now bound in C. C. C. C., 162 (S. 5).

2. Cottonian Cod., Julius E. VII, Brit. Mus. (Wanley, p. 186), *Inter. Sige. in Gen.* is here found as No. 37 of Ælfric's *Saints' Lives.* This Cod. probably belongs in the second quarter of the eleventh century.

3. Cod. Junii 23, Bodleian Lib. Oxford (Wanley, p. 36).

---

[1] See Bibliography, 1883.

The contents are selected from the *Cath. Hom.* I-II, the *Saints' Lives,* and the sermons, probably by Ælfric, in C. C. C. C., Cod. 162.

This Cod. was evidently written when Ælfric's original order was being forgotten. The date is undoubtedly in the last quarter of the eleventh century.

4. Cod. Junii 24, Bodleian Lib. Oxford (Wanley, p. 40). This Cod. is a volume of sermons for saints' and week-day festivals, taken with a few exceptions from Ælfric. *Inter. Sigè. in Gen.* is here associated with three others from the *Saints' Lives.*

5. C. C. C. 303 (S. 17), (Wanley, p 133). A mixed Cod. of the twelfth century, mutilated at the beginning. The aim of the scribe must have been to make a full edition of Ælfric's homilies. *Inter. Sige.* is in a group from the *Saints' Lives.*

Besides the above five MSS.; there is a transcript by Junius (Cod. Junii 104, Bodl. Lib.) of the third of these.

Two MSS. of Alcuin's Latin *Inter. Sige.* are in the Bodl. Lib. MSS. Barlow 35, and Laud. 437 (Laud. F. 134). In the latter are the lives of five saints. These Latin Codd. add to the testimonies that the Inter. was long and widely used in theological school-books, and further, that it had in some way become connected with the lives of saints.

The O. E. MSS. of *Inter. Sige.* are all of L. W. S. and indicate the composition of the work as about 1000 A. D.

II. The *final Creed and Doxology* are contained in only two of the MSS. But the contents of the appendix favors its authenticity. It is alliterative and thus harmonizes in form with the *Inter.* and the *Saints' Lives.* The subject matter could almost be replaced word for word from other passages in Ælfric. The probable indirect source of this form of the creed was Isidore, an author whom Ælfric used during this period of his life in his *Glossary* and in his treatise *On the Old and New Testaments.* It is most probable that some early copyist, knowing of Ælfric's repetitions about the Trinity, or wishing to save labor and parchment, ended his copy at the good stopping-place afforded by the remark, 'We will not speak further about this, because we have now written the most necessary questions.'

III. *The Question of Authorship.* The chief difficulties of the critics sprang from their treatment of the *Inter.* as an independent treatise.

1. *The External Evidence.*

The *Inter.* is bound without exception with Ælfric's Codd. The best hypothesis to explain all the phenomena of the MSS. is that Ælfric wrote the *Inter.*

2. *The Internal Evidences.*

The *form* of the *Inter.*, in its alliteration, poetic passages, and even punctuation, is a strong argument for the integrity of the longer version and the Ælfrician authorship.

The language and dialect, so thoroughly L. W. S., and without any substantial traces of *early* L. W. S., show that Bouterwek's supposition that it dates from a monk in the ninth century, is untenable. A comparison of its vocabulary and forms of expression with those of the *Blickling Homilies,* a specimen of pre-Ælfrician literature, renders it probable that no earlier date than Ælfric's time can be assigned for it.

In the light of the exigencies of translation and alliteration, the correspondences between the *Inter.* and the parallel passages from Ælfric make a deep impression as to common authorship.

There is a probable direct reference in the *Inter.*, in one of those personal explanatory remarks so characteristic of Ælfric, to a similar remark in his *De Temporibus.* At *Inter.*, l. 114, he writes, 'I will say *now* that about which I kept silent some time *before* on account of the unwontedness of the lay understanding.' He then gives, ll. 115-144, a translation of cap. XII, *De Cursu Planetarum,* of Bede's *De Natura Rerum.* In the *De Temp.* the author is following closely cap. XI, *De Stellis,* of the same book of Bede's. He closes the chapter with: 'Though we should speak more of the heavenly constellations, still the unlearned may not learn their luminous course.' In the *Inter.* it must be the same author who, upon the simple mention by Alcuin of the counteracting influence of the heavens and the planets, reverts to his former omission in the *De Temp.* He makes his longest insertion in Alcuin from Bede, at the very point where he began to omit in the *De Temp.* In the *Saints' Lives,* according to the preface, he was opening more than ever before subjects with which the laity were unacquainted.

3. *The Translation is Ælfrician.* It shows a master's hand in its general literalness, combined with freedom of arrangement and English idioms.

4. *The Subject.* The Creation was a favorite subject with Ælfric. The choice of questions and passages from Alcuin displays an author of Ælfric's caution about giving all the narratives of *Gen.* to the public of his time. Also the insertions from other authors are Ælfrician.

5. *The Sources are Alcuin and Bede.* Traces of Gregory the Great and Isidore appear. The translator of *Inter.* was thoroughly at home among the sources of Alcuin's originals.

A. Tessman has compared the texts of the five manuscripts of the *Interrogationes* in regard to the following points: 1. Characteristics common to the language of all the manuscripts: a. vowels of root syllables; b. vowels of middle and final syllables; c. consonants; d. inflection. 2. Peculiarities of the single manuscripts. 3. Relation of the manuscripts to each other. He has also considered the metrical form of the work. The text of MacLean is criticised in accordance with Tessman's collation of the manuscripts. The fragment in Codex Harley 3271, British Museum, is printed,[1] and the text of the whole is given, with variant readings in footnotes.

V.

An investigation of the sources of the legendary homilies of the first volume of the *Lives of the Saints* has been made

---

[1] See *Mod. Lang. Notes*, 1887, 378-9.

by J. H. Ott.[1] Of the twenty-three homilies in this volume, enumerated on page 9, there are therefore omitted from the study Nos. I, XII, XIII, XVI, XVII, and XVIII. From the dissertation by Ott we take the following:

Ælfric names as sources, Ambrose, in the life of St. Agnes; Terence, in the Superscription of the life of Gallicanus; Marcellus, in the life of Petronilla; Jerome, in ·the life of the four evangelists; Bede, in the life of Ætheldred; Landferth, in the life of Swithun.

No collection of Latin legends furnished Ælfric with originals, but he has gathered from different books.

His additions are of three sorts: (1) metrical, the most common; (2) explanatory; (3) homiletic.

The results in respect to each of the seventeen homilies considered are given on pp. 8-60 of Dr. Ott's dissertation.

VI.

The authorship of the Old English homily on the book of Judith is considered by Assmann in *Anglia*, 10. 76 ff., where he gives in detail the reasons for claiming Ælfric as its author. The subject is treated in the following order:

I. Introduction. Dietrich concludes that this homily does not belong to Ælfric, because in the work on the Old Testament he makes no claim for it, but says only of the book of Judith, 'sēo ys ēac on Englisc on ūre wīsan gesett.' These last three words both Dietrich and Assmann understand to refer to poetical expression, but the former understands Ælfric to refer in all that he says to the well-known poem of *Judith*, first published by Thwaites.

Assmann reaffirms what he has said in his study of Ælfric's book of *Esther*, that the uncertain statement in the work on the Old. Testament is not sufficient ground for rejecting Ælfric's authorship of the *Judith*

II. Manuscripts. This work is found in two manuscripts:

---

1 See Bibliography, 1892.

1. The MS. in Corpus Christi College, Cambridge, No. 303. Wanley describes this and gives the beginning of the *Judith* as found there. A full description of this MS. is given by MacLean in *Anglia* 6. 446-447. The *Judith* has the last place in this defective MS., and lacks a conclusion.

2. The MS. in Otho B, 10, in the Cotton MSS. in London. Wanley describes the *Judith* in this as follows: '*Tractat autem Historiam Judithæ et Holofernis, et de S. Malcho;*' and gives the first seven lines, and seven lines at the end. This MS. suffered greatly by the fire which, in 1731, injured the Cotton collection. Lines 62-123 and 384-445 of the *Judith* were· deciphered by Assman. From this MS. it appears that a history of the life of Malchus was appended to the work.

The whole homily had perhaps five hundred and twenty lines, of which the first four hundred and forty-five are extant, and also the last seven lines, preserved by Wanley.

III. Authorship. Both MSS. consist chiefly of writings of Ælfric. More satisfactory proofs of his authorship are

A. The Relation of the *Judith* to its sources. The first ten lines are derived, not from the book of Judith, but from II Chronicles. This corresponds with Ælfric's efforts elsewhere for the laity; he always tries to bring together such materials as will give his readers a correct view of his narrative in its different relations.

To this translation the author adds an allegorical explanation in reference to the heroine from a Latin source, and magnifies chastity, Ælfric's favorite theme.

The *Judith* shows Ælfric's method:

1. In reference to omissions. The author omits names of unimportant persons, genealogies, extended descriptions, exact note of time, passages of unnecessary length, repetitions, digressions from the main subject.

2. In reference to additions. He adds a second name if a person has two names; he adds references to faith in the true God, and emphasizes that faith in persons for whom he wishes to awaken sympathy; he also adds that which will make the meaning clearer.

3. In reference to manner of translating. The *Judith* has the same clearness and simplicity which the writings of Ælfric show. It has his free, not slavish, translation of the Latin. This appears in changes of order in the matter translated; in the use of indirect discourse for the direct found in the original; in the poetical means, which consist only in the use of descriptive language. Ælfric's expletive words, sōðlice, hwaet, etc., are found in the *Judith*. There are also mistakes in translation similar to those found in his writings.

B. If this work is by Ælfric it must be written in poetical form, since he says the book of *Judith* is composed, on 'ūre wīsan.' It is found that it can be arranged in rhythmical form with the greatest ease. In the manuscript there are numerous points, and though their use is not a certain criterion for the presence of rhythmical form, yet the points here correspond exactly with the divisions of the half-lines. Of the 890 half-lines, 857 can be read as four-stressed metre. The others are either too long or too short. This result corresponds in general with that found in *Esther,* and in the second and the seventh of the *Saints' Lives.*

C. Vocabulary. Only three words are found in the *Judith* which are not in Ælfric.

D. The Phraseology is Ælfrician. This is seen in an arrangement of parallel passages from the *Judith* and the work, *On the Old Testament.*

E. Date of Composition. It must have been written between the *Heptateuch* (997) and *De Veteri Testamento.*

BIBLIOGRAPHY.

1. 1558. BALE, JOHN: *Illustrium Majoris Britanniæ Scriptorum. . . .* Ipswich. See article Alfric.

2. 1566 or 1567. *A Testimony of Antiquitie* Shewing the Ancient Faith in the Church of England touching the sacrament of the body and blood of the Lord. London. This book contains *Hom.* II. 262-282, and extracts from Ælfric's letter for Wulfsige, with English translations of both; also an extract from the 2d Latin letter for Wulfstan. All the above-named contents treat of the Paschal Lamb. The Lord's Prayer and a short creed are printed here. A preface discusses the question of Ælfric's identity, and of the value of these documents in the history of the belief of the early English church. The 3d edition in 1623, (see no. 6). Reprint, 1688: *No Antiquity for Transubstantiation.* London. Reprint, 1849; 2d edition of this reprint, 1875, (see no. 71).

3. 1570. FOX, JOHN: *Ecclesiastical History.* London. 2d ed. This contains the homily on the Paschal Lamb, and extracts from *Pastoral Letters*, (see no. 2). 1838. *Acts and Monuments*, V. 273-289: the same as the above.

4. 1605. CAMDEN, WILLIAM: *Remaines of a Greater Worke, concerning Britaine,* etc. London. 4th ed., pp. 76 and 234.

5. 1610. FREHER, M.: *Decalogi, Orationis,* etc.: contains the *Lord's Prayer.*

6. 1623. L'ISLE, WILLIAM: *A Saxon Treatise concerning the Old and New Testament,* written about the time of King Edgar by Ælfricus Abbas. London. To this book was appended a reprint of *A Testimonie of Antiquitie* (see no. 2).

7. 1624. GUILD, M. WILLIAM: *Three Rare Monuments of Antiquitie,* or Bertram, Priest, a French-man, of the Bodie, and Blood of Christ. . . . Ælfricus, Archbishop

of Canterburie, an Englishman, His Sermon of the Sacrament.
. . . and Maurus Abbot, a Scots-man, His discourse of the
same. . . . With translation, Aberdeen.

8. 1638. L'ISLE, WILLIAM: *Divers Ancient Monuments in
the Saxon Tongue.* London. New edition of No. 6.

9. 1643. WHELOC, ABRAHAM: *Historiae Ecclesiasticae
Gentis Anglorum,* Libri V. a venerabili Beda. . . . Scripti.
Cambridge. This book contains a large number of homilies and
long extracts from homilies, with Latin translations. Pp.
41-50: *Hom.* I. 274-292; 61: II. 260; 62: I. 16; 62 f.: II. 6; I.
18 f.; 462-479: II. 262-282; and other extracts from the Homilies; 332 f.: *Pastoral Letter for Wulfsige;* 495-498: *Prayers*
and *Confessions* by Ælfric.

10. 1659. SUMNER, WILLIAM: *Dictionarium Saxonico-
Latino-Anglicum* voces phrasesque praecipuas Anglo-Saxonicas
. . . Accesserunt Ælfrici Abbatis *Grammatica Latino-
saxonica,* cum *Glossario* suo ejusdam generis. Oxford.

11. 1670. SHERINGHAM, ROBERT: *De Anglorum Gentis
Origine Disceptatio* . . . Cambridge. Pp. 310 ff.: Extracts from Ælfric's *Homilies,* with English translation.

12. 1676. SAMMES, AYLETT: *Britannia Antiqua Illus-
trata.* London. Pp. 448 ff.: the same extracts from Ælfric's
Homilies. as in no. 11.

13. 1688. CAVE, WILLIAM: *Scriptores Ecclesiastici.* London, 1688; Basel, 1745. II. 108-112. (On p. 109 the view of
Archbishop Usher is given).

14. 1689. WHARTON, HENRY: *Auctarium Historiae Dog-
maticae Jacobi Userii* . . . de scripturis et sacris verna-
culis. London. Pp. 380-386: Ælfric's Preface to *Genesis,*
with Latin translation by Hickes.

15. 1691. WHARTON, HENRY: *Anglia Sacra.* London.
I. 125-134: *Dissertation De Elfrico Archiepiscopo Cantuar-,
utrum is fuerit Elfricus Grammaticus.*

16. 1698. THWAITES, EDWARD: *Heptateuchus, Liber Job,*
etc. Oxford.

17. 1709. ELSTOB, ELIZABETH: *English-Saxon Homily*

on the *Birthday of St. Gregory,* with English translation. London.

18. 1715. ELSTOB, ELIZABETH: *The English-Saxon Homilies of Ælfric Archbishop of Canterbury.* . . . Now first printed, and translated into the language of the present times. Oxford. Only thirty-six pages were printed.

19. 1721. WILKINS, DAVID: *Leges Anglo-Saxonicae Ecclesiasticae et Civiles.* London. Pp. 153-160: *Pastoral Letter for Wulfsige;* 161-172: *Pastoral Letters for Wulfstan.*

20. 1737. WILKINS, D.: *Concilia Britannia.* London. I. 250-255: *Pastoral Letter for Wulfsige;* Discussion of Ælfric's identity.

21. 1759. WARNER, F.: *The History of England as it Relates to Religion and the Church.* London. I. 220-223: Of Ælfric's *Canons,* and of his teaching on the eucharist.

22. 1778. STRUTT, JOSEPH: *Chronicle of England.* II. 280: a part of the first chapter of *Genesis* with interlined English translation.

23. 1789. MORES, EDWARD ROWE: *Ælfrico, Dorobernensi Archiepiscopo, Commentarius.* London.

24. 1798. OELRICHS, JOH.: *Angelsächsische Chrestomathie.* Hamburg and Bremen. Pp. 19-21: *Gen.* IX. 1-17; 22-24: *Gen.* XLV. 1-16; 24-26: *Ex.* XX. 1-17; 26-28; *Deut.* I. 6-21; 28-30: *Lev.* XIX. 3-37; 31-33: *Num.* XVI. 1-35; 33-40: *Deut.* XXXII. 1-43; 40-42: *Judges* VII. 2-25. A German translation accompanies each extract.

25. 1817. RASK, R. K.: *Angelsaksisk Sproglaere.* Stockholm. Pp. 142-151: Selections from Ælfric's *On the Old and New Testament.*

26. 1820-4. GORHAM, G. C.: *History and Antiquities of Einesbury and St. Neot in Huntingdonshire.* Contains *Life of St. Neot.*

27. 1821. STRYPE, JOHN: *The Life and Acts of Archbishop Parker.* Oxford. I. 472-476; II. Bk. IV. Sect. II: Account of publication of Ælfric's Easter sermon, and of the labors of Archb. Parker in preserving Old Eng. writings.

28. 1830. RASK, E.: *A Grammar of the Anglo-Saxon Tongue.* Copenhagen. Pp. 193-201: Selections from Ælfric's *On the Old and New Testament.*

29. 1830. SOAMES, H.: *An Inquiry into the Doctrines of the Anglo-Saxon Church.* Bampton Lectures. Oxford. Pp. 126-134: *Hom.* I. 364-370; 384-388, 421-442: Of Ælfric's teaching on the eucharist, with illustrative extracts.

30. 1830. GURNEY, ANNA: *Ancient History, English and French, exemplified in a Regular Dissection of the Saxon Chronicle. . . .* London. Wharton's *Dissertation* is here reprinted. Pp. 226-239: *Colloquium* (contains only the Old English).

31. 1835. LEO, HEINRICH: *Angelsächsische Sprachproben.* Halle. Pp. 20-32: *Hom.* II. 132-154; 1-11: *Colloquium;* 11-15: Preface to *Genesis;*

32. 1835. MÜLLER, LUD. CHR.: *Collectanea Anglo-Saxonica.* Copenhagen. Pp. 1-4: *Abgarus.*

33. 1838. LEO, HEINRICH: *Altsächsische und Angelsächsische Sprachproben.* Halle. This book contains the same writings of Ælfric's as no. 31: pp. 23-32; 6-15; 15-18.

34. 1838. PHILIPPS, THOMAS: *A Fragment of Ælfric's Anglo-Saxon Grammar, Ælfric's Glossary, etc.,* discovered among the Archives of Worcester Cathedral. London.

35. 1839. LANGLEY, L.: *Introduction to Anglo-Saxon Reading.* London. Contains Ælfric's homily on the *Birthday of St. Gregory.*

36. 1840. THORPE, BENJAMIN: *Ancient Laws and Institutes of England.* II. 342-363: *Pastoral Letter for Wulfsige,* with translation; 364-389 and 390-393: *Pastoral Letters for Wulfstan,* with translations.

37. 1840. PETHERAM, J.: *Historical Sketch of Anglo-Saxon Literature.* London. Pp. 13-16: Ælfric's life and works.

38. 1841. WRIGHT, THOMAS, and HALLIWELL, J. ORCHARD: *Reliquiae Antiquae.* London. I. 276-282: *Hom.* II. 332-348.

39. 1841. WRIGHT, THOMAS: *Popular Treatises on Science* written during the Middle Ages. London. Pp. 1-19: *De Temporibus.*

40. 1842. WRIGHT, THOMAS: *Biographia Britannica Literaria.* A.-S. Period. London. Pp. 480-495: Discussion of Ælfric's identity and writings.

41a. 1845. LINGARD, JOHN: *History and Antiquities of the Anglo-Saxon Church.* London. II. 311-320; 452-477: The questions of Ælfric's identity and of his teaching on the eucharist are discussed.

41b. 1844-1846. THORPE, BENJAMIN: *The Homilies of the Anglo-Saxon Church.* The first part, containing the *Sermones Catholici* or Homilies of Ælfric, in the original Anglo-Saxon, with an English version. 2 vols. London: printed for the Ælfric Society. II. 596-601: *Prayers* and *Confessions* by Ælfric.

42. 1846. VERNON, E. J.: *A Guide to the Anglo-Saxon Tongue.* London. Pp. 109-116: Extracts from *Genesis* and *Exodus.*

43. 1846. THORPE, BENJAMIN: *Analecta Anglo-Saxonica.* London. 2d edition. Pp. 18-36: *Colloquium;* 36-44: *Hom.* II. 446-460; 44-52: *Hom.* II. 116-132; 52-63: *Hom.* II. 132-154; 63-73: *Hom.* I. 274-294; 73-80: *Hom.* II. 72-88; 119-126: *St. Edmund,* from *Lives of Saints.* The first edition (1834) contained Preface to *Genesis.*

44. 1846. UNGER, C. R.: *Annaler for Nordisk Old-kyndighed.* . . . Copenhagen. Pp. 67-81: Fragment af en allitereret angelsaxisk Homili. . . . *On False Gods,* from *Lives of Saints.*

45. 1847. EBELING, F. W.: *Angelsächsisches Lesebuch.* Leipzig. Pp. 46-57: *Colloquium.*

46. 1848. GOODWIN, C. W.: *The Life of Saint Guthlac.* London.

47. 1848. KEMBLE, JOHN M.: *Dialogue of Salomon and Saturnus.* London. Pp. 120-125: A large part of the homily *On False Gods,* from the *Lives of the Saints,* with English translation.

204   *Bibliography.*

48. 1849. KLIPSTEIN, LOUIS F.: *Analecta Anglo-Saxonica.* I. 195-214: *Colloquium;* 245-247: Extracts from *De
Temporibus;* 318-323: *Pastoral Letter for Wulfsige;* II.
74-80: Extracts from *On the Old and New Testaments.*
49. 1849. KLIPSTEIN, LOUIS F.: *Natale Sancti Gregorii
Papæ.* Collateral Extracts from King Ælfred's Version of
Bede's *Ecclesiastical History* of the Anglo-Saxons, and from
the *Saxon Chronicle,* with a full rendering into English. . . .
New York.
50. 1849. NORMAN, H. W.: *The Anglo-Saxon Version
of the Hexameron of St. Basil.* London. Pp. 1-29: The
Hexameron; 31-57: *Admonitio ad Filium Spiritualem.*
With translation, notes, and account of the presumed author.
51. 1850. JOHNSON, JOHN: *A Collection of the Laws
and Canons of the Church of England.* Oxford. Pp. 388-
407: English translation of *Pastoral Letter for Wutfsige,*
with notes.
52. 1850. ETTMÜLLER, LUDWIG: *Engla and Seaxna
Scōpas and Bōceras.* . . . (Also vol. XXVIII of the *Bibliothek
der Gesamten Deutschen National-Litteratur*). Quedlinburg
and Leipzig. Pp. 61-63: Homily on *Albanus;* 63-69: *Hom.*
II. 262-282; 70-76: *Hom.* I. 274-294; 76-77: *Hom.* I.
110-114; 77-83: *Hom.* II. 132-154; 84-92: *Hom.* II. 132-154;
43 and 92: short extracts from the homilies; 3-7: *Job.*
53. 1851. HARDWICK, C.: *Early English Poetry, Bal-
lads, and Popular Literature of the Middle Ages.* Pub. of
Percy Society. London. Vol. 28. Pp. 2-29: *Passion of
St. George,* from the *Lives of the Saints.*
54. 1853. MIGNE, J. P.: *Patrologia Latina.* Paris.
Vol. 139. pp. 1455-1460: Historical Notes on Ælfric of Canterbury who is considered to be Ælfric the Grammarian (from
Mabill. *Acta SS. Bened.* VIII. 55); 1459-1470: Wharton's
Dissertation; 1469-1376: *Canones Ælfrici ad Wulfinum
Episcopum* (in Latin), through section 35.
55. 1853. STEPHENS, G.: *Tvende Old-Engelske Digte
med Oversættelser og Tillæg.* Copenhagen. Pp. 15-21:

Abgarus (*L. of S.* Pt. III. 58-66), with English and Danish translations.

56. c.1855. MÜLLER,THEODOR:*AngelsächsischesLesebuch.* 'This book was not all printed, but was well known.' Pp. 1-9: *Gen.* I. 42-45; 14-32: *Colloquium;* 72-79: *Hom.* I. 258-274; 79-88: *Hom.* II. 498-518.

57. 1855-1856. DIETRICH, EDWARD F.: *Zeitschrift für die Historische Theologie.* Gotha. XXV. 487-594: Ælfric's Writings; The Teachings of the Old English Church according to Ælfric's Writings; XXVI. 163-256: Ælfric's Education and Character; Ælfric's Life.

58. 1856. SOAMES, HENRY: *The Anglo-Saxon Church.* London. Pp. 184-205: Ælfric's Life and Writings; 261-281: Translation of 2d *Pastoral Letter for Wulfstan.*

59. 1858. BOUTERWEK, C. W.: *Screadunga.* Elberfeld. Pp. 17-23: *Sigewulfi Interrogationes in Genesin;* 23-31: *De Temporibus.*

60. 1858. STEVENSON, JOSEPH: *Chronicon Monasterii de Abingdon.* Rolls Series. London, Pp. 255-266: Ælfric's *Life of Æthelwold.*

61. 1660. HOOK, W. F.: *Lines of the Archbishops of Canterbury.* London. I. 434-449: Discussion of Ælfric's identity, and quotations from his works.

62. 1861. RIEGER, MAX: *Alt-und Angelsächsischen Lesebuch.* Giessen. Pp. 189-197: *Hom.* II, 116-132.

63. 1864-9. COCKAYNE, O.: *The Shrine.* London. Pp. 12-17: *Life of St. Neot.*

64. 1866. COCKAYNE, O.: *Leechdoms, Wortcunning and Starcraft of Early England.* London. III. pp. XIV.-XXIX.: treats of Ælfric's life; pp. 232-283: *De Temporibus.*

65. 1868. MORRIS, R.: *Old English Homilies and Homiletic Treatises.* First Series. 1150-1230 A. D. London. Appendix II. pp. 296-304: *De Octo Vitiis*, from *Lives of Saints.* In this collection of a time later than Ælfric are three of his sermons transliterated to the language of the day: pp. 87-100: *Hom.* I. 310-328; 101-119: *De Octo Vitiis* (the one

14

in Appendix II); 216-230: *Hom.* I, 8-28 (slightly abridged); also, 242-245: fragment of a text, *Hom.* I. 338.

66. 1870. BIRLINGER, ANT.: *Bruchstück aus Ælfric's Angelsächsischer Grammatik,* in Pfeiffer's *Germania,* XV. 359.

67. 1870. CORSON, Hiram: *Handbook of Anglo-Saxon and Early English.* P. 57 f.: extract from preface to *Cath. Hom.* I.; 59-62: *Hom.* I. 238-244; 62-67: *Hom.* I. 180-192; 68-76: *Hom.* II. 116-132.

68. 1870. HUTCHINS, JOHN: *The History and Antiquities of Dorset.* Westminster. IV. 24-26: An account of Ælfric, considered as Archbishop of Canterbury, and of his writings.

69. 1871. MORRIS, RICHARD: *Legends of the Holy Rood;* London. Pp. 98-107: *The Finding the Cross* from *Lives of Saints,* with English translation.

70. 1872. GREIN, CHRISTIAN W. M.: *Bibliothek der Angelsächsischen Prosa.* I. *Ælfrik de vetere et novo Testamento, Pentateuch, Josua, Buch der Richter and Hiob.* Cassel and Göttingen.

71. 1875. THOMPSON, E.: *Select Monuments of the Doctrine and Worship of the Catholic Church in England Before the Norman Conquest.* London. This book contains a reprint of *A Testimony of Antiquitie* (See No. 2); pp. 94-102: Extracts from *Hom.* I. 364 f.

72. 1876. SWEET, HENRY: *Anglo-Saxon Reader.* Oxford. Pp. 56-74: *On the Old Testament;* 75-87: *Hom.* I. 58-76; 87-94: *Hom.* I. 76-90; 95-102: *Life of Oswald* from *Lives of the Saints'.* The 7th edition (1894) omits the first selection.

73. 1877. TEN BRINK B.: *Geschichte der Englischen Litteratur.* Berlin. Pp. 133-140: Of Ælfric's life and writings. English transl. by H. M. Kennedy (1883), pp. 103-111.

74. 1878. CARPENTER, STEPHEN H.: *An Introduction to the Study of the Anglo-Saxon Language.* Boston. Pp. 78-87: *Hom.* II. 116-132; 108-112: I. 8-29; 112-120: II. 58-77.

75. 1879. GREIN, C. W. M.: *Ælfric's Extract from the Book of Judges,* metrically arranged, *Anglia* 2. 141-152. Halle.

76. 1879. BRENNER, O.: *Angelsächsische Sprachproben.* Munich. Pp. 7-15: Account of Samson from *Book of Judges;* 50-53: Extracts from *Hom.* II. 132-154.

77. 1879. MARCH, FRANCIS A.: *Anglo-Saxon Reader.* New York. Pp. 13-32: Extracts from Ælfric's *Colloquium;* 35-38: *Hom.* II. 116-132.

78. 1880. ZUPITZA, JULIUS: *Ælfric's Grammatik und Glossar.* Erste Abteilung: Text und Varianten. Berlin.

79. 1880. *Sammlung Englischer Denkmäler.* Berlin. Contains Ælfric's *Grammar.*

80. 1880. KÖRNER, KARL: *Einleitung in das Studium des Angelsächsischen.* Zweiter Teil. Heilbronn. Pp. 8-11: History of Joseph, from the *Heptateuch;* 12-17: Samson, from *Book of Judges;* 16-29: *Life of St. Oswald.* A German translation is given with each selection.

81. 1881. SKEAT, WALTER W.: *Ælfric's Lives of Saints.* Vol. I. Pt. I. London; 1885. Vol. I. Pt. II.; 1890. Vol. II. Pt. III.: Text and English translation.

82. 1883. MacLEAN, G. E.: *Ælfric's Version of Alcuini Interrogationes Sigewulfi in Genesin.* Halle; also in *Anglia* 6. 425-473; 7, 1-59.

83. 1883. NAPIER, ARTHUR: *Wulfstan; Sammlung der Ihm Zugescriebenen Homilien.* Berlin. Pp. 50-60: Forms I. and II. of homily on the *Sevenfold Gifts of the Spirit.*

84. 1884. WRIGHT, THOMAS: *Anglo-Saxon and old English Vocabularies.* 2d edition. Edited and collated by R. P. Wülcker, London. I. 89-103: *Colloquium*; 306-336: *Glossary.*

85. 1885. GREIN, C. W. M.: *Bibliothek der Angelsächischen Prosa,* continued by R. P. Wülker with others. III. edited by Bruno Assmann. Cassel. Pp. 1-12. Homily addressed to Wulfgeat of Ylmandune; 13-23. *Homily on Chastity* addressed to Sigefyrth; 24-48: *Homily on the Nativity of the*

Virgin Mary; 49-64: *Homily for a Saint's Day,* translated at the request of Bishop Æthelwold II: 65-72: *Homily on John XI.* 47-54; 73-80: *Homily on John XVI.* 16-22; 81-91: Fragment of the *Preface to the Old Testament;* 92-101: *On Esther;* 102-116: *Homily on Judith.*

86. 1885. Assmann, B.: *Abt Ælfric's Angelsächische Bearbeitung des Buches Esther.* Halle. In *Anglia* 9. 25-38, the author adds further observations, and prints the text in metrical lines.

87. 1885. Sweet, H.: *Selected Homilies of Ælfric.* Oxford. Pp. 1-6: Latin and English prefaces of *Hom.* I.; 6-17: I. 8-28; 17-24: I. 44-56; 24-33: I. 104-120; 34-41: I. 152-164; 41-50: I. 166-180; 50-55: I. 180-192; 55-64: II. 116-132; 64-74: II. 132-154.

88. 1885. Wülker, Richard: *Grundriss zur Geschichte der Angelsächsischen Litteratur.* Leipzig. Pp. 452-481: A summary of information concerning Ælfric and his works.

89. 1886. Wohlfahrt T.: *Die Syntax des Verbums in Ælfric's Ueber des Heptateuch und des Buches Hiob.* Munich.

90. 1887. Schrader, B.: *Studien zur Ælfrischen Syntax.* Jena.

91. 1887. Ebert, A.: *Allgemeine Geschichte der Litteratur des Mittelalters in Abendlande.* Leipzig. III. 509-516: Of the life and works of Ælfric.

92. 1887. Breck, E.: *A Fragment of Ælfric's Translation of Æthelwold's De Consuetudine Monachorum and its Relation to other MSS.* Leipzig.

93. 1888. Zimmermann, D.: *Die Beiden Fassungen des dem Abt Ælfric zugeschriebenen Angelsächsischen Traktats über die Siebenfältigen Gaben des Heiligen Geistes.* Leipzig.

94. 1888. Morley, Henry : *English Writers.* London. II. 310-314; Ælfric's life and writings.

95. 1888. Assmann, B. : *Abt Ælfric's Angelsächsische Homilie über das Buch Judith. Anglia* 10. 76-104. Halle.

96. 1888. Reum, A.: *De Temporibus Ein Echtes Werk des Abtes Ælfric. Anglia.* 10. 457-498. Halle.

97. 1888. MITCHELL, FRANCES H.: *Ælfric's Sigewulfi Interrogationes in Genesin.* Critical revision of the text of MacLean. Zurich.

98. 1889. KÜHN, P. T.: *Die Syntax des Verbums in Ælfric's Heiligenleben.* Leipzig-Reudnitz.

99. 1889. FISCHER, FRANK: *The Stressed Vowels of Homilies* I. *Pub. of Mod. Lang. Assoc. in America.* Vol. IV. No. 2.

100. 1890. BRAUNSCHWEIGER, M.: *Flexion des Verbums in Ælfric's Grammtik,* Marburg.

101. 1891. TESSMANN, A.: *Ælfric's Altenglische Bearbeitung der Inter Sig. Pres. in Gen. des Alcuin.* Berlin.

102. 1891. WYATT, A. J. and JOHNSON, H. H.: *A Glossary of Ælfric's Homilies.* London.

103. 1892. FÖRSTER, MAX: *Über die Quellen von Ælfric's Homiliae Catholicae;* I., Legenden. Berlin. 1894. II. Exegetical Homilies, *Anglia* 16. 1-61. Halle.

104. 1892. BRÜHL, C.: *Die Flexion des Verbums in Ælfric's Heptateuch und des Buches Hiob.* Marburg.

105. 1892. OTT, J. H.: *Ueber die Quellen der Heiligenleben in Ælfric's Lives of Saints.* I. Halle.

106. 1893. MACLEAN, G. E.: *Old and Middle English Reader.* New York. Pp. 39-45: Extracts from Ælfric's *Genesis* and *Judges.*

107. 1893. SMITH, C. A.: *The Order of Words in Anglo-Saxon Prose; Pub. of Mod. Lang. Assoc. of Amer.,* 8. 210-244. The subject is illustrated from Ælfric's writings.

108. 1893. SCHWERDTFEGER, G.: *Das Schwache Verbum in Ælfric's Homilies.* Marburg.

109. 1895. COOK, Albert S.: *A First Book in 'Old English.* Boston. Pp. 125-128: Extract from Ælfric's *Genesis;* 129-136: from the *Colloquium;* 189-199: from the *Hexameron.*

110. GORRELL, J. H.: *Indirect Discourse in Anglo-Saxon; Pub. of Mod. Lang. Assoc. of Amer.* 10. 342-485: The subject is treated in reference to Ælfric's *Homilies* and other texts.

111. 1897. TUPPER, J. W.: *Tropes and Figures in Anglo-Saxon Prose.* Baltimore. The subject is treated in reference to the *Catholic Homilies,* and other Old English Prose. **112.** 1897. ZUPITZA, J.: *Alt-und Mittelenglisches Uebungsbuch.* Revised by A. Schipper. Vienna and Leipzig. Pp. 66-71: Selections from Ælfric's *Genesis and Judges.* **113.** 1898. COOK, Albert S.: *Biblical Quotations in Old English Prose Writers.* London and New York. Pp. LXIV.-LXXVI.: Ælfriç's life and identity; MSS. and editions of Ælfric's *Pentateuch, Joshua, Judges* and *Job.* Pp. 76-257: Old English Biblical quotations from Ælfric's *Homilies* with the corresponding Latin of the *Vulgate.*

---

114. *Catholic Homilies.* a. A. NAPIER. *A Fragment of Ælfric's DeInit. Creat., Mod. Lang. N.,* 1893, 398-400. b. E. MENTHEL: *Zur Gesch. des Otfrid. Verses in Engl., Anglia.* 8. 50-53. c. A. S. COOK: *Notes on the Vocalism of L. W. S., Trans. of Amer. Phil. Assoc.* 1889, 175-6. **115.** *Colloquium.* a. J. ZUPITZA: *Die Ursprüngliche Gestalt von Ælfric's C., Zs. f. D. A,.*[1] 31. 32-45. b. E. SCHRÖDER: *Colloquium Ælfrici, Zs.f.D.A.,*[1] 41.283–290. **116.** *The Lives of the Saints.* a. A. NAPIER: *A Fragment of the Life of St. Basil, Mod. Lang. N.,* 1887, 378-9. b. J. ZUPITZA: *Bemerkungen zu Ælfric's L. of S. I., edited by Skeat, Zs. f. D. A.*[1] 17. 269-96. c. B. WELLS: *List of Strong Verbs in L. of S.* I., II., *Mod. Lang. N.* 1888, 1. 18-185, 256-262. d. A. S. COOK: *A List. of the Strong Verbs in L. of S.* II., *Mod. Lang. N.* 1897, 117-8. e. E. HOLTHAUS: *Ælfric's L. of S.* I. (an examination of their metrical form), *Anglia* 6. Anz.104-117; cf. E. Einenkel: *Schipper, Englische Metrick, Anglia* 5. Anz. 31 f.; M. Trautmann: *Otfrid in England, Anglia* 7. Anz. 211-5; E. Menthel: *Zur Geschichte des Otfridischen Verses in Englischen, Anglia* 8. Anz. 52-53. **117.** *Job.* a. B. ASSMANN: *Ælfric's A.-S. Bearbeitung*

---

1. *Zeitschrift für Deutsches Alterthum.*

des Buches Hiob (comparison of Grein's text with the MS.), *Anglia* 9. 39-42; b. M. FÖRSTER. Comparison of the *Job* in Grein's text with *Hom.* II. 446 ff., *Anglia* 15. 473-7.

118. *Judith.* a. B. WELLS: *Strong Verbs in J., Mod. Lang. N.,* 1888, 13-15. b. A. S. COOK: Comparison of the O.E. poem *Judith* with Ælfric's homily on the same subject, *Judith,* pp. LXXI.-LXXIII.

CLASSIFIED BIBLIOGRAPHY.

I. BIOGRAPHICAL AND CRITICAL:

    Nos. 1, 2, 4, 6, 8, 13, 15, 20, 23, 30, 37, 40, 41 a, 50, 54, 57, 58, 61, 64, 68, 71, 73, 88, 113.

II. GRAMMATICAL:

    Nos. 89, 90, 98, 99, 100, 104, 107, 108, 110, 111, 114 b, c, 116c, d, e, 118 a.

III. ÆLFRIC'S WRITINGS:

    1. *Catholic Homilies:*

        Complete edition: No. 41 b;

        Separate homilies: Nos. 2, 3, 6, 7, 8, 9, 11, 12, 17, 18, 29, 31, 33, 35, 38, 43, 49, 52, 56, 62, 65, 67, 71, 72, 74, 76, 77, 87;

        Miscellaneous: 27, 41 a, 57, 88, 99, 102, 103, 107, 108, 110, 111, 113, 114.

    2. *De Temporibus:*

        Editions: Nos. 39, 59, 64;

        Criticism: No. 96.

    3. *Grammar:*

        Editions: No. 10, 34, 66, 78, 79.

    4. *Glossary:*

        Editions: Nos. 10, 34, 78, 84.

5. *Colloquium:*
    Editions of the whole or of a part: Nos. 30, 31, 33,
        43, 45, 48, 56, 77, 84, 109;
    Critical: No. 115.

6   *Lives of the Saints:*
    Complete edition: No. 81 (see p. 131 n. 2);
    Separate homilies: Nos. 32, 43, 44, 47, 52, 53, 55,
        59, 65, 69, 72, 80, 82, 116 a;
    Critical: 82, 97, 98, 101, 105, 116 b, c, d, e.

7. Homilies which do not belong to any volume:
    Editions: Nos. 26, 50, 63, 83, 85.

8. *Translations of the Bible:*
    Editions: Nos. 14, 16, 22, 24, 31, 33, 42, 52, 56,
        70, 75, 76, 80, 85, 86, 95, 106, 109, 112; ˙
    Critical: 89, 104, 113, 117, 118.

9. *On the Old and New Testaments:*
    Editions of the whole or of a part: Nos. 6, 8, 25, 28,
        48, 70, 72.

10. *Canons* or *Pastoral Letters:*
    Editions of the whole or of a part: a. *Letter for
        Wulfsige:* Nos. 2, 3, 6, 8, 9, 19, 20, 36, 48, 51,
        54, 71; b. *Letters for Wulfstan:* Nos. 2, 3, 6, 8,
        19, 36, 58, 71.

11. *Life of Æthelwold:*
    Edition: No. 60.

SUPPLEMENTARY CLASSIFIED
BIBLIOGRAPHY

Caroline White's chronological list of work on Ælfric up to 1898 (nos. 1–113) has been left unaltered, since it serves as a valuable guide to the history of Ælfric studies. The classified bibliography which follows combines material from this list (cited by number) with works published since 1898, together with a few earlier items which were missed by Miss White or for which her original references need supplementing or correcting. The bibliography is intended to be reasonably comprehensive for the twentieth century, but unprinted dissertations and their printed summaries have not been included, and only the more substantial reviews of books devoted to Ælfric are listed. The few major points in which Caroline White's views on Ælfric's life and work need to be corrected or supplemented have been noted at appropriate points in the classified bibliography; but her work (closely based of course on that of Dietrich and other scholars) has stood the test of time remarkably well.

M. R. GODDEN

University of Liverpool

BIOGRAPHICAL AND CRITICAL

The main biographical details remain little changed. Caroline White's view (pp. 52–3) that Ælfric remained at Cerne until moving to Eynsham, rather than returning to live at Winchester, seems to have been generally accepted. It should, however, be noted that Ælfric may have died earlier than 1020–25; none of his works can be definitely dated much beyond 1006, and there is no definite mention of him in any of the charters of the period; see the studies by Clemoes ('Chronology') and Whitelock below.

Mores, E.R., 1789: no. 23 above.

Dietrich, Eduard, 1855–6: no. 57 above.

Gem, S.H: *An Anglo-Saxon Abbot: Ælfric of Eynsham*. Edinburgh, 1912.

Dubois, Marguerite-Marie: *Ælfric, Sermonnaire, Docteur et Grammairien*. Paris, 1943.

Whitelock, Dorothy: 'Two notes on Ælfric and Wulfstan: 1, the date of Ælfric's death', *Modern Language Review* 38, 1943.

Clemoes, P.A.M: 'The chronology of Ælfric's works', *The Anglo-Saxons: Studies presented to Bruce Dickins*, ed. Peter Clemoes. London, 1959. Major and detailed study of the Ælfric canon and the chronology of all his writings.

Clemoes, P.A.M: 'Ælfric', *Continuations and Beginnings*, ed. E.G. Stanley. London, 1966.

Hurt, James: *Ælfric*. New York, 1972 (Twayne English Authors Series).

Books containing accounts of Ælfric's life and work:

Nos. 1, 2, 4, 6, 8, 13, 15, 20, 30, 37, 40, 41a, 58, 61, 64, 68, 73, 88, and 113 above, and the following:

Ward, Sir A.W., and A.R. Waller (ed.): *The Cambridge History of English Literature*, vol I. Cambridge,

1907. Chapter 7, by J.S. Westlake, includes account of Ælfric.

Wardale, E.E : *Chapters on Old English Literature.* London, 1935. Pp. 266–72 on Ælfric.

Anderson, George K : *The Literature of the Anglo-Saxons.* London, 1949. Ch. 9 summarizes Ælfric's work.

Greenfield, Stanley B : *A Critical History of Old English Literature.* New York, 1965; London, 1966. Pp. 47–52 on Ælfric.

Wrenn, C.L : *A Study of Old English Literature.* London, 1967. Pp. 224–37 on Ælfric.

ÆLFRIC'S WRITINGS

The Ælfric canon has been established and listed in detail by P.A.M. Clemoes, 'The chronology of Ælfric's works' (above, p. 214) and John C. Pope, *Homilies of Ælfric,* pp. 136–45. The additions to the canon since Caroline White's time are the twenty-one homilies edited by Pope, the five others edited by Belfour and the one edited by Brotanek (see below p. 221f), and a few very short pieces listed at the end of this section. The Lives of St Neot and St Guthlac, discussed above p. 134, are not now thought to be by Ælfric. On chronology, the main changes are that Thorpe's text of the *Catholic Homilies* is no longer thought to represent a second, expanded edition issued by Ælfric after 1016 (see Sisam, 1931–3, below p. 218), and the letters for Wulfstan are now dated *c.* 1005–6, not 1014 or later (cf. above, p. 68; the laws of Æthelred borrow from the letters, not vice-versa). For further details, see Clemoes. For linguistic, stylistic and palaeographical studies, see the separate sections below.

Catholic Homilies

Edited Benjamin Thorpe, 1844–6: no. 41b above.

Eliason, Norman, and Peter Clemoes (eds) : *Ælfric's First Series of Catholic Homilies: BM Royal 7 C xii.* Copenhagen, 1966 (Early English Manuscripts in Facsimile vol. 13). Facsimile of the earliest MS of the First Series, with detailed introduction demonstrating that the MS was produced under Ælfric's direction and corrected by him.

Editions of selected homilies :

Nos. 2, 3, 6, 7, 8, 9, 11, 12, 17, 18, 29, 31, 33, 35, 38, 43, 49, 52, 56, 62, 65, 67, 71, 72, 74, 76, 77, and 87 above, and the following :

Warner, Rubie D.-N. (ed.) : *Early English Homilies from the Twelfth Century MS Vespasian D. xiv.* Early English Text Society, O.S. 152, London, 1917. Text only. Includes numerous items from the *Catholic Homilies*, plus other items by Ælfric and anonymous homilies and tracts. For full analysis of contents see Förster and Ker, below p. 237f.

Raith, Josef : *Altenglisches Lesebuch (Prosa).* Munich, 1940; revised 1958. Includes Old English prefaces to the *CH* and the Second Series homilies on Easter Day (omitted in 2nd edn) and St. Gregory.

Bolton, W.F : *An Old English Anthology.* London, 1963. Includes *De Initio Creaturae* (part) and homily for Mid-Lent Sunday from the First Series.

Whitelock, Dorothy (ed.) : *Sweet's Anglo-Saxon Reader.* Oxford, 1967 (15th edn). Includes homilies for Innocents and Septuagesima, with selected variants from all MSS. For earlier editions of Sweet's *Reader*, see no. 72 above.

Cassidy, Frederick G., and Richard N. Ringler (eds) : *Bright's Old English Grammar and Reader.* New York, 1971 (3rd edn, revised). Includes homily on Assumption of St John, printed from Royal MS with selected variants from Cambridge MS Gg.3.28 and comments on sources and MS alterations.

Only the more important editions in readers have been listed.

Secondary works:

Wyatt, A.J., and H.H. Johnson: *A Glossary to Ælfric's Homilies.* London, 1891. Glossary to Sweet's edition (no. 87 above), not to Thorpe's.

Förster, Max: *Über die Quellen von Ælfrics Homiliae Catholicae: 1, Legenden.* Berlin, 1892. *And* 'Über die Quellen von Ælfrics exegetischen *Homiliae Catholicae*', *Anglia* 16, 1894. See above pp. 185–8.

Napier, A.S: 'Fragments of an Ælfric MS', *Modern Language Notes* 8, 1893. Brasenose College, Oxford, MS containing fragment of *De Initio Creaturae* from the First Series.

Cook, Albert S: *Biblical Quotations in Old English Prose Writers.* Series I & II, London and New York, 1898–1903. For Series I see no. 113 above. Series II prints the biblical passages omitted in Thorpe's edition of the *Catholic Homilies*, taken from A.S. Napier's supplement to Series I in *Archiv* 101–2, 1898–9.

Förster, Max: review of Cook, Series I, with discussion of versions of the Bible used by Ælfric in the *Catholic Homilies. Englische Studien* 28, 1900.

Stephan, A: 'Eine weitere Quelle von Ælfrics Gregorhomilie', *Anglia Beiblatt* 14, 1903.

Mosher, J.A: *The Exemplum in the Early Religious and Didactic Literature of England.* New York, 1911. Pp. 29–37 on Ælfric.

Fehr, Bernhard: 'Über einige Quellen zu Ælfric's *Homiliae Catholicae*', *Archiv* 130, 1913. On homilies for St Bartholomew (First Series) and Epiphany and Mid-Lent (Second Series).

Liebermann, F: 'Ein staatsrechtlicher Satz Ælfrics aus lateinischer Quelle', *Archiv* 139, 1919. On the First Series homily for Palm Sunday.

Sisam, Kenneth: 'MSS Bodley 340 and 342: Ælfric's *Catholic Homilies*', *Review of English Studies* 7–9, 1931–3; reprinted in K. Sisam, *Studies in the History of Old English Literature*, Oxford, 1953, with additional note on the order of Ælfric's early books. Corrects earlier views of Thorpe's text as Ælfric's second edition of the *Catholic Homilies* (cf above pp. 103–4), discusses the date of composition, and demonstrates the existence of three different authentic versions of the First Series.

Wright, C.E: 'Two Ælfric fragments', *Medium Ævum* 7, 1938. Fragments of First Series homilies for St Stephen and Assumption of St John in British Museum MS Harley 2110.

Davis, Charles R: 'Two new sources for Ælfric's *Catholic Homilies*', *Journal of English and Germanic Philology* 41, 1942. On homilies for St Andrew and St Matthew.

Davis, Charles R: 'A note on Ælfric's translation of Job I. 6', *Modern Language Notes* 60, 1945.

Loomis, Laura H: 'The St Mercurius legend' (see below p. 226). Includes discussion of First Series homily on the Assumption of the Virgin.

Jost, Karl: 'The legal maxim in Ælfric's homilies', *English Studies* 36, 1955.

Cross, J.E: 'A source for one of Ælfric's *Catholic Homilies*', *English Studies* 39, 1958. On the First Series homily for All Saints.

Smetana, Cyril L.: 'Ælfric and the early medieval homiliary', *Traditio* 15, 1959. On Paul the Deacon's homiliary as a source-book for Ælfric, with discussion of the sources of nearly all the exegetical homilies.

Temple, Winifred M: 'The weeping Rachel', *Medium Ævum* 28, 1959. On the use of Rachel as a type in medieval texts, including Ælfric's Innocents homily.

Schelp, Hanspeter: 'Die Deutungstradition in Ælfrics *Homiliae Catholicae'*, *Archiv* 196, 1960.

Smetana, Cyril L: 'Ælfric and the homiliary of Haymo of Halberstadt', *Traditio* 17, 1961. Demonstrates the use of Haymo's homiliary as a source for numerous of the *Catholic Homilies*. (The homiliary is now thought to be the work of Haymo of Auxerre.)

Ker, N.R: 'The Bodmer fragment of Ælfric's homily for Septuagesima Sunday', *English and Medieval Studies presented to J.R.R. Tolkien*, ed. Norman Davis and C.L. Wrenn. London, 1962. Gives text and discussion.

Cross, J.E: 'Ælfric and the medieval homiliary— objection and contribution', *Scripta Minora Lundensis* 1961–2. Responds to 1959 article by Smetana, and establishes sources for First Series homilies on St Stephen, the Catholic Faith and the Church of St. Michael, and Second Series homilies for Christmas, a Confessor, and the Dedication of a Church.

Cross, J.E: 'Bundles for burning—a theme in two of Ælfric's *Catholic Homilies*, with other sources', *Anglia* 81, 1963. On the First Series homilies for the 3rd Sunday after Epiphany and 21st Sunday after Pentecost.

Gatch, Milton McC: 'MS Boulogne-sur-Mer 63 and Ælfric's First Series of *Catholic Homilies'*, *Journal of English and Germanic Philology* 65, 1966. On a source for part of the First Series homily on St Paul.

Pearce, T.M: 'Name patterns in Ælfric's *Catholic Homilies'*, Names 14, 1966. On Ælfric's use of name-interpretations.

Cross, J.E: 'More sources for two of Ælfric's *Catholic Homilies'*, *Anglia* 86, 1968. On the First Series homily on the Lord's Prayer and the Second Series homily on St Peter.

Godden, M.R: 'The sources for Ælfric's homily on St. Gregory', *Anglia* 86, 1968.

Cross, J.E: 'Ælfric—mainly on memory and creative method in two *Catholic Homilies*', *Studia Neophilologica* 41, 1969. On the homilies for Innocents and Septuagesima.

Becker, W: *Studien zu Ælfrics Homiliae Catholicae.* Marburg, 1969 (inaugural dissertation). Mainly on Ælfric's translating technique.

Wrenn, C.L: 'Some aspects of Anglo-Saxon theology', *Studies in Language, Literature and Culture of the Middle Ages and later*, ed. E. Bagby Atwood and Archibald A. Hill. Austin, Texas, 1969. Discusses Ælfric's treatment of the Eucharist in the Second Series homily for Easter Day.

Cross, J.E: 'Source and analysis of some Ælfrician passages', *Neuphilologische Mitteilungen* 72, 1971. On the Second Series homilies for St Stephen and Monday and Tuesday in Rogationtide, and homily XI in Pope's *Homilies of Ælfric.*

Cross, J.E: 'The literate Anglo-Saxon—on sources and disseminations', *Proceedings of the British Academy* 58, 1972, and separately. Discusses Ælfric's use of sources, especially for the Second Series homily for Monday in Rogationtide.

Szarmach, Paul E: 'Three versions of the Jonah story: an investigation of narrative technique in Old English homilies', *Anglo-Saxon England* 1, 1972. Partly on the First Series homily for Rogationtide.

Godden, M.R: 'The development of Ælfric's Second Series of *Catholic Homilies*', *English Studies* 54, 1973. Mainly on the numbering of the homilies (cf above p. 102 and Sisam 1930).

Besserman, L.L: 'A note on the source of Ælfric's homily on the Book of Job', *English Language Notes* 10, 1973.

Later Homilies

Norman, H.W. (ed.) : *The Anglo-Saxon Version of the Hexameron of St Basil, and Admonitio ad Filium Spiritualem* (1849). No. 50 above.

Napier, A.S. (ed.) : *Wulfstan* (1883). No. 83 above; reprinted with bibliographical supplement by K. Ostheeren, Berlin, 1967. Items VII (*De septiformi spiritu*) and XXXI (exemplum) are by Ælfric.

Assmann, Bruno (ed.) : *Angelsächsische Homilien und Heiligenleben.* Kassel, 1889 (no. 85 above) ; reprinted with supplementary introduction by Peter Clemoes, Darmstadt, 1964. For earlier editions by Assmann of items VIII and IX (*Esther* and *Judith*) see nos. 86 and 95 above.

Belfour, A.S. (ed.) : *Twelfth-century Homilies in MS Bodley 343.* Early English Text Society, O.S. 137, London, 1909; reprinted 1962. Items 1–4, 7–9, 13 and 14 are by Ælfric, but 1 and 2 have since been re-edited from all the MSS by Pope (below) and 13 and 14 are extracts from Second Series homily XXX and Pope's homily VI respectively. Includes translation.

Brotanek, R. (ed.) : 'Zwei Homilien des Ælfric', in Brotanek's *Texte und Untersuchungen zur altenglischen Literatur und Kirchengeschichte.* Halle, 1913. Only the first homily is by Ælfric.

Crawford, S.J. (ed.) : *Exameron Anglice.* Hamburg, 1921 (Bibliothek der Angelsächsischen Prosa 10) ; reprinted Darmstadt, 1968. Ælfric's *Hexameron*, previously edited Norman (no. 50). Includes introduction, notes and translation.

Braekman, W. (ed.) : 'Ælfric's Old English homily *De Doctrina Apostolica*', *Studia Germanica Gandensia* 5, 1963. Same as Pope's XIX.

Braekman, W. (ed.) : '*Wyrdwriteras* : an unpublished Ælfrician text in MS Hatton 115', *Revue Belge de Philologie* 44, 1966. Same as Pope's XXII.

Pope, John C. (ed.) : *Homilies of Ælfric: a Supplementary Collection.* Early English Text Society 259–260, London, 1967–8. Contains twenty-one homilies and some shorter pieces, with extensive introduction and apparatus and full glossary. Reviewed by N. Eliason, *Speculum* 43, 1968; E.G. Stanley, *Notes and Queries* 17, 1970 (pp. 262–6) ; J.E. Cross, *Studia Neophilologica* 43, 1971 (with supplementary notes on sources) ; M.R. Godden, *Anglia* 89, 1971.

Secondary works :

Zimmermann, D., 1888 : no. 93 above. On *De Septiformi Spiritu.*

Förster, Max : 'Altenglische Predigtquellen II : 9, Martin von Braga und Ælfric's *De Falsis Deis*', *Archiv* 122, 1909. On Pope's XXI.

Holthausen, F : 'Quellenstudien zu englischen Denkmälern', *Englische Studien* 46, 1913. Identifies homilies of Haymo as sources for homilies V and VI in Assmann's edition.

Emerson, O.F : 'Notes on Old English: I, Ælfric's *Hexameron*', *Archiv* 145, 1923.

Temple, Winifred M : 'The song of the angelic hosts', *Annuale Mediaevale* 2, 1961. Refers to Pope's XXVII.

Colgrave, Bertram, and Ann Hyde : 'Two recently discovered leaves from Old English manuscripts', *Speculum* 37, 1962. Leaf from Assmann's homily IV (*In natale unius confessoris*) in Kansas University Library.

Taylor, Arnold : '*Hauksbók* and Ælfric's *De Falsis Deis*', *Leeds Studies in English* New Series 3, 1969. On Pope's homily XXI.

Meaney, Audrey L : 'Æthelweard, Ælfric, the Norse Gods and Northumbria', *Journal of Religious History* 1970. Partly on Pope's homily XXI (*De Falsis Deis*).

Ross, A.S.C : 'Some alliterative phrases in the Bodley homilies', *Notes and Queries* 17, 1970. On the homilies in Bodley 343 edited by Belfour, including some by Ælfric.

Cross, J.E: 'Source and analysis of some Ælfrician passages', *Neuphilologische Mitteilungen* 72, 1971. Partly on Pope's homily XI.

Grammar

Edited Sumner (no. 10 above) and Zupitza (nos. 78 & 79), and fragments in nos. 34 and 66. Zupitza's edition, no. 78, is reprinted Berlin, 1966, with a preface by H. Gneuss; reviewed by Fred C. Robinson, *Anglia* 86, 1968.

Liebermann, F: 'Aus Ælfrics *Grammatik* und *Glossar*', *Archiv* 92, 1894. Prints extracts from Bodleian MS Barlow 35.

Williams, Edna R: 'Ælfric's grammatical terminology', *Publications of the Modern Language Association of America* 73, 1958.

Collins, Rowland L: 'Two fragments of Ælfric's *Grammar*: the kinship of Ker 384 and Ker 242', *Annuale Mediaevale* 5, 1964.

Paroli, Teresa: 'Le opere grammaticali di Ælfric', *Annali dell' Istituto Universitario Orientale* (Naples) 10, 1967.

Bolognesi, Giancarlo: *La grammatica latina di Ælfric*. Paideia, 1967. Discusses Ælfric's sources and his treatment of them.

Paroli, Teresa: 'Rapporto preliminare sugli aspetti linguistici e culturali della grammatica latina in anglosassone di Ælfric', *Arts libéraux et philosophie au moyen âge: Actes du quatrième congrès international de philosophie médiévale*. Montreal, 1969.

Glossary

Edited Zupitza (no. 78 above, reprinted Berlin, 1966)
and Wright (no. 84, reprinted Darmstadt, 1968), and
fragment in no. 34. The glossary in no. 10 is not Ælfric's but the so-called *Archbishop Ælfric's Vocabulary*
(see p. 121 above, and C.A. Ladd, *Review of English
Studies* New Series 11, 1960).

Colloquy

Garmonsway, G.N. (ed.) : *Ælfric's Colloquy.* London, 1939 (Methuen's Old English Library) ; revised
1947. The only separate edition.

The text is also printed in nos. 30, 31, 33, 43, 45, 48,
56, 77, 84 and 109 above, and the following :

Wyatt, A.J : *An Anglo-Saxon Reader.* Cambridge,
1919. Old English text only.

Stevenson, W.H. (ed.) : *Early Scholastic Colloquies.*
Oxford, 1929. Also includes colloquies of Ælfric Bata.

Raith, Josef: *Altenglisches Lesebuch (Prosa).* Munich, 1940, revised 1958.

Secondary works :

Zupitza, J : 'Die ursprüngliche Gestalt von Ælfric's
Colloquium', Zeitschrift für Deutsches Altertum 31,
1887.

Schroeder, E : 'Colloquium Ælfrici', *Ibid.* 41, 1897.

Whitbread, L : 'Notes on Ælfric's Colloquy', *Notes
and Queries* 184, 30 January 1943.

Garmonsway, G.N : 'The development of the colloquy', *The Anglo-Saxons: Studies presented to Bruce
Dickins,* ed. P. Clemoes. London, 1959.

Colledge, E : 'An allusion to Augustine in Ælfric's
Colloquy', Review of English Studies New Series 12,
1961.

De Temporibus Anni

Henel, Heinrich (ed.) : *Ælfric's De Temporibus Anni*. Early English Text Society 213, London, 1942. Includes introduction, notes, sources and parallels.

Also printed in nos. 39, 59 and 64 above. Extracts in Vatican MS Reg. Lat. 1283 printed E. Steinmeyer, *Zeitschrift für deutsches Altertum* 24, 1880.

Studies:

Reum, A., 1888: no. 96 above. For summary see pp. 188–92 above.

The Lives of Saints

Skeat, W.W. (ed.) : *Ælfric's Lives of Saints*. Early English Text Society O.S. 76, 82, 94 and 114, London, 1881–1900; reprinted as 2 volumes, 1966. Introduction, notes and translation. Items XXIII, XXIIIB, XXX and XXXIII are not by Ælfric.

Editions of selected items:

Nos. 32, 43, 52, 53, 55, 69, 72 and 80 above, and the following:

Earle, J. (ed.) : *Gloucester fragments*. London, 1861. Fragments in Gloucester Cathedral Library of Lives of St Swithin and St Mary of Egypt (Skeat XXI and XXIIIb). Includes translation and facsimile.

Needham, G.I. (ed.) : *Ælfric: Lives of Three English Saints*. London, 1966 (Methuen's Old English Library). Saints Oswald, Edmund and Swithin. Includes introduction, notes and glossary. Reviewed by P. Clemoes, *Anglia* 86, 1968.

Sweet, Henry: *An Anglo-Saxon Primer*. Oxford, 1882; revised Norman Davis, 1953 (9th edn). Includes Life of St Edmund.

Fowler, Roger: *Old English Prose and Verse.* London, 1966. Includes Life of St Oswald.

The Life of St Oswald is also included in the collections of Sweet, Raith, Bolton and Bright listed above p. 216. A twelfth-century copy of part of Skeat XVI (*De Memoria Sanctorum*) is printed in Warner's edition, above p. 216.

Studies:

Zupitza, J: 'Bemerkungen zu Ælfric's *Lives of Saints*', *Zeitschrift für Deutsches Altertum* 29, 1885.

Napier, A.S: 'A fragment of Ælfric's *Lives of Saints*', *Modern Language* Notes 2, 1887. Part of Life of St Basil from Bodleian MS Rawlinson Q.e.20 (detached from British Museum MS Cotton Otho B x).

Herzfeld, G: 'Bruchstücke von Ælfric's *Lives of Saints*', *Englische Studien* 16, 1891. Part of Lives of St Agnes and St Agatha, from British Museum MS Royal 8 c vii.

Ott, J: *Über die Quellen der Heiligenleben in Ælfrics Lives of Saints I.* Halle, 1892. See above pp. 195–6.

Förster, Max: 'Altenglische Predigtquellen I', *Archiv* 116, 1906. 2, 'Pseudo-Augustin und Ælfric', is on Skeat XVII (*De Auguriis*).

Gerould, Gordon H: 'Ælfric's legend of St. Swithin', *Anglia* 32, 1909.

Gerould, Gordon H: 'Ælfric's Lives of St Martin of Tours', *Journal of English and Germanic Philology* 24, 1925.

Loomis, Grant: 'Further sources of Ælfric's saints' lives', *Harvard Studies and Notes in Philology and Literature* 13, 1931.

Loomis, Grant: 'The growth of the St Edmund legend', *Ibid.* 14, 1932.

Bethurum, Dorothy: 'The form of Ælfric's *Lives of Saints*', *Studies in Philology* 29, 1932.

Prins, A.A: 'Some remarks on Ælfric's *Lives of Saints* and his translations from the Old Testament', *Neophilologus* 25, 1940. Suggests that the *Lives of Saints* collection originally included further Old Testament narratives.

Loomis, Laura H: 'The Saint Mercurius legend in medieval England and in Norse saga', *Philologica: the Malone Anniversary Studies*, ed. T.A. Kirby and H.B. Woolf. Baltimore, 1949. Refers to Life of St Basil.

Collins, Rowland L: 'An Ælfric MS fragment', *Times Literary Supplement* 2nd September 1960. Reports that Indiana University MS Poole 10 contains end of Skeat XXII and beginning of Skeat XXIV.

Wolpers, Theodor: *Die Englische Heiligenlegende des Mittelalters: eine Formgeschichte des Legendenerzählens von der spätantiken lateinischen Tradition bis zur Mitte des 16. Jahrhunderts.* Tübingen, 1964. Pp. 131–51 on Ælfric, and *passim*.

Cross, J.E: 'Gregory, *Blickling* homily X and Ælfric's *Passio S. Mauricii* on the world's youth and age', *Neuphilologische Mitteilungen* 66, 1965.

Cross, J.E: 'Oswald and Byrhtnoth', *English Studies* 46, 1965. On *The Battle of Maldon* and Ælfric's Life of St Oswald.

Clark, Cecily: 'Ælfric and Abbo', *English Studies* 49, 1968. On the Life of St Edmund.

Hurt, James R: 'A note on Ælfric's *Lives of Saints* no XVI', *English Studies* 51, 1970.

Bolton, W.F: 'The Alfredian Boethius in Ælfric's *Lives of Saints* I', *Notes and Queries* 19, 1972 (pp. 406–7).

Farrar, Raymon S: 'Structure and function in representative Old English saints' lives', *Neophilologus* 58, 1973. Refers to Ælfric's Lives of St Agnes, St Agatha and St Cecilia.

Interrogationes Sigewulfi
Edited: Bouterwek (no. 59 above), MacLean (no. 82), and Tessmann (no. 101).

Pastoral Letters
Fehr, Bernhard (ed.): *Die Hirtenbriefe Ælfrics.*
Hamburg, 1914 (Bibliothek der angelsächsischen Prosa 9); reprinted with supplement to the introduction by Peter Clemoes, Darmstadt, 1966. Reviewed by W. Vietor, *Anglia Beiblatt* 27, 1916, and Fred C. Robinson, *Anglia* 86, 1968.

Selections:
Nos. 2, 3, 6, 8, 9, 19, 20, 36, 48, 51, 54, 58 and 71 above.

Studies:
Fehr, Bernhard: 'Augustins Lehrsatz über die Willensfreiheit bei Ælfric', *Anglia Beiblatt* 34, 1923. On the 1st Latin letter for Wulfstan.

The Old English Heptateuch
A composite collection containing an Old English version of the Pentateuch which is partly by Ælfric, together with his preface to Genesis, and Ælfric's paraphrases of the Books of Joshua and Judges. For the most recent comments on the extent of Ælfric's contribution to the Pentateuch see the studies of the Ælfric canon by Clemoes and Pope (above p. 214f); but the question is not yet settled.
Edited: Thwaites (no. 16 above), Grein (no. 70), and:
Crawford, S.J: *The Old English Version of the Hep-*

tateuch, *Ælfric's Treatise on the Old and New Testament, and his Preface to Genesis.* Early English Text Society O.S. 162, London, 1922; reprinted with text of two additional MSS transcribed by N.R. Ker, 1969.

Selections:
Nos. 14, 22, 24, 31, 33, 42, 43, 56, 75, 76, 80, 106, 109, and 112 above, and the following:

Sweet, Henry: *An Anglo-Saxon Primer.* Oxford, 1882; revised by Norman Davis, 1953 (9th edn). Includes extracts from *Judges* and, in revised edition, Ælfric's *Preface to Genesis.*

Chase, F.H: 'A new text of the Old English prose *Genesis*', *Archiv* 100, 1898. Prints 6 chapters from British Museum MS Claudius B iv and Cambridge MS Ii.1.33, and discusses the different versions of the translation.

Craigie, W.A: *Specimens of Anglo-Saxon Prose.* 3 parts, Edinburgh, 1923–9. Includes numerous extracts from the *Heptateuch* (and from the homilies).

Raith, Josef: *Altenglisches Lesebuch (Prosa).* Munich, 1940, revised 1958. Includes *Preface to Genesis* and part of text of *Genesis.*

Studies:
Förster, Max: 'Ælfric's s.g. Hiob-übersetzung', *Anglia* 15, 1893. Shows that the paraphrase of the *Book of Job* included in Thwaite's and Grein's editions of the *Heptateuch* is simply a copy of the homily on Job in *Catholic Homilies* Series II.

Crawford, S.J: 'The Lincoln fragment of the Old English version of the *Heptateuch*', *Modern Language Review* 15, 1920.

Jost, Karl: 'Unechte Ælfrictexte', *Anglia* 51, 1927. On Ælfric's contribution to the translation of the Pentateuch.

Raith, Josef: 'Ælfric's share in the Old English *Pentateuch'*, *Review of English Studies* New Series 3, 1952.

Hargreaves, Henry: 'From Bede to Wiclif: medieval English Bible translations', *Bulletin of the John Rylands Library* 48, 1965.

Shepherd, Geoffrey: 'English versions of the Scriptures before Wiclif', *The Cambridge History of the Bible* vol II, ed. G.W.H. Lampe Cambridge, 1969. Pp. 374–7 on Ælfric.

Homiletic paraphrases by Ælfric of other Books of the Old Testament: *Job* in the Second Series of *Catholic Homilies; Kings* and *Maccabees* in the *Lives of Saints* ed. Skeat; and *Esther* and *Judith* in nos. 85, 86 and 95 above.

Letter to Sigeweard, on the Old and New Testament

Printed in nos. 6, 8, and 70 above, and in Crawford, *The Old English Heptateuch*.

Extracts in nos. 25, 28, 48 and 72.

Life of St Æthelwold

Edited Stevenson, 1858 (no. 60 above) and:

Winterbottom, Michael (ed.): *Three Lives of English Saints*. Toronto, 1972. Lives of Æthelwold by Ælfric and Wulfstan, and Life of St Edmund by Abbo.

Translated S.H. Gem, *An Anglo-Saxon Abbot: Ælfric of Eynsham* (Edinburgh, 1912) and Dorothy Whitelock, *English Historical Documents* vol I (London, 1955).

Studies:

Fisher, D.J.V: 'The early biographers of St Ethelwold', *English Historical Review* 67, 1952. Argues that Ælfric based his Life on that by Wulfstan the precentor (cf the contrary view above pp. 156–8).

Letter to the Monks of Eynsham

(including the so-called *Excerpts from the De Consuetidine Monachorum*, discussed above pp. 159–64, now considered to be part of the letter).

Edited by Mary Bateson as 'Excerpta ex institutionibus monasticis', in *Compotus Rolls of the Obedientiaries of St Swithun's Priory*, ed. G.W. Kitchin, London, 1892, pp. 171–98.

Miscellaneous Short Texts

De Duodecim Abusivis. Printed in Morris (no. 65 above) and Warner (above p. 216).

De Sanguine Prohibito. Ed. F. Kluge, *Englische Studien* 8, 1885, p. 62ff.

De Infantibus, and *De Cogitatione.* Ed. A.S. Napier, *Anglia* 10, 1887, pp. 154–5. For the attribution of these last three texts, see John C. Pope, *Homilies of Ælfric*, p. 145.

Decalogus Moysi, and *De Septem Gradibus Aecclesiasticis.* Printed Fehr, *Die Hirtenbriefe Ælfrics* (see above p. 228), pp. 190–203 and 256–7. For attribution see Pope, *Homilies of Ælfric*, p. 145, and Clemoes in supplement to Fehr. On the latter text, see Roger E. Reynolds, '*The De Officiis VII Graduum*: its origin and early medieval development', *Medieval Studies* 34, 1972.

The Ely Charter. Ed. John C. Pope, 'Ælfric and the Old English version of the Ely privilege', *England before the Conquest: Studies in Primary Sources presented to Dorothy Whitelock,* ed. Peter Clemoes and Kathleen Hughes, Cambridge, 1971. Presents detailed evidence for attributing text to Ælfric.

Admonitions, prayers, creeds and blessings printed at the end of Thorpe's edition of the *Catholic Homilies* (no. 41b above).

Miscellaneous Studies

Fehr, Bernhard: 'Das Benediktiner-Offizium und die Beziehungen zwischen Ælfric und Wulfstan', *Englische Studien* 46, 1913.

Menner, R.J: 'Two notes on mediaeval euhemerism', *Speculum* 3, 1928. Discusses Ælfric briefly.

Henel, Heinrich: 'Planetenglaube in Ælfrics Zeit', *Anglia* 58, 1934.

Raynes, Enid M: 'MS Boulogne-sur-Mer 63 and Ælfric,' *Medium Ævum* 26, 1957. Suggests that part of this MS is "copied from a MS which Ælfric kept for his personal use, and in which he entered Latin sermons for translation and other items of interest". See also article by Gatch, above p. 219.

Ure, J.M. (ed.): *The Benedictine Office: an Old English Text.* Edinburgh, 1957. Suggests that the prose parts of the *Office* were adapted by Wulfstan from a lost Old English text by Ælfric.

Clemoes, P.A.M: '*The Old English Benedictine Office,* Corpus Christi College, Cambridge, MS 190, and the relations between Ælfric and Wulfstan: a reconsideration', *Anglia* 78, 1960. Argues against Ure's suggestion, and considers more generally Wulstan's use of texts provided by Ælfric.

Cross, J.E: 'Aspects of microcosm and macrocosm in Old English literature', *Comparative Literature* 14, 1962; reprinted in *Studies in Honor of Arthur G. Brodeur*, ed. Stanley B. Greenfield, Eugene (Oregon), 1963. Discusses various of the *Catholic Homilies, Lives of Saints* XII and XIII and the *Hexameron.*

Nichols, Ann E: '*Awendan*: a note on Ælfric's vocabulary', *Journal of English and Germanic Philology* 63, 1964. On Ælfric's distinction between translation and paraphrase.

Nichols, Ann E: 'Ælfric's prefaces: rhetoric and genre', *English Studies* 49, 1968.

Robinson, Fred C: 'The significance of names in Old English literature', *Anglia* 86, 1968. Pp. 16–24 on Ælfric. Cf also article by Pearce p. 219 above.

Cross, J.E: 'The ethic of war in Old English', *England before the Conquest: Studies in Primary Sources presented to Dorothy Whitelock*, ed. Peter Clemoes and Kathleen Hughes, Cambridge, 1971.

LANGUAGE

Nos. 89, 90, 98, 99, 100, 104, 107, 108, 110 and the following:

Wells, B: 'Strong verbs in Ælfric's *Judith* and *Saints*', *Modern Language Notes* 3, 1888.

Brüll, Hugo: *Die altenglische Latein-Grammatik des Ælfric: Eine sprachliche Üntersuchung.* Berlin, 1904.

Gottweis, Reinhard: 'Die Syntax der Präpositionen ÆT, BE, YMB in den Ælfric-Homilien und andern Homiliensammlungen', *Anglia* 28, 1905.

Wilkes, J: *Lautlehre zu Ælfrics Heptateuch und Buch Hiob.* Bonn, 1905.

Wilkes, J: *Der i-Umlaut in Ælfrics Heptateuch und Buch Hiob.* Bonn, 1905.

Schüller, O: *Lautlehre von Ælfric's Lives of Saints.* Bonn, 1908.

Glaeser K: *Lautlehre der Ælfricschen Homilien in der HS. Cotton Vesp. D. xiv.* Leipzig, 1916.

Ropers, K: *Zur Syntax und Stilistik des Pronominalgebrauchs bei Ælfric.* Kiel, 1918.

Anger, R: *Aktionsarten des Verbums in Ælfrics Homilien.* Prague, 1924.

Halvorson, Nelius O: *Doctrinal Terms in Ælfric's Homilies.* Iowa City, 1932 (University of Iowa Studies, Humanistic Series 5).

Gohler, T: *Lautlehre der AE. Hexameron-Homilie des Abtes Ælfric.* Munich, 1933.

Meissner, P: 'Studien zum Wortschatz Ælfrics', *Archiv* 165–6, 1934–5.

Andrew, S.O: *Syntax and Style in Old English.* Cambridge, 1940. Includes discussion of sentence-structure in the *Catholic Homilies*, and suggests changes in punctuation of some sentences in Thorpe's edition.

Shook, L.K: 'A technical construction in Old English', *Medieval Studies* 2, 1940. On word-formation in Ælfric's *Grammar*.

Anderson, George K: 'Notes on the language of Ælfric's English *Pastoral Letters*, in Corpus Christi College 190 and Bodleian Junius 121', *Journal of English and Germanic Philology* 40, 1941.

Jost, Karl: *Wulfstanstudien.* Bern, 1950. Includes discussion of Ælfric's linguistic usage as evidence for authorship.

Barrett, C.R: *Studies in the Word-Order of Ælfric's Catholic Homilies and Lives of the Saints.* Cambridge,

1953 (Department of Anglo-Saxon Occasional Papers III). Reviewed by M.L. Samuels, *Review of English Studies* New Series 5, 1954.

Funke, Otto: 'Some remarks on late Old English word-order with special reference to Ælfric and the Maldon poem', *English Studies* 37, 1956.

Williams, Edna R: 'Ælfric's grammatical terminology', *Publications of the Modern Language Association of America* 73, 1958.

Gradon, Pamela: 'Studies in late West-Saxon labialization and delabialization', *English and Medieval Studies presented to J.R.R. Tolkien*, ed. Norman Davis and C.L. Wrenn. London, 1962. Based on manuscripts of Ælfric's homily for the Assumption of St John and his *De Temporibus Anni*.

Reszkiewicz, Alfred: *Ordering of Elements in Late Old English Prose in Terms of their Size and Structural Complexity*. Wroclaw (Poland), 1966. Based on Ælfric.

Barrett, C.R: 'Aspects of the placing of the accusative object in Ælfric', *AUMLA* (Journal of the Australasian Universities Language and Literature Association) 28, 1967. Based on the *Catholic Homilies* and *Lives of Saints*.

STYLE

Holthaus, E: Review of W.W. Skeat, *Ælfric's Lives of Saints*, with extensive examination of their metrical form. *Anglia* 6, 1883, *Anzeiger* 104–117.

Brandeis, Arthur: *Die Alliteration in Ælfric's metrischen Homilien.* Vienna, 1897. Included in *Jahresbericht der K.K. Staatsrealschule im vii Bezirke in Wien für 1896–7.*

Tupper, J.W: *Tropes and Figures* (1897). No. 111 above.

Gerould, G.H: 'Abbot Ælfric's rhythmic prose', *Modern Philology* 22, 1924–5.

Bethurum, Dorothy: 'The form of Ælfric's *Lives of Saints*', *Studies in Philology* 29, 1932. Partly on the rhythmical prose.

McIntosh, Angus: 'Wulfstan's prose', *Proceedings of the British Academy* 35, 1949, and separately. Includes analysis of Ælfric's rhythmical prose.

Funke, Otto: 'Studien zur alliterierenden und rhythmisierenden Prosa in der älteren altenglischen Homiletik', *Anglia* 80, 1962. On alliterative prose before Ælfric.

Kisbye, Torben: 'Zur Pronominalen Anrede bei Ælfric', *Archiv* 201, 1965.

Lipp, Frances R: 'Ælfric's Old English prose style', *Studies in Philology* 66, 1969.

Clemoes, Peter: *Rhythm and Cosmic Order in Old English Christian Literature.* Cambridge, 1970 (inaugural lecture). Discusses Ælfric's rhythmical style.

Nichols, Ann E: 'Ælfric and the brief style', *Journal of English and Germanic Philology* 70, 1971.

See also the major study of Ælfric's rhythmical prose in John C. Pope's *Homilies of Ælfric* (see above p. 222).

MANUSCRIPTS AND FORMS OF PUNCTUATION

Förster, Max: 'Der Inhalt der altenglischen Handschrift Vespasianus D. xiv', *Englische Studien* 54, 1920. On contents of MS printed in full by Warner (see above p. 216).

Sisam, Kenneth: 'MSS Bodley 340 and 342: Ælfric's *Catholic Homilies*'. See above p. 218.

Willard, Rudolf: 'The punctuation and capitalization of Ælfric's homily for the first Sunday in Lent', *Studies in English* 29, 1950.

Sisam, Celia: 'The scribal tradition of the *Lambeth Homilies*', *Review of English Studies* New Series 2, 1951.'On Lambeth Palace MS 487, edited by R. Morris and including late twelfth-century adaptations of homilies by Ælfric; see no. 65 above.

Clemoes, Peter: *Liturgical Influence on Punctuation in Late Old English and Early Middle English Manuscripts*. Cambridge, 1952 (Department of Anglo-Saxon Occasional Papers I). Partly on Ælfric's punctuation.

Ker, N.R: *A Catalogue of Manuscripts containing Anglo-Saxon*. Oxford, 1957. Contains detailed descriptions of all MSS, tables listing the MSS in which each item of the *Catholic Homilies* appears, and an index listing the MSS of each work by Ælfric.

Needham, Geoffrey: 'Additions and alterations in Cotton MS Julius E vii', *Review of English Studies* New Series 9, 1958. On the main MS of the *Lives of Saints*.

Harlow, C.G: 'Punctuation in some manuscripts of Ælfric', *Review of English Studies* New Series 10, 1959.

Richards, Mary P: 'On the date and provenance of MS Cotton Vespasian D. xiv ff. 4–169', *Manuscripta* 17, 1973. Sets out evidence that the MS was produced at Rochester in the 2nd quarter of the 12th century.

See also introductions to editions by Eliason and Clemoes (p. 216 above) and Pope (p. 222 above).

INDEX.

Abbey, of Glastonbury, 20-2; of Abingdon, 24-7; of Winchester, 27-8, 36-43; of Ely, Peterborough, and Thorney, 30, 33; of Ramsey, 32-3; of Cernel, 47-9; of Eynsham, 60-3.

Abbo, see Fleury.

Abdias Legends, a source of Ælfric's Homilies, 104.

Abdon and Sennes, homily on, 128.

Abgarus, see Bibliography, no. 55.

Abingdon Abbey, destroyed by Danes, founded anew, 24; Æthelwold abbot of, 25-7; monks of, 28; school of, 33.

Ælfhere, of Mercia, seeks to overthrow the monks, 43-4.

Ælfric, his life, 35-70; education, 71-6; characteristics as a writer, 56, 64, 71-2, 76-9, 83, 84, 134, 144, 148-9, 157, 188, 189-90, 194-5, 197-8; as a teacher, 74-81, 84-6; his patriotism, 58, 78-9, 90, 151; his humility, 81.

Ælfric, Archbishop of Canterbury, Ælfric identified with, 89-93, 99.

Ælfric Bata, quoted, 98; *Colloquium* revised by, 122-124; what is known of, 122; Ælfric's writings ascribed to, 143-4, 184; perhaps author of appendix of the *De Temporibus*, 191.

Ælfric Puttoc, Archbishop of York, Ælfric identified with, 93-95, 99-100.

Ælfric, Bishop of Crediton, Ælfric identified with, 88, 98-9.

Ætheldred, St., homily on, 127.

Æthelmær, endows Cernel Abbey, 47-50; founds Eynsham Abbey, 53, 60-62, 182; Ælfric writes for, 53, 57; death, 69.

Æthelnoth, perhaps pupil of Ælfric, 56; Archbishop of Canterbury, 56, 69.

Æthelstan, King mentioned by Ælfric, 79, 147; Dunstan and Æthelwold at court of, 20, 24.

Æthelweard, friend of Ælfric, his identity, 47-8, 57; Ælfric writes for, 51-3, 57, 102, 126, 147-8; counsels payment of Danegelt, 54: sent by King Æthelred to King Olave, 55; death, 57.

Æthelwin, of East Anglia, patron of Oswald, 32; heads a monastic party, 43-4, 86; death, 54.

Æthelwold I., 14, 19; his early life, 21; life at Glastonbury, 21-4, 157; Abbot of Abingdon, 25-7; Bishop of Winchester, 27-31, 33, 34, 36-7, 43-5; as a teacher, 39-40, 56; his connection with the Benedictine Rule, 27, 39, 159-64; biographies of, 65, 90, 156-9.

Æethlwold II., Ælfric writes homily for, 67, 93, 106, 109.

Alban, St., homily on, 127.

Alcuin, his treatise on Genesis, 131-2; a source of Ælfric's *Homilies*, 104, 187.

Aldhelm, Ælfric compared with, 80, 87.

Alfred, his educational work, 17-18, 50, 52; translations, 18; mentioned by Ælfric, 50, 79, 147.